MAY IT PLEASE
YOUR LORDSHIP

May It Please Your Lordship

E. S. TURNER

London

MICHAEL JOSEPH

First published in Great Britain by
MICHAEL JOSEPH LTD
52 Bedford Square
London, W.C.1
1971

7181 0737 3

Set and printed in Great Britain by
Tonbridge Printers Ltd, Peach Hall Works, Tonbridge, Kent
in Baskerville eleven on twelve point on paper supplied by
P. F. Bingham Ltd, and bound by James Burn
at Esher, Surrey

CONTENTS

ILLUSTRATIONS

Illustrations

The author is grateful to The National Portrait
Gallery for permission to reproduce the portrait
of Sir William Scroggs; *Punch* for the cartoons
facing pages 129, 160 and 192; *Vanity Fair* for
the drawings facing page 225; and The Radio
Times Hulton Picture Library for the remainder.

INTRODUCTION

First, a few facts about judges.

In the eyes of the Ministry of Social Security, a judge is a self-employed person. In practice, he is nothing of the sort. A judge of the High Court receives a steady £11,500 a year, with a pension on retirement, and is subject to none of the occupational ups-and-downs which beset authors, comedians and barrow boys. He is classed as a self-employed person only in order to support the concept that he is not a servant of the State which pays him his salary.

According to the Table of Precedence, a judge of the High Court ranks far below a bishop. He dwells in that social no-man's-land between the eldest son of a baron and the younger son of a viscount. This is not the most suitable place for the man who, traditionally, 'stands equally between the Sovereign and the Executive, between the Executive and the people'. Even the Lord Chief Justice of England is outranked by the meanest bishop, though as a life peer he stands a little above himself. The Lord Chancellor precedes the Prime Minister and takes duchesses in to dinner.

A High Court judge receives an automatic knighthood. No one grudges him this privilege, though why a judge should be granted an *ex officio* honour when, say, a lieutenant-general is not is hard to discern; unless one concedes that sentencing bank robbers is a nobler task than forcing beach-heads. If a judge resigns to enter the City he keeps his knighthood.

In many countries a school leaver can train to be a judge, but not in Britain. A judgeship is an honour which descends, at the Lord Chancellor's instigation, on a successful barrister. It

9

may involve him in financial loss, but a Bench, as the unfortunate Lord Westbury said, 'is a damned fine thing to sit on'. From this point onwards he is not supposed to look for promotion, though conceivably he may be raised to the peerage. On the other hand he has no fear of dismissal, so long as he does nothing to inflame both Lords and Commons. 'We have put him in a position in our constitution where the only possible object of his honourable ambition is to leave a reputation for impartiality. He has nothing else to gain.'*

Although the Bench is not a career, 'it is not too difficult for a hard-working man to be some kind of judge by the age of fifty', according to an anatomist of the times.† For 'man' read 'barrister'. It is no handicap to have been to Oxford or Cambridge, since these universities provide three judges out of four. If the hard-working aspirant has not become a judge by the age of seventy-five he should turn to something else, for that is now the judicial retiring age. A judge can claim a pension after fifteen years, or at seventy if he feels his powers failing.

It is assumed that a man who has spent most of his life arguing one side of a problem will have no difficulty in seeing both sides when he becomes a judge; and that all the knowledge which he vainly strove to amass when a barrister will suddenly impregnate him as he ascends the Bench. The system works astonishingly well. 'There are no bad judges,' says a veteran of the Bar. 'There have been bad judges and there will be bad judges, but there are no bad judges.'‡

Many sacrifices are expected of a judge, the least of which is that he may not serve his country on a jury. He is debarred from sitting in the House of Commons. He is also discouraged from criticising Parliament, or from making too many barbed references to 'the wisdom of Parliament', in return for which Parliament usually refrains from criticising him. He is expected to concern himself with what Parliamentary draftsmen have laid down, not to speculate on what may have been in the legislators' minds at the time. He is supposed to refrain from making political statements, a difficult feat when almost any controversy is liable to become politically charged.

A judge's function, briefly and starkly, is to discover the facts,

*Sir John Simon, *Hansard*, June 23, 1927.
†Anthony Sampson: *Anatomy of Britain Today*.
‡F. J. de Verteuil: *Fifty Wasted Years*.

interpret the law and then administer it. As Socrates said, he should hear courteously, answer wisely, consider soberly and decide impartially. It is also his duty to suppress prolixity and irrelevance. He must not allow himself to brood on the thought that the parties endlessly bickering before him have taken out an insurance policy on his life, for fear he tiresomely drops dead and involves them in heavy expenses. Having given of his best, the judge must not take it amiss when superior judges reverse his decisions, reduce his sentences and question his common-sense, his learning, his application and his sense of propriety. In few learned professions do superiors so publicly reprehend the apparent shortcomings of their inferiors.

Sir Winston Churchill, who said hard words about judges in his time, observed that they were required to lead 'a form of life and conduct far more severe and restricted than that of ordinary people'. What, he asked, would be thought of a Lord Chief Justice if he won the Derby, a feat which was perfectly permissible in a Prime Minister?* Well, we have had a Lord Chief Justice who wrote for the *News of the World,* which would seem a more dubious feat than winning the Derby, and we have had a Lord Chancellor who frequented not only English race-tracks but French casinos. However, it remains true that a judge must be content to forego many pleasures to which others look forward, like attending parties at which distinguished criminals may be present. If he wants to join Bohemian clubs and tell racy stories, there are precedents, though not very good ones (about one judge in four belongs to the Athenaeum). On circuit a judge may not put up at the fascinating hotel of his choice, but must stay at appointed lodgings, with his own marshal, butler and cook, safe from importunity and contamina-tion; if he does not care for his lodgings (and often he does not) there is a complaints book on the premises. As the price for circumscribing his social life, he must be prepared to be accused of living out of touch with common humanity. If he is convicted of driving with too much alcohol in his blood, as was a Lord Justice in 1969, he will receive the help of the Sunday news-papers in deciding whether or not to resign. The Judge in question remained in office. No judge will be expected to resign for being involved in a divorce.

Francis Bacon said, 'A popular judge is a deformed thing and

Hansard, March 23, 1954.

plaudits are fitter for players than magistrates.' A variation on
this by the late Lord Justice MacKinnon is, 'He is the best judge
whose name is known to the fewest readers of the *Daily Mail*.'*
Some of us can remember when no list of 'Sayings of the Week'
was complete without an aphorism about women by the
'Bachelor Judge', Mr Justice McCardie, or a witticism by Mr
Justice Darling. The witty and opinionated judges seem to have
vanished, along with the truculent and tyrannous ones, to be
replaced by men of sound if unremarkable views. Headline-
hunting is no longer a judicial recreation. Occasionally we have
a divorce judge, perhaps only a commissioner, whose disserta-
tions on what went on, or failed to go on, beneath the bed-
clothes so fascinate the newspapers as to leave the parties concerned little option but to emigrate. It may be that in such
cases the judge did not intend to create headlines and that any
fault lies with a prurient press; but judges should know the sort
of press we have.

Whether a judge is remembered by posterity often depends on
fortuitous incidents and exchanges. To Mr Justice Eve fell the
task of deciding whether a spiritualistic medium enjoys the copy-
right of automatic writing; if a judge cannot make a name for
himself on an issue like that he has himself to blame. Lord
Justice Scrutton wrote *The Contract Of Affreightment As
Expressed In Charterparties And Bills Of Lading,* a work of
quiet fascination which ran through many editions, but he tends
to be remembered as the judge who rebuked Mr Justice
McCardie for knowing too much about women's underclothes.
A county court judge called Willis survives because he said
testily to the future Lord Birkenhead, 'What do you suppose
I am on the Bench for, Mr Smith?' and received the reply,
'It is not for me, your Honour, to attempt to fathom the in-
scrutable workings of Providence.'† There are judges of great
learning and mellifluity who have achieved fame because they
said things like, 'Are you sure?' thus giving counsel the opportunity to reply, 'Cock, my Lord.' It is as well for our modern
judges that they are not faced by some of the wickedly insolent
barristers of old. Lord Clare, sitting on the Irish Bench, was well
aware to whom the advocate Curran was referring when he said,
'I know that error is in its nature flippant and compendious; it

*F. D. MacKinnon: *On Circuit.*
†Lord Birkenhead: *Life of F. E. Smith.*

hops with airy and fastidious levity over proofs and argument
and perches upon assertion, which it calls conclusion.'* It is very
difficult to achieve a quick and crushing *riposte* to that sort of
thing, couched in the same airy and fastidious vein, and Lord
Clare did not try.

Even off the Bench, no critics of judges are harsher or more
censorious than fellow-judges and lawyers. Last century Lord
Campbell's biographies of Lord Chancellors were said to add
a new terror to death, as much for their inaccuracies as for
their asperities; and his fellow Whig, Lord Cockburn, was not
much kinder to the Scots judiciary. A recent Lord Chief
Justice was not long in his grave before he was called the worst
judge of the century. The *Dictionary of National Biography* has
some harsh appraisals of judges, also some puzzling ones. Of
Mr Justice Byles it says, '. . . his mind was marked by a defect
singular in one of his indubitable ability. He displayed a serious
want of readiness in his perception of the facts of a case . . .' To
a layman this unfortunate lack seems to render the Judge's
ability more than dubitable. And what is the non-lawyer to make
of this by Lord Dunedin : 'No judge is always right, but Lindley,
even if he were wrong, was consistently sound?'†

This book is an attempt to tell the judicial story from the days
when a man was as likely to be hanged by an abbot as by a
judge. It describes how the King's courts and assize circuits were
built up, how judges were repeatedly purged for corruption and
extortion, how they were thrown into dungeons by barons and
lynched in peasant risings; how they resisted, or failed to resist,
the encroachments of the royal prerogative; how, after 1688
they ceased to be the royal jackals and became the watchdogs
of the people; how they attempted to suppress the ideas liberated
by the French Revolution; how they fell foul of the trade
unions and were accused of laying down inequitable 'judge-made
law', which Parliament could have changed if it had wanted to;
and how, after nine centuries, they reluctantly allowed themselves to become political neuters.

For reasons partly of space the book concentrates on judges
at High Court level. It deals with certain law reforms as they
affected the Bench, but does not pretend to be a history of the

*W. H. Curran: *Life of J. P. Curran.*
†*The Times,* February 18, 1932.

law. It is not concerned with explaining arcane legal customs or *minutiae* of dress. What it aims to do is to give some idea of what it was like to be a thief up before the justiciar Ralph Basset, a Roman Catholic up before Sir William Scroggs, a libeller up before Lord Ellenborough, a Parliamentary reformer up before Lord Braxfield or a Luddite up before Baron Alderson.

I

THE KING'S JUSTICE

It was once the habit of political firebrands, when at odds with the law, to remind the Bench that King Alfred had hanged forty-four judges in one year for various errors; also that, in an earlier day, Cambyses had flayed an unjust judge and upholstered the judgment seat of Persia with his skin, as a warning to successors. The enemies of Lord Chief Justice Scroggs took pains to bring this information to his notice. Maurice Margarot, not the most endearing of martyrs, cited these precedents to the ferocious Lord Braxfield, before whom he was convicted of sedition in Edinburgh in 1794. 'Orator' Hunt, who was gaoled after the affray at Peterloo, helped to perpetuate the same legend. King Alfred, in the view of radicals, was a sovereign who had the right idea about judges.

The story of Alfred's purge comes from a law-book called *The Mirror of Justices,* the work of many unscrupulous pens, among them that of Andrew Horn (d. 1320). Sir Edward Coke seems to have accepted much of its contents, but modern scholarship regards it is an 'enigmatical treatise'* in which insolence joins hands with romance. The names of the forty-four judges are thought to be invented, so it is more than likely that the crimes attributed to them are invented too. These include : 'judging a man to death' for a non-mortal offence, for escaping from prison, for killing a man by misadventure; judging to death without the consent of all the jurors, or without swearing the jurors, or on a prohibited day; judging to death a madman and a person under twenty-one; and judging to death on various technicalities or 'after sufficient acquittal'. The *Mirror of Justices*

---

*F. W. Maitland: *The Mirror of Justices* (Selden Society).

would have us believe that Alfred not only hanged judges who wrongly hanged others but also hanged judges who wrongly refrained from hanging others. 'And besides this the coroners, officers, assessors and those who tortured folk and those who could have disturbed the false judgments but did not do so, were hanged whenever the justices were hanged . . .'

All of which suggests that hanging was already a national obsession; as indeed it was. The country was replete with gallows, both public and private, and remained so after the Norman Conquest, when hanging for a while gave way to maiming.

One statement in *The Mirror of Justices* sounds credible enough : no persons could be judges if they were women, serfs, open lepers, idiots, lunatics, attorneys, deaf mutes, criminals, excommunicated persons, non-Christians or under twenty-one.

Under the Normans the concept of royal justice began to dislodge that of private or community justice. The King's Court, where the monarch sat in council, was an all-purpose body. Its members might be barons, bishops, soldiers or Household officers; but whatever they were, they undertook as required the duties of legislators, administrators, revenue collectors, courtiers and judges. In its role as legal tribunal, the King's Court generally confined itself to wrangles between the King and his most powerful subjects. For petty disputes, and for most infractions of the law, there were already courts enough. There were the courts of the hundred and the shire, where the sheriff held sway; there were the manorial and seigneurial courts, in which a lord had the right to hang a thief caught red-handed on his lands; there were ecclesiastical courts, newly founded for the punishment of adulterers, fornicators, blasphemers, heretics and all misbehaving clerics; there were forest courts, for the discouragement of deer-slaying; and there were 'pie-powder' courts to discipline persons who misbehaved at fairs (from *pieds poudreux*, because those who attended usually had dusty feet).

Gradually the judicial function of the King's Court was handed over to specialists, men versed in the common law. Barons often lacked the judicial instinct and bishops were too apt to confuse sin with crime, besides which the Church forbade them to sit in secular courts. However, literacy was hard to come by other than through the Church, so those who wielded judicial

power continued to be drawn from the ranks of clerics and to
hold on to their Church appointments.

It was not enough for the King's judges to sit in grave state
at Westminster. The Conqueror sent them into the shires to teach
the new laws, to stiffen those petty courts which needed stiffen-
ing, to challenge those barons and abbots who were abusing
their powers and to smell out all malpractices which affected
the King's pocket. The arrival of the itinerant royal judges
aroused as little pleasure in the populace as it did in the ranks
of corrupt sheriffs and baronial hangmen. 'The louder the talk
of law and justice, the greater the injustices committed,' says *The
Anglo-Saxon Chronicle* in 1086. Occasionally a judicial visitation left a whole community maimed and orphaned. The
Chronicle tells how in 1124 the King's 'justiciar', Ralph Basset,
descended on Huncote, in Leicestershire, and hanged more
thieves than had ever been hanged there before (curiously, the
total was forty-four, the number of judges Alfred is supposed to
have despatched). Not content with the work of execution, this
low-born Norman avenger put out the eyes of six men and
deprived them of their testicles. Many honest men, thought
the chronicler, felt that a great injustice had been done to Huncote. 'A very distressful year this was! He who had any money
was deprived of it by violent extortions and the oppressive
courts; he who had none died of hunger.'*

The Normans kept much of Saxon law and added French
refinements. Trials by ordeal still survived. Suspects were invited
to pluck stones from cauldrons of boiling water, or were thrown
into ponds which had been commanded in God's name to cast
out the wicked (the innocent sank, the guilty floated). For centuries to come the floating test was applied to suspected witches.
In trial by oath a litigant would be ordered to find a body of
men willing to swear to the justice of his cause, the assumption
being that dread of Hell-fire would discourage perjury. Neither
of these systems found much favour in the eyes of the con-
querors, but long distrust of human justice had driven men to
seek divine arbitraments. The Normans introduced the irrational,
but chivalrous, trial by battle, a system of determining land
disputes between knights, in which it was supposed that God
would favour the right. While the King's judges watched from a
sort of grandstand, champions appointed by the parties be-

*G. N. Garmonsway (tr.): *The Anglo-Saxon Chronicle*.

laboured each other with staves from sunrise until the stars appeared in the sky, or until one of them conceded he was recreant, or craven. Leather 'armour' was worn and the outcome was rarely lethal. If the encounter was a draw, the decision went to the sitting tenant. For the populace, it was a rude entertainment and for the King's judges the 'hearing' posed no great intellectual challenge. No doubt there are those today who enjoy lands secured by an ancestor's proxy who blinded another man's proxy with blood.

What the Normans began the Plantagenets perfected. Henry II did much to spread his own justice through the realm, pouncing on lawless sheriffs, barons and abbots. Here was a king who was prepared to come to his subjects instead of waiting for them to come to him. He established fixed circuits for his itinerant judges, who were empowered to hear civil disputes as well as to try major criminals. By various enactments Henry laid down that murder, robbery, receiving, forgery and arson were for the King to punish; in other words, if men were to be hanged it was the King who was going to hang them. Moreover, as the Assize of Clarendon made clear, it was the King who was going to have their chattels. The King's judges, being men of like mind and training, and free from local pressures, were able to enforce a uniformity of justice, severe though it often was. The King's task as law-giver and law-enforcer was made no easier by the Church, which sought constantly to extend Canon Law and to shield its own teeming wrongdoers from civil justice.

To Henry goes the credit for fostering the dual system of juries which lasted into our own times. It became the sheriff's function to summon a grand jury of responsible citizens to consider the prosecution evidence against a suspect. If they thought the evidence strong enough to justify putting him on trial, they returned a 'true bill' of indictment and the case was then heard by a common jury. If they thought the evidence inadequate, the bill of indictment was thrown out (the grand jury system, which still exists in America, was abolished in Britain in 1933).

Henry was chided for accepting gifts from those who hoped to expedite the course of justice, though he is unlikely to have allowed his decision to be swayed thereby. John, who enjoyed hearing suits, is said, perhaps wrongly, to have accepted a more substantial gift – 3,000 marks* – to reach a favourable decision in an action involving the barony of Mowbray. His vindictive and jealous temperament would seem to have ill qualified him to occupy the Bench, but the public were eager to have their actions tried before him and he is reputed to have shown notable indulgence towards the downtrodden. Magna Carta, signed by him, proudly lays down : 'To no one will we sell, to no one will we refuse or delay right or justice.' It also says : 'We will appoint as justices, constables, sheriffs or bailiffs only such as know the law of the kingdom and mean to observe it well.' The use of torture was forsworn. For long years to come these promises were all too often honoured in the breach.

Those who enforced the royal justice at its highest levels needed to be men of great versatility. It was an advantage to have been trained as a soldier, since one was always liable to be seconded to fight the Welsh or the Scots. Alternatively one might be invited to join the King on a Crusade, under penalty of a heavy fine for refusal. It was equally an advantage to have been trained as a cleric, for if disgrace came, as it often did, one could always resume the tonsure, against the onset of better days. The King's principal judicial officer, or justiciar, had to be a man of enough learning, presence and administrative talent to act as viceroy during his master's absence; or, if he had the necessary skills and graces, he might be sent on diplomatic missions. Two of William the Conqueror's justiciars, William de Warenne and Richard de Clare, suppressed an insurrection of nobles while the King was in France and cut off the right feet of the prisoners, which they felt was what their master would have wished. The first man to hold the title of Chief Justiciar of England, under Henry I, was Roger, Bishop of Salisbury. Before he ascended the throne Henry stopped at Caen to hear mass and was so impressed by the speed with which Roger, the chaplain, got through the service that he took him on forthwith, as steward. On his accession, Henry made the young man Chancellor and Bishop of Lincoln in quick succession. Roger then administered the realm while the King was absent, obeying with alacrity all orders transmitted from France. When the King called for action against coiners, Roger's men scoured the kingdom and concentrated as many as they could find at Winchester. Then, says *The Anglo-Saxon Chronicle*, 'they were

*A mark was worth 13s. 4d.

taken one by one and each deprived of the right hand and the testicles below'. The chronicler conceded that something had to be done, since money had become almost valueless. Roger built various castles, three of which he kept in the family. The next King, Stephen, said that Roger was welcome to half the kingdom if he wanted it, but later took up arms against the family and shut his Chief Justiciar, temporarily, in a cow-house. Roger had a rare talent for administration, not only of the country but of the courts; and if administration meant leaving a trail of left-handed eunuchs he was not one to shrink from the task.

If justiciars and judges kept their records clean they qualified for substantial rewards – manors, heiresses, licences to build castles, captured vessels, wardships and much else. William de Braose, one of Henry II's itinerant judges, was well rewarded for his skilful murder of a large company of Welshmen whom he invited to a feast in the Castle of Abergavenny. Under John he failed to turn in certain revenues, as a punishment for which his wife and eldest son were taken to Windsor and starved. William escaped to France as a beggar, possibly receiving that courtesy he had always extended to the poor, if not to hungry Welshmen.

Greed and ambition toppled many a chief justiciar. Richard I put up the office for sale and a successful bid came from a churchman who had sired three bastards by three mothers at the age of twenty-five, and who, as Archdeacon of Winchester, had kept a harem on Church premises. This was Hugh Pusar, Bishop of Durham, whose efforts to obtain a return on his judicial investment were so unconscionable that the King appointed William de Longchamp as co-justiciar. Having disposed of his rival, William also gave way to the intoxication of power and seized revenues which were not his. On the run he was spotted in female attire waiting for a ship on Dover beach, where his awkwardness of gait and inability to speak English had aroused suspicion. But he was later restored to favour.

Some extravagant rogues served in the legal ranks. John at one time employed Falkes de Breauté, adventurer, extortioner, depopulator and despoiler extraordinary, a man said to have been consumed by a fierce resentment of orderly adminstration. In the reign of Henry III he was sufficiently carried away to declare personal war on the King's judges. Three of them had been sent to Dunstable to hear complaints against him of 'forcible disturbance', and they fined him £1,000 on each of thirty charges. In a fury Falkes urged his brother William and a band of knights to kidnap the judges. Two of them escaped, but the third, Henry de Braybroc, was imprisoned in Bedford Castle, where he suffered indignities. The prisoner's wife set off for Northampton, where the King was sitting in council, and demanded action, but the King needed no urging. He marched on Bedford and besieged the Castle for two months, then summarily hanged the whole garrison, including William and numerous knights. Falkes was taken in a church at Coventry and threw himself on the mercy of the King, reminding him of his past brutal services and offering to give up all his possessions. His life was spared but he was banished. The King of France took a strong dislike to him and, according to Foss, his life was 'terminated by poison administered in a fish at St Ciriac'.* Henry de Braybroc, the judge freed from captivity, was given the satisfying task of razing Bedford Castle and distributing the materials in accordance with the King's pleasure; after which he resumed his duties as itinerant justice in Buckinghamshire and Bedfordshire.

The chief justiciar who sentenced Falkes de Breauté, Hubert de Burgh, himself clashed with Henry III, as the powerful usually did. When first appointed justiciar he defended Dover Castle against the French and won a sea battle against them, which made him the Nelson of his day; but his mutilations of London rioters swung popularity into hatred. When he fell from grace and took refuge in Merton Priory a mob of 20,000 were ready to storm it, at the risk of 20,000 excommunications. Later the King's men seized him from a chapel at Brentwood and, when the Bishop of London threatened to excommunicate the King, put him back again. His food was gradually cut off and Hubert decided the Tower was preferable. Handed over for safe keeping to four earls, he escaped from Devizes Castle to a church. Again he was dragged from sanctuary, again restored under threats of excommunication and again they tried to starve him out. He escaped to join the King's enemies and was outlawed. His career underlines the difficulties of law enforcement in a land where the Church made its own rules, based on no discernible pattern of natural justice.

*Edward Foss: *A Biographical Dictionary of Judges.*

2

DISGRACE ABOUNDING

Edward I, alias the English Justinian, inherited and strengthened a system of courts which was to last for six hundred years. His judges sat in Westminster Hall, that glorious barn built by Rufus. The foremost judgment seat was the King's Bench, where the King still had the right to sit. It heard actions involving the Crown, but later opened its doors to profitable private suits. At its head was the former Chief Justiciar, now the Chief Justice of the King's Bench and the forerunner of the Lord Chief Justice of England. Next was the Court of Common Pleas, established primarily to hear disputes between private individuals, provided they were willing to hand over their quarrels to serjeants-at-law, who alone had the right to plead there. Thirdly, there was the Court of Exchequer, which heard matters affecting the Revenue but which also began to compete for private suits; its justices were called barons. These three tribunals had all been hived off from the original King's Court. A fourth court was slowly evolving : the Court of Chancery, which was to become the fount of equity under the Lord Chancellor, as 'keeper of the King's conscience', with the aid of the Master of the Rolls. Its duty was to rectify the grievances of those who could not obtain justice at the other three courts, usually because the common law was too inflexible or was incapable of meeting new situations. Inevitably, in discharging this duty, the Court of Chancery was to earn the jealousy of the other courts.

Edward regarded his judges not only as instruments of justice but as instruments of government. Usually, though not invariably, he had enough respect for the principles of justice not to try to coerce judges into giving judgments against their con-

science. Chief Justice Ralph de Hengham resisted the King on a
point of procedure involving the litigious Countess of Albemarle.
To a judicial colleague he said, in Edward's presence : 'The law
wills that no one be taken by surprise in the King's Court. But,
if you had your way, this lady would answer in court for what
she has not been warned to answer by writ . . .' The King, who
was an interested party, commented, 'I have nothing to do with
your disputations, but God's Blood! you shall give me a good
writ before you arise hence.'*

Under the three Edwards the country came to respect, and
soon to dread, the visitation of Justices in Eyre. A General Eyre
was an administrative inquisition, designed in great part to
inflate the royal revenue by fining the incompetent, the usurping
and the sticky-fingered; at the same time the justices heard civil
actions and tried criminals. In other words, it was a session of
accountancy to the sound of trumpets, with a little hanging on
the side. As a rule, a town suffered an Eyre only once every
seven years; then all the official rolls for the preceding years had
to be minutely examined. Sheriffs, coroners, bailiffs – all were
called to account and penalised for the smallest infractions.
Profiteers were disciplined, cheats had their scales smashed and
bad liquor was poured down the nearest drain, if any. So long
as they sat, the Justices in Eyre enjoyed plenary powers and not
even the courts at Westminster could override them. On the
judicial side some belated justice was no doubt done, but often
the memories of offences committed five or six years earlier must
have been defective. Sometimes weaker citizens fled the town
when they heard that an Eyre was due; of those who stayed,
few escaped being dragged into the proceedings. At harvest time
the justices might see fit to suspend operations until the crops
were gathered in. When it was all over, the community, smarting
from its fines, returned to its time-honoured corruptions. By the
days of the third Edward, the Eyre had become 'a terror and an
abomination in the sight of all men'.† From then on the
institution was allowed to lapse.

Gradually the legal profession began to take corporate shape.
The serjeants-at-law formed their own Inn of Court and set
about consolidating and extending their privileges. The Order
of Serjeants was sometimes known as the Order of the Coif,

*W. S. Holdsworth: *A History of English Law.*
†W. C. Bolland: *The General Eyre.*

from the white silken hood worn by its members. This headgear was also worn by judges until wigs became the style in the seventeenth century. The Order was essentially a trade union and the members addressed each other as 'brother', a usage adopted by the judges who were now increasingly drawn from its ranks. Inevitably it became a conspiracy against the laity, its proceedings being conducted in a jargon made up of bad English, bad Latin and bad French, but mostly bad French. The serjeants assumed responsibility for the education of newcomers, which is to say that they allowed students the privilege of hearing them argue causes in court. Fortunately in Edward I's reign the great jurist, Henry de Bracton, assisted the cause of legal education by compiling his *De Legibus Angliae,* a much-needed systematic exposition of the common law. In addition there began to appear Year Books containing reports of actions. As a profession the law began to rival the Church; and like the Church it offered wealth and unpopularity.

From the Year Books it is evident that words were not minced in Edward's courts. The learned Henry Spigurnel tells a suitor that his claim fails because he was begotten in fornication. Excess is punished by excess. A woman identified only as Alice has been 'forcibly ravished against the peace and dignity of the Crown'; the man responsible is given the option of marrying her or having his eyes put out and his testicles cut off. Spigurnel, as precedent for burning a girl of thirteen who has killed her mistress, points out that a boy of ten has been hanged for killing because it was obvious he knew the difference between good and evil, 'and so malice makes up for age'. For those who refuse to plead, there is *peine forte et dure,* or pressing to death. Most of the cases deal with wranglings over land or infringements of rights. Sir Reginald de Grey and his wife Maud resent an attempt by *quo warranto* to deprive them of their gallows, which has been in the family a long time.*

The Year Books do not convey the atmosphere of the court but their editor assures us that the advocates of the day already had a well-established set of tricks and mannerisms, some of them not unfamiliar today. These 'rules' were laid down by Guillaume Durand, of Provence, in his *Speculum Juris.* Obeisances should be graduated according to the rank of the judge. 'Do not laugh causelessly before the judge,' says Durand.

*Alfred J. Horwood (ed.): *Year Books of Edward I.*

'When the judge speaks, listen respectfully and then laud his wisdom and eloquence.' He does not recommend the idea of whispering frequently to the judge, in the hope that the opposing advocate will think he is under discussion and become flustered. He notes that some advocates rise with arrogance, rubbing the face, pushing the hair back behind the ears, blowing the nose loudly, examining their hands and dress; others alternately lift their eyes heavenward or bow the head. There is a right moment, and a wrong moment, for slowly and wearily rising as if from sleep. 'If the judge be literate,' says Durand, he may be trusted to make any necessary explanations to the other side; but 'if the judge be illiterate (for he may be a baron or count)', the advocate should explain the law.

Edward's problem was that which faced all the Angevin kings: how to find honest men to put on the Bench, men who could be relied upon to maintain the dignity of a royal emissary yet who would exact only a decent minimum of hospitality from their hosts on circuit. The judges received astonishingly low salaries, which were often paid years in arrears. They were entitled to augment their income by charging certain fees, but all too often they seem to have resorted to accepting gifts, to soliciting bribes and to extortion. It was an age when a man made what he could while the going was good; the Church was a prey to ravening pluralists. If gold rusts, what shall iron do? The lesser men of the law – sheriffs and so on – leagued themselves with the judges in a confederacy which anticipated the Mafia by half a millenium. Inevitably some were caught out. In 1275 John de Lovetot was shut in the Tower and fined a reputed 3,000 marks for extortion. Three years later William de Brompton, a judge of the Common Pleas, went to the Tower not only for corruption but for ordering a prisoner in Newgate to be severely used. He was fined a reported 6,000 marks. These penalties were often exaggerated and may have been only a tenth of the quoted figure. Even so, they were large sums to pay out of a salary of between £30 and £80 a year; and any judge who was able to pay them must, by so doing, have confirmed the allegations against him.

In 1289 Edward, returning from France, heard such tales of judicial malpractice that he set up a special tribunal of investigation composed of men of his own Household. The result was the most spectacular purge the Bench has ever undergone. In the

King's Bench six out of eight judges were disgraced and retribution of one form or another overtook many scores of dishonest officials throughout the country. Outstanding among the fallen judges was Thomas of Weyland, Chief Justice of the Common Pleas. Arraigned on a charge of suborning murder and shielding the murderers, this one-time deacon of the Church escaped from custody and took refuge in a Franciscan priory at Bury St Edmunds, where he pleaded both sanctuary and benefit of clergy. By a special order of the King, little or no food reached him. Edward demanded to know of the Franciscans why they admitted rogues to their order; they did not ask him why he admitted rogues to the King's Bench. At length the Chief Justice surrendered and was shut in the Tower, where he was given the choice of being put on trial, imprisoned for life without trial, or exile. The last fate seemed the most agreeable. He was required to walk barefoot and penniless from prison to the beach at Dover, scene of William de Longchamp's embarrassment. Thence he embarked carrying a cross, leaving behind 100,000 marks to the King, enough to pay the salaries of honest judges for a very long time to come.

Fierce mulcts were imposed on the other judges. Solomon of Rochester, a justice in eyre, had to pay about 4,000 marks. Adam de Stratton, whose precise role in the Court of Exchequer is unclear, was said to have amassed greater wealth than the King; the loot in his house included a great stock of bullion and a royal crown. He was fined a reported 32,000 marks and imprisoned on charges of forgery, fraud and extortion. Even the much-respected Ralph de Hengham, Chief Justice of the King's Bench, fell from grace, thanks in part to his mistaken kindness in falsifying a court record in order to save a poor suitor the consequences of a heavy fine. Edward is supposed to have extracted from Hengham enough money to build a clock tower at New Palace Yard. In due course Hengham was restored to favour and made Chief Justice of the Common Pleas. It has been suggested that he would have been more lightly treated if he had not defended himself so vigorously; for if the judge was in the right the Sovereign must be in the wrong. One judge who dreaded the royal wrath, Henry de Bray, tried to drown himself on the way to the Tower and later succeeded in ending his life.

For the common man, it was an enjoyable purge, yet for many reigns to come judicial corruption flourished. It was one thing to pass Statutes of Westminster, it was quite another to enforce them. There could be no efficient central control of what went on in assize towns or anywhere else. Each community was a pool of peccancy on its own. The King's judges who came to deliver the gaols and to hold Commissions of Oyer and Terminer (hear and determine) no doubt inflicted condign punishment on those rogues who had not influence enough, or literacy enough, to beat the gallows, or the abhorred shears; but the biggest rogues who suborned, and connived, and condoned, and browbeat, and encroached, and filched and twisted the law to their own ends were less easily caught.

Late in his reign, Edward appointed a new type of itinerant judge, under an Ordinance of Trailbaston. The King's Highway was beset by discharged soldiers and ruffians of all kinds who trailed 'bastons' (large sticks) with which to belabour travellers. In suitable areas the judges of trailbaston held summary courts to deal with violent breaches of the peace. Under Edward's son violence did not noticeably diminish and even judges were at risk. An Exchequer judge was ambushed and murdered near Melton Mowbray by four well-born brothers, one of them a chaplain, and all of them outlaws. With some fifty followers, they continued to waylay travellers. Soon afterwards they seized another judge, accused of selling the law, and demanded a ransom of 1,300 marks. Probably Edward's unluckiest judge was Hugh Cressingham, an itinerant justice of the northern counties who was promoted to be Treasurer of Scotland. In this role he had to don armour to fight Wallace's rebels, who seized him at Cambuskenneth and flayed his fat body. Wallace is said to have helped himself to as much skin as would make a sword belt.

It would be fatiguing, as well as unfair, to list all the judges who were reputed to have 'sold the laws like cows' during the Plantagenet years. The year 1350 was memorable, however, as the year when the Chief Justice of the King's Bench was sentenced to death for corruption. Sir William de Thorpe was shown to have received bribes from suitors at Lincoln Assizes in order to delay proceedings. A Commission headed by three earls ordered him into the Tower and declared his possessions forfeit. This did not satisfy Edward III, who had already dismissed five judges for malpractice. He reminded the Commissioners of the rule that judges should take no rewards save their three robes a year from the King and, when travelling, accept only food and drink of little worth. The Chief Justice had sworn his oath accepting these terms on the cross of the Archbishop of Canterbury and the penalty for breaking that oath was death. Therefore, said the King, the Chief Justice must be condemned to die. The death sentence was accordingly passed. Having won his point, the King pardoned the offender, seized his lands, detained him in prison for a few months and then – for judges were rarely left permanently in disgrace – made him a baron of the Exchequer.

A chief justice had escaped the executioner, but another chief justice was to be less fortunate. The notorious Sir Robert Tresilian became Chief Justice of the King's Bench in 1381 in place of Sir John de Cavendish, whose head was carried on a pike through Bury St Edmunds in the course of the Peasants' Revolt. Wat Tyler's men had marauded in London, displaying especial enmity towards lawyers and judges, whom they regarded as the fount of injustice. In Essex, where the poll-tax commissioner had been beaten and stoned, the Chief Justice of the Common Pleas, Sir Robert Bealknap, attempted to open a Commission of Trailbaston to punish the offenders. The mob overcame his pikemen, forced him to kneel and swear never to hold another commission, and then beheaded his clerks along with various tax assessors and paraded their heads through the countryside. More fortunate than Cavendish, Bealknap fled back to London.

The peasants insisted that they had no quarrel with their young King, Richard II, whose courageous intervention had checked them in the capital. But Richard sat beside his new Chief Justice, Sir Robert Tresilian, when the ringleaders were tried by Special Commissions at Chelmsford and St Albans. Tresilian's procedure in the latter town was to force a reluctant jury of twelve to present the names of ringleaders according to a list drawn up in advance. A second jury of presentment was then empanelled to confirm the choice of the first, and a third jury was called on to confirm the choice of the second. It was a Bloody Assize of the kind later made famous by Lord Jeffreys. Estimates of the numbers hanged range from 150 to 1,500, but the lesser figure is the more probable. After a successful example had been made the young monarch declared an amnesty.

Tresilian lived only five more years to enjoy his unpopularity.

In 1386 he was involved in the attempt by Parliament to wrest control from the King and to rule by Commissioners. As a judge he held that his allegiance lay with the Sovereign, however weak and spendthrift. At the request of the King's favourites the Chief Justice called his fellow judges to Shrewsbury and Nottingham, then presented them with a questionnaire designed to show that the country's new Commissioners were in breach of the royal prerogative and guilty of treason. Either voluntarily, or under pressure, they signed. Sir Robert Bealknap had to be threatened severely by the Duke of Ireland and the Earl of Suffolk; as he gave in he said, 'Now here lacketh nothing but a rope that I may receive a reward worthy of my desert.' When the plot was discovered the royal favourites were themselves charged with treason and coercion of the justiciary. All the judges, save one who had been too ill to sign, were sent to the Tower, where they pleaded that they had been victims of *force majeure*. It seems unlikely there was any serious intention to hang, draw and quarter the entire Bench of England, but the life of Tresilian was demanded. By this time he was in hiding, but anxious to know what was afoot he went to London in disguise and lodged in an ale-house opposite the royal palace. Recognised by a squire of the Duke of Gloucester, he pretended to be a farmer trying to obtain redress for wrongs. When arrested he refused to speak. What then happened is not clear, except that the Chief Justice was put to death, either by beheading or hanging. Meanwhile, the Bench of Bishops had very civilly pleaded for the lives of the Bench of Judges, and so had the Queen. The offenders received sentence of banishment for life, mostly to various parts of Ireland. Bealknap was confined to an area of three miles circumference with its centre at Drogheda, and was given a modest annuity to support him. From this rustication he was delivered by a reversal of the judgment against the judges.

The King's justice, for all the frailty of those who administered it, was superior to the offhand hanging which disfigured the baronial courts. Increasingly the right to erect gallows was reserved to the King; those barons and abbots who still claimed the power to hang thieves caught red-handed were called to account for such irregularities as hanging men in the absence of the coroner. Another blow was struck at baronial pride by an enactment of Richard II in 1396. 'No man,' it said, 'shall sit upon the Bench of Assize. Item, the King doth will and forbid that no lord, nor other of the county, little or great, shall sit upon the Bench with the justices to take assizes.'* The independence of a judge was clearly compromised if overbearing nobles or local notabilities hedged him in and played to the gallery. Yet sheriffs and others were to be found sitting beside judges six hundred years later.

The royal judges could not be everywhere at once, but by now – thanks to Edward III – every county had its local magistrates, or justices of the peace. These were chosen from 'the most worthy men of the county, with some learned in the law'. Their function was primarily a peace-keeping one, but they had powers to bind over and punish offenders at sessions four times a year; hence 'quarter sessions'. As time passed their responsibilies multiplied, among these being control of alehouses, rounding up of vagrants and binding of apprentices. Part of the duty of the assize judges was to keep the justices of the peace on their mettle. It was from these worthy men that the grand jurors who presented criminals for trial at assizes were drawn.

When a judge was not being harried by king, barons or mob, how did he spend his day? Sir John Fortescue, Chief Justice of the King's Bench, gives a somewhat idealised picture in his *De Laudibus Legum Angliae,* compiled in 1468-71. The judge, it appears, sits in court for only three hours, from eight in the morning until eleven; then, after refreshing himself, he passes the rest of the day studying the nation's laws, reading the Holy Scriptures, indulging in innocent amusements and contemplating whatever is to be contemplated. It is a quiet life, free from all worry and worldly cares. 'Nor was it ever found,' said Fortescue, 'that any judge has been corrupted with gifts or bribes.' This may have been true of Fortescue's contemporaries, but the Chief Justice cannot have been ignorant of the murky history of the judicial Bench. There is a tales-told-to-the-children quality about this treatise and it was, in fact, compiled for the benefit of Edward, Prince of Wales, son of Henry VI. The idea was to help his character and acquaint him of the duties of a patriot monarch. 'A King of England,' warns Fortescue, 'cannot, at his pleasure, make any alteration in the laws of the land, for the nature of his government is not only regal, but political.' He must not burden his subjects against their wills with 'strange

Notes and Queries III.

impositions' (a statement cited in the ship money controversy of Stuart times). Fortescue sets out the terms of the judge's oath, which is administered by the Master of the Rolls, in the Lord Chancellor's presence. He is to do equal justice to all subjects, rich and poor, and is to be influenced by none. Even if he receives letters from the King, containing express directions or personal commands, he is to disregard them. He is to take no gifts from pleaders; the only hospitality he may accept is 'meat and drink, and that of little value'. On appointment he is not to 'make an entertainment', for his post is not a degree in law but only an office 'determinable on the King's good pleasure'.

Fortescue advances the interesting notion that the virtue of judges is reflected in the prosperity of their children. A greater number of leaders and magnates have sprung from the loins of judges than from any other estate of men. This is in accordance with the pronouncement of God's prophet who says, speaking of the just, 'Their children shall be blest.' Scarcely any judges die without issue, 'which is like a great and, as it were, an appropriate benediction of God'. Possibly these words found no great favour among childless judges.

The Chief Justice believed that 'the more you criticise the laws of England, the more they shine', which was to be the view of Sir William Blackstone in the eighteenth century. He compares them shudderingly with those of France, where torture was a licensed method of extracting information and men were 'examined in the King's chamber or other private place', forced to confess, stitched up in sacks and handed to the Provost-Marshal for drowning.*

He could have mentioned that in 1442 Juliana Quick, charged before an English court with high treason in speaking contemptuously of the King, suffered *peine forte et dure,* or pressing to death, which was the penalty under English law for those who stood mute and refused to plead.

---

*A. Amos (ed.) *De Laudibus Legum Angliae* (125).

3

TOOLS OF THE KING

The judges believed that the laws of England were rooted in Christianity. It was a proposition on which they did not begin to voice doubts until late in the nineteenth century. The Christian God had ordained kings to have dominion over their subjects, who were required to love, fear and obey them; and the judges were there to deal with those subjects who failed to do so. If the King whom God had ordained went intermittently off his head and a would-be usurper was encamped in his palace, what then? This was the situation in 1460, at the height of the Wars of the Roses, and the judges, to their alarm and embarrassment, were invited to express the view that the Duke of York, who had seized effective power, was fit and proper to be an anointed King, in place of the sad Henry VI. Prudently, they informed the Lords that this was a matter above the law and beyond their learning, 'wherefore they durst not enter into any communication thereof . . . for it pertained to the Lords of the King's blood . . .' In brief, they begged to be 'utterly excused' of giving an opinion. They then bent their heads and waited for the Wars of the Roses to subside.

In 1485 God's new vice-regent in this kingdom picked up his crown from a bramble bush on Bosworth Field and became Henry VII. Slowly, craftily, he began to build up the central power in his ravaged realm: a realm scourged not only by rapacious and oppressive magnates but by hordes of criminals who sheltered under the dingy skirts of the Church, escaping retribution by pointing to their tonsures. Henry inherited a legal system which, while boasting a reasonable integrity, was incapable of dealing with all the new abuses of the times. To

meet this need the King's Council, or Privy Council, hived off
yet another court, to be known as the Court of Star Chamber.
Primarily it was aimed at aggressors: those great lords who
went about with armed retainers, maintained law-breakers and
seized lands by force. Secondly, it was directed at those who
preferred cheating to bullying; for example, those who engaged
in manipulations of the grain market, cornering of goods and
various forms of profiteering which are now normal commercial
practice; those who were guilty of cozenage, 'an offence whereby
anything is done guiltily in or out of contracts, which cannot
fitly be termed by any other name'; and those who spread false
reports of wars overseas and pretended that the seas were im-
passable, in order to force down the price of woollen goods.
The Court undertook to settle what should happen 'if an enemy
take a ship from an Englishman and another Englishman taketh
it from him again'; and it was prepared to hear actions by a
foreign merchant who had been robbed at sea by Englishmen,
always provided that his country was in amity with the King.
The Court was concerned also with 'routs and riots', a rout consisting of three or more persons setting out forcibly to commit
an unlawful act. It had power to punish justices of the peace
who took inadequate steps to arrest rioters; and it was ready
to impose additional fines on those already fined in lower courts.
Other insolences under the Court's jurisdiction were libels,
especially against the King and his friends, peers, archbishops,
bishops and judges; the practice of going overseas without permission; abducting a girl under sixteen; brawling by persons of
position; trickery by quacks; and any excess of adminstrative enthusiasm, as when the Masters of Bridewell were fined 'a large
summe' for whipping a pregnant woman who, as a result, 'fell
to travail before her time'.*

The Court of Star Chamber has been called a criminal court
of equity; 'in theory it supplemented the shortcomings of the
common law in criminal matters, just as the Court of Chancery
was supposed to supplement or control it in civil proceedings'.†
Since it wielded the King's prerogative, since it was directed at
powerful law-breakers, it had to be powerfully manned. The two
chief justices sat there, to ensure a measure of traditional legal
form; but they were strengthened, and often overborne, by

*William Crompton: *Star Chamber Cases* (1630).
†Arthur Underhill in *Shakespeare's England*.

B

members of the Privy Council in varying numbers – peers, bishops, and officers of the Household. The Court met in a room with a star-spangled ceiling in the Palace of Westminster and in full session it made an imposing, not to say intimidating, sight.

Under Wolsey as Chancellor the new Court humbled many a powerful oppressor, at the same time swelling the revenue with some tremendous fines. It even succeeded on occasions in the rare feat – for those days – of oppressing the rich at the instance of the poor. The cases which came before it required no subtle knowledge of the law and the members of the court were at liberty to devise their own penalties. If John Skelton is to be believed, in *Why Come Ye Not To Court,* Wolsey tyrannised over the proceedings:

> He is set so hye
> In his ierarchy
> Of frantic frenesy
> And folyshe fantasy,
> That in the Chambre of Starres
> All maters there he marres;
> Clappyng his rod on the borde,
> No man dare speke a worde,
> For he hath all the sayenge,
> Without any renayenge . . .

Unfortunately the Court which had been set up to fight tyranny and outrageous behaviour in high places became increasingly an instrument of oppression. It began by cuffing the ears of barons and was to end, as we shall see, by hacking off the ears of pamphleteers.

One power which the new court lacked was that of putting offenders to death. When the traditional processes were not suitable, Henry VIII resorted to a device which eliminated the judiciary altogether, along with any element of justice; he persuaded Parliament to pass a bill of attainder, which progressed quietly through both Houses, without any tiresome disclosures, and the victim went to the block unheard. If publicity was desired, then the offender underwent a spectacular state trial. Nobody doubted what the result would be, for if the King wanted someone out of the way it was virtually treason to impugn his witnesses. On these occasions Westminster Hall was taken over and turned into one huge amphitheatre. The

Commissioners, composed of leading nobles, Privy Councillors and Household officers, sat in the seats of honour and the judges were distributed below them, at their feet, as if to emphasise their subservience. The lesser judges took a completely passive part in the proceedings and the Chief Justices and the Chief Baron knew that this was no time for splitting legal hairs. In supreme authority was the Lord Chancellor, in the guise of Lord High Steward of England, with a white wand of office. Dwarfed by this dazzling and powerful assembly, the prisoner on his platform defended himself as best he might, without counsel, without any assistance whatever. When found guilty he could expect to hear a homily from the Chief Justice of the King's Bench on the wickedness of attempting the overthrow of a most sacred and anointed king, the very nonpareil and jewel of princes. To a prisoner of high birth such homilies from a common lawyer must have seemed insupportable; but the chances were that the sentence of hanging, drawing and quartering would come from the Lord High Steward himself. At the close, that dignitary broke his white wand, the lords and ladies departed and Westminster Hall was restored to its ordinary wranglings.

The Lord Chancellor's post had become one of great power and prestige, as also of peril, but the law was not yet his principal concern. It was still an appointment for a cleric. In the Court of Chancery, as keeper of the King's conscience, Wolsey was alert to redress grievances against the common law and to determine issues never envisaged by that law. John Skelton would have us believe that the Cardinal ran the Court of Chancery as he ran the Court of Star Chamber :

> In the Chauncery where he syttes,
> But suche as he admyttes,
> None so hardy to speake;
> He sayth, Thou huddypeke,*
> Thy lernynge is too lewde,
> Thy tonge is not well thewde
> To seke before our grace;
> And openly in that place
> He rages and he raves,
> And calls them cankerd knaves.†

*Blockhead.
†A. Dyce (ed.): *Poetical Works of John Skelton* (1828).

The operation on which Wolsey was engaged, though no one would gather it from the foregoing, was nothing less than the marrying of all the laws of God, man and Nature with the wishes of the Sovereign; and the result was called equity. In attempting this extravagant task the Chancellor had no sympathy from the common lawyers, to whom equity was all too loose and subjective a concept. An aphorism by the disreputable Mr Justice Manwood, of a later reign, gives an indication of how lawyers regarded the system of courts : 'In the Common Pleas there is all law and no conscience; in the Queen's Bench both law and conscience; in the Chancery all conscience and no law; and in the Exchequer neither law nor conscience.'* The grievances of a new world emerging flowed ever faster into Chancery. Wolsey, having encouraged suits, found he had no time to handle them and a formidable backlog awaited his successor, Sir Thomas More. By then some of the causes were in their third decade. More, who was wary of accepting gifts, promised to do justice on the principle that if his father stood on one side and the Devil on the other, the Devil, if he could show a better cause, should have the decision.

To be keeper of the conscience of Henry VIII was no task for the fastidious; whoever kept it had no room for a conscience of his own. The religious schisms following the breach with Rome, the question of the supremacy, the King's perennial marital problems – these were matters on which no Lord Chancellor could take other than his master's view. Sir Thomas More failed to make the necessary accommodation and went to the block. 'Loyalty was honoured and rewarded,' says Froude; 'the traitor, though his crime was consecrated by the most devoted sense of duty, was dismissed without a pang of compunction to carry his appeal to another tribunal.'† For those who could adjust, there were rewards in plenty. Thomas Audley, later Baron Audley, who took the Great Seal after More's execution and held it through, as Foss says, twelve disgraceful years of royal divorces, executions of two queens and 'innumerable judicial and remorseless murders', enjoyed rich plunder in the shape of monastic lands. Audley is said to have admitted that he was glad not to have been highly educated, since too much learning brought moral scruples. Whether the job called for

*D.N.B.

†J. A. Froude: *A History of England.*

helping a colleague and friend to the block, exterminating a few friars or pressing a Queen for the names of her lovers, Audley could be depended upon, in sickness and in health.

One of the darker duties of the Lord Chancellor was to transmit orders to rack suspects. Chief Justice Fortescue had given thanks that English law did not recognise torture, which was specifically banned by Magna Carta, but under the Tudors it was held to be justified by such 'extraordinary considerations' as the need to discover evidence in plots against the throne. 'Exorbitant offences' were adjudged as being beyond the jurisdiction of common law. A law officer, not necessarily a judge, was required to be present at the examination. Rumour, possibly malicious, says that Lord Chancellor Wriothesley helped to operate the rack on Anne Askew, with the assistance of Sir Richard Rich, himself destined to be a Lord Chancellor. After being stretched she is supposed to have sat on the floor of the torture chamber for two hours arguing with the Lord Chancellor whether bread could turn into Christ's flesh; hence, if Wriothesley and Rich did turn the screws, they probably did not turn them far. After being tried at Guildhall, Anne was burned at the stake, the loyal Lord Mayor giving the order to light the pyre and crying 'Fiat justitia'.

The Chief Justices, also, were drawn into the King's marital affairs. Sir Edward Montagu, in particular, was set some nasty conundrums. Was the King's marriage to Anne of Cleves valid if he had entertained misgivings at the time? Would the law infer that Catherine Howard had committed adultery, from the facts which in the case of a common person would afford no such inference? The answers were not to be discovered in Bracton, but it was obvious what the answers must be. Sir Edward Montagu found it all something of a strain and asked to be demoted to the Common Pleas. However, he picked up some abbey lands on the way.

Froude describes as 'abominable nonsense' the much-quoted statement that 72,000 persons were hanged during Henry VIII's reign, 10,000 of them at Tyburn. He traces the report back to a dubious enough authority. 'Judges and magistrates,' he says, 'could not easily send a poacher or a vagrant to the gallows while a notorious murderer was lounging in comfort in a neighbouring sanctuary, or having just read a sentence from a book at the bar in arrest of judgment had been handed over to an apparitor of the nearest archdeacon's court and been set at liberty for a few shillings.' Injustice arising from sanctuary and benefit of clergy cried to the skies. The test of whether a man qualified for such benefit was one of literacy, since literacy could normally be obtained only by serving the Church; so, if he could read, or pretend to read, the first verse of the Fifty-First Psalm, known as the 'neck verse' since it saved innumerable necks, he was handed over to the Church, which either let him escape or freed him if he could raise a panel of persons to attest his good character. However, an Act of Henry VII said that a felon could plead benefit of clergy only once, so the courts took to branding an offender on the hand with a suitable letter. The irons were kept in court, for use with a brazier, and the judge's marshal was required to report, 'Good mark, my Lord.' Some country justices were said to regard a burn as unsatisfactory unless it made a hole through the hand, but as time passed the judges connived at the use of a cold iron. Benefit of clergy was as cynical a feature of jurisprudence as could be conceived in a thousand years. The lives it saved were often of less value than the lives of those who did not know their alphabets and – in the absence of a clement judge – were hanged.

The judges who rode on circuit often held court in an atmosphere of intimidation, both from violent nobles who hoped, in spite of the Star Chamber, to overawe the court and save their dependents, and from gangs of criminals and ruffians. The sessions at Bridgwater and Taunton were forcibly broken up in 1535 by such gangs, which were rapidly extending their influence in the West Country. Eventually a dozen culprits were caught and hanged. But colonies of felons still held out on church premises, living at the expense of the neighbouring countryside. In conditions like these the judges got on with an unenviable task as best they could, commending the Sovereign's virtues to the grand jury, making known his commands, rejecting over-generous gifts and, if they were wise, concealing their religious inclinations. From excess of zeal a man might find himself sitting on a heresy-hunting commission, or helping to sift immigrant anabaptists, or performing some other task which might bring him enemies when the climate changed. Happily for them, the assize judges were not called upon to order the burning of heretics, who were handed over direct to the sheriffs by the bishops' courts (in 1540 a boy of fifteen was burned in

London by direction of Bishop Bonner). A Lord Chancellor might have to sign warrants for burning his fellow men, but that was the penalty for rising to the top.

Under the boy King, Edward VI, the Star Chamber netted a fat legal fish in the person of the Master of the Rolls, Sir John Beaumont, who was accused of champerty. He made a bargain with a suitor in his court, Lady Anne Powis, who was trying to recover lands from the Duke of Suffolk, that she would sell the title to himself, if the suit succeeded. To assist this arrangement he forged the Duke's signature on a deed. He was also accused of appropriating more than £20,000 from the court of wards. At this time the Judge had been in office for little more than a year. Under pressure he denied, confessed, retracted and confessed again. In the end most of his property went to the King. He might well have met a harsher fate under Henry VIII who – save where his own affairs were concerned – believed in immaculate justice.

Two of Edward VI's judges were unlucky enough to become co-opted in the plot to break the Tudor line and put Lady Jane Grey on the throne. They were Sir Edward Montagu, then Chief Justice of the Common Pleas, and Sir Thomas Bromley, of the same court, both of whom were members of the King's council of regency. The Duke of Northumberland, pleading that the country would be in peril under a Roman Catholic queen, sought the judges' aid in preparing a legal instrument to bar Mary from the succession. Both said that such an act would be a breach of the statutes and constitute high treason. Northumberland, in a great rage, stormed at them, offering to fight anybody in his shirt, and the young King ordered them to 'dispatch the matter'. On the promise of a pardon if anything went wrong, the judges gave in. Bromley contrived not to witness the document, but Montagu, less devious perhaps, signed. When Mary acceded, and the Reformation went into reverse, Montagu was in instant disgrace; he was sent to the Tower, fined £1,000 and suffered some forfeitures, while his crafty colleague was made Chief Justice in his place.

Less fortunate than Montagu was Mr Justice Hales, who had been a member of the court which deprived Gardiner of his bishopric. At Kent Assizes, just after Mary's accession, he informed the grand jury that the laws against nonconformists stayed in force and were not to be relaxed in favour of Roman

Catholics. The Queen renewed his patent as judge of the Common Pleas, but when he reported to Westminster Hall to swear his oath, Gardiner, now Lord Chancellor, declined to administer it, saying, 'Ye stand not well in Her Grace's favour.' Hales pleaded that conscience would not allow him to make the necessary 'purgation', which brought the taunt that he preferred his own religion to that of the Queen. 'Seeing you be at this point, Master Hales,' said the Lord Chancellor, 'I will presently make an end of you. The Queen's Highness shall be informed of your opinion and declaration . . . Until such time ye may depart as ye came, without your oath; for as it appeareth ye are scarce worthy the place appointed.'* The Judge was then bandied from one London prison to another. In the Fleet the Warden put him in fear of the torments which awaited heretics; and a visit from the Bishop of Chichester and a fellow judge, Mr Justice Portman, did nothing to relieve his anxieties. Half-converted, he made an unsuccessful attempt to kill himself with a penknife. He was allowed to go to his home, whence, in an un-balanced state, he went out and drowned himself in a shallow stream near Canterbury. Mr Justice Portman, who was 'of the old way of thinking' in religious matters, became a chief justice the same year.

Sir Thomas Bromley, though he escaped the Queen's wrath for his share in the Northumberland plot, nevertheless earned it for his conduct, as Lord Chief Justice of the King's Bench, at the trial of Sir Nicholas Throckmorton, accused of high treason. Normally the mere accusation was enough to guarantee a con-viction, but the Guildhall jury, showing astonishing temerity, returned a verdict of not guilty. In the prosecution view Bromley had given the accused man too much latitude in his defence; and during the inexpert summing up Throckmorton had prompted the Judge 'as if he had been a disinterested spectator'. The jury's verdict stung Bromley to anger. 'Remember yourselves better,' he said to the foreman, 'have you considered substantially the whole evidence in sort as it was declared and recited? The matter doth touch the Queen's Highness, and yourselves also. Take good care what you do.' In the face of this threat the foreman, whose name was Whetston, replied, 'We have found him not guilty, agree-able to all our consciences.' When the Judge had acquitted Throckmorton and ordered his committal on other charges, the

*State Trials.

Attorney-General asked that the jury 'which have strangely acquitted the prisoner of his treasons, whereof he was indicted,' be bound in a recognisance of £500 each 'to answer to such matters as they shall be charged with in the Queen's behalf'. Whetston said, 'Let us not be molested for discharging our consciences truly. We be poor merchant men.' The court sent all the jurors to prison. Eight of them were brought before the Star Chamber and the other four apologised for doing their duty.* Heavy fines were also imposed but were not exacted in full. It was a reminder that, although the law could prevent the intimidation of juries by barons, it could not prevent their intimidation by the Crown. Judges are expected to make no comment on what they regard as perverse verdicts, but every age furnishes its own examples to the contrary.

The judges lay low while the bishops ordered their bonfires of martyrs. The church courts, reactivated by Gardiner, were given arbitrary powers to root out heresy; and special commissions were set up to try the more influential offenders. The first court of the persecution sat in St Mary Overy's Church, Southwark, under six bishops, and claimed Hooper and Rogers for its victims. In St Mary's Church, Oxford, Town and Gown dutifully attended the episcopal denunciations of Cranmer, Ridley and Latimer. The bishops had their own prisons, where their victims were starved or had their limbs macerated; which was a privilege the judges had never enjoyed. Never had the sheriffs seen such a busy reign. From the judges they accepted the normal quota of miscreants for hanging; from the bishops they accepted a superior class of persons for burning and exploding (gunpowder was inserted in the pyres to shorten suffering, though it did not always do so). At intervals the fanatical Queen urged her bishops to greater efforts against those with 'naughty opinions'. It was to be noticed that those who died for denying transubstantiation tended to be more and more the poor and friendless. Armed with their own excellent reasons for non-intervention, Parliament, Town, Gown, Bench and the military tried not to retch at the smell of roasting flesh; and tens of thousands of ordinary people got up early to watch the murder of twos and threes.

Under Elizabeth the Reformation recovered its course and the late persecutors were persecuted. It was a sign of loyalty to

*State Trials.

hunt down popish recusants, who were treated as revenue-fodder. One judge on gaol delivery found four hundred recusants waiting for him at Hampshire Assizes, another was greeted by six hundred in Lancashire.* For the more efficient persecution of Roman Catholics – and, increasingly, of Puritans – the church courts were strengthened and the High Commission, founded originally to defend the doctrines of the Reformation, developed the functions of a court. Elizabeth was a Tudor and did not shrink from using the rack. In 1571, authorising the torture of two of the Duke of Norfolk's servants, she wrote, 'We warrant you to cause them both, or either of them, to be brought to the rack . . . and to find the taste thereof . . .' One of her loyal servants was Richard Topcliffe, gentleman of Lincolnshire and Member of Parliament, a freelance torturer who claimed to have helped more traitors to Tyburn than all the nobles of the Court. He was in the pay of Sir William Cecil (Lord Burghley), who authorised him to have a private rack 'to torment priests in his house in such manner as he shall think good'.† As a volunteer Topcliffe spared the Government the embarrassment of dirtying its own hands. In principle the Queen was against the lighting of religious bonfires, but scheming Jesuits had to be put down and the usual means adopted was to charge them with treason. The trial of Edmund Campion shows Elizabethan justice at its most dubious. On the instigation of the Church, Campion had been racked three times in an effort to make him recant. He had taken part in public disputations with Protestant divines, who had been unable to undermine his convictions. Somehow this dangerous missionary had to be removed. The best way to do so, in the eyes of the Privy Council, was to convict him of having tried to engineer the death of the Queen. When asked to plead he could not raise his arm without assistance. Lord Chief Justice Wray, who had presided over many State trials, sentenced the priest to be hanged, drawn and quartered. The Judge must have known that he was an instrument in a judicial murder, but in matters which involved – or could be shown to involve – the safety of the Tudors normal standards of justice and morality did not apply.

Three years after Campion's death Lord Chief Justice Wray passed a like sentence on Dr William Parry, lawyer and Member

*Lingard: *History of England.*
†Hugh Ross Williamson: *The Gunpowder Plot.*

of Parliament, for seeking 'the destruction of a most sacred and an anointed Queen, thy Sovereign and mistress, who hath shewed thee such favour as some, thy betters, have not obtained'. But it was obvious who should really have been in the dock. Wray continued :

'The Pope pretendeth that he is a pastor when as in truth he is far from feeding the flock of Christ, but rather as a wolf seeketh but to feed on and to suck out the blood of true Christians and as it were thirsteth for the blood of our most gracious and Christian Queen.'*

The sentence in full on traitors at this period was: 'Thou shalt be had from hence to the place whence thou didst come, and so drawn through the open city of London upon an hurdle to the place of execution, and there to be hanged and let down alive, and thy privy members cut off and thy entrails taken out and burned in thy sight; then thy head to be cut off and thy body to be divided into four parts and to be disposed of at Her Majesty's pleasure; and God have mercy on thy soul.'†

Judges did not lightly defy Queen Elizabeth, but Mr Justice Monson did so and was gaoled for his pains. The Puritan John Stubbs had been sentenced to mutilation for a pamphlet deprecating a report that the Queen was to marry the Duke of Anjou and suggesting, among other things, that she was too old to bear children. His conviction was secured under an Act passed in the previous reign to prevent libels on Queen Mary's husband. Many thought the Act was being unreasonably stretched and Robert Monson said so. Although detained in prison for only a few months, he never returned to the Bench.

The Queen was reluctant to confer knighthoods on judges. They were a mixed lot. Not all of them came from 'good' families and some had sown the wildest of oats in youth. Mr Justice Manwood was the son of a Sandwich draper yet he was one of those who sat in judgment on Mary Queen of Scots; he twice failed, however, to buy a chief justiceship. Lord Chief Justice Popham, who lived to send royal favourites to their death, was said to have been an associate of highwaymen in his youth and even to have dabbled in the game himself; he grew to be a great foe of the fraternity, as also of bawds, whom he threatened to drive from Southwark to the sound of trumpets.

*State Trials.
†Ibid.

The law was a profession in which talent mattered very much more than birth; the Inns of Court taught such civilised graces as were necessary. For judges who did not aspire too high, and who got through the work without delay and demur, there might be such practical rewards as a grant from the royal kitchen of a buck in summer and a doe in winter, which was the privilege of Mr Justice Flowerdew. For others, virtue was its own reward. Mr Justice Dyer became unpopular with the gentry on the Midland Circuit, where his impartial justice was not appreciated. One of his detractors eventually found himself in trouble in the Star Chamber.

In London the Queen's justice was open to everyone in Westminster Hall, where it was administered on the fringes of a sea of hubbub. Occasionally the hubbub was increased by the ancient practice, gratefully borrowed by the Star Chamber, of parading convicted persons, or even refractory lawyers, round the courts with labels on their persons attesting their offences. Nor was it unknown for such offenders to be mounted back to front on an unsaddled horse. The courts – King's Bench, Common Pleas, Exchequer and Exchequer Chamber* – were unenclosed except by low partitions. In the central area jostled clerks, cryers, attorneys, prisoners in custody, students, vendors of legal requisites, servants and sightseers. In one corner a man might be sentenced to death while in another parties squabbled over a right of way. This was how it had been under the Plantagenets and this was how it would be under the Hanoverians. The Common Pleas, being near the main entrance, was unusually draughty and noisy; a well-meant effort, in the next century, to have it moved into a quieter adjacent room was blocked by Chief Justice Bridgeman, on the grounds that Magna Carta required the court to sit in *certo loco,* and that to move it an inch from this place would invalidate its jurisdiction. In the vicinity of Westminster Hall, and also in the area of the Temple, lurked professional false witnesses, or men of straw, so called from the straw tucked into a boot which was the sign of their trade. It can hardly have been a regular occupation, unless all the judges were exceptionally short-sighted.

---

*A court in which all the judges sat to decide questions of law and to correct errors.

4

TWELVE ON THEIR KNEES

The judges had faced humiliations enough under the Tudors, but the first of the Stuarts was not happy until he had all twelve judges of England grovelling on their knees, craving forgiveness for defying him. Among them was the Lord Chief Justice, who attempted some justification but was rebuked for sophistry.

For the judiciary it was the most degrading hour in the long-drawn constitutional battle which was to end in regicide. The judges were bruised and bloodied at almost every twist of the plot. Their most combative member, Sir Edward Coke, was ahead of many Members of Parliament in realising the perils to the nation's liberties from the loose and intemperate use of the royal prerogative. Disgrace overtook him, if being dismissed by James I counts as disgrace; but black ignominy overwhelmed his principal opponent, Francis Bacon, who had taken more trouble to defend the King's honour than he had to guard his own.

Coke had made his name as a priest-hounding attorney-general under the ageing Elizabeth. The post was one which Bacon had wanted desperately, but the Queen, distrusting him, would not even make him solicitor-general. To Coke fell the task of prosecuting the Queen's one-time favourite, the Earl of Essex. Under James he led the attack on Sir Walter Raleigh ('Thou art a monster! Thou hast an English face but a Spanish heart!'); and he prosecuted the Gunpowder Plot conspirators. Faithfully he served the ends of both sovereigns in their prerogative court, the Star Chamber. The turning-point of his life was his appointment in 1606 as Chief Justice of the Common Pleas. From then on he battled to prevent the laws from being over-ridden by the King to whom he had sworn his oath. Elizabeth had often exceeded her powers in the judicial field, as by issuing proclamations and signing torture warrants, but she had never hanged a thief out of hand, as did James on his journey south to claim the throne. James had lost little time in giving other signs of his conviction that *Rex* was *lex*. Exactly when Coke first became seized of the danger is not clear. He was bellicose and unpredictable, always keen for a jurisdictional squabble, but under his turbulent qualities lay a reverence for the common law which could lead him even to justify the symbolic indecencies involved in hanging, drawing and quartering. At all events, as soon as he took his seat in the Common Pleas, he began to express views about the royal power which, if he had been a Puritan pamphleteer, would have cost him his ears. The Lord Chancellor, Lord Elles-mere, did not disguise his view that Coke's pronouncements verged on treason. Nor did the King. Bacon, who at last had the royal favour, advanced a more welcome concept, which he expressed in his essay *Of Judicature:* 'Let judges . . . remember that Solomon's throne was supported by lions on both sides; let them be lions, but yet lions under the throne; being circumspect that they do not check or oppose any points of sovereignty.' Policy and law, he wrote, were like spirits and sinews, each moving with the other.

The King's view, all too frequently made known, was that as God's vice-regent his prerogative must prevail and that to oppose it showed impiety and high contempt. Boldly Coke argued that the common law was a higher force than the prerogative. This was the essence of the dispute, though Coke kept enlarging the battlefield. Like an earlier monarch, John, James took pleasure in sitting in his courts and fancied his abilities as a judge. Coke contended that he should not sit even in his prerogative courts. When the King argued that the law was founded on reason and that 'I and others surely have reason too,' Coke read him a curtain lecture. 'True it is, please your Majesty, that God has endowed your Majesty with excellent science as well as great gifts of Nature; but your Majesty will allow me to say with all reverence that you are not learned in the laws of this your realm of England, and I crave leave to remind your Majesty that causes which concern the life or inheritance, or goods or fortune, of your subjects are not to be decided by natural reason but by the artificial reason and judgment of the law; which law is an art which requires long study and experience before that a man can attain to the cognisance of it.' By now in a great rage, the King said, 'Then I am to be under the law, which it is treason to affirm.' Coke took refuge in Bracton, who wrote that the King 'ought not to be under man but under God and the laws'.

Apart from one or two notorious appearances in the Star Chamber, James made no serious efforts to sit in judgment. That his qualifications were no better than those of the layman is suggested by his confession : 'I could get on very well hearing one side only, but when both sides have been heard, by my soul I know not which is right.'

Coke was quick to challenge the jurisdiction and pretensions of the church courts. Bishops, he thought, had no more right to give judgments than had kings. He also joined sporadic battle with the Court of Chancery, denying its right to interfere with common law judgments. This, too, was a prerogative court with no fixed rules, values or precedents; in practice the King's conscience, which it sought to exercise, was the King's prerogative.

Thanks to Bacon's scheming, Coke was promoted to the chief justiceship of the King's Bench, in which role it was thought he would be 'more obsequious'. It was a bad miscalculation. For Coke, one of the first challenges in his new role arose from the case of the Puritan clergyman, Edmond Peacham. Foolish writings had been found in Peacham's possession, suggesting to the suggestible that some sort of attempt on the King was contemplated. When James ordered that he be tortured in order to discover the names of other conspirators, Bacon, by now Attorney-General, agreed that 'in the highest cases of treason' the rack was permissible, 'for discovery and not for evidence'. Despite his reverence for the common law, Coke seems to have raised no objection. Peacham, an elderly man, was questioned 'before torture, in torture, between tortures and after torture,' Bacon being present throughout. As it became clear that Peacham would not talk, the King instructed Bacon to approach the judges individually to ask them whether, in their view, a charge of treason could be sustained. This was the sort of mischief-making errand Bacon enjoyed. He can scarcely have been surprised, though he may have been secretly pleased, when Coke refused to co-operate, holding that the 'particular and auricular taking of opinion' in this manner was without precedent and dangerous. His brethren, he said, would adopt the same attitude. Unfortunately for Coke, they did not. Mr Justice Doddridge was reported by Bacon as 'very ready to give opinion in secret, every judge being bound expressly by his oath to counsel His Majesty when called'. The other King's Bench judges replied similarly. In view of the terms of the oath Coke was in a weak position. The serpentine Bacon kept calling on him, full of courtier-like graces and devious arguments, then carrying a poisoned report back to the King. Finally he had to return with the message that, in Coke's view, Peacham was not guilty of treason. The King took this badly. Peacham was put on trial, convicted and sentenced to death, but saved a great deal of trouble by dying in gaol.

The scene in which the twelve judges fell to their knees occurred in the course of a dispute originating from the Court of Exchequer, where a temerarious serjeant had disputed the Crown's right to grant certain church preferments. In some anger the King asked for the proceedings to be stayed until he reached London. Coke refused to give any such order. As Attorney-General Bacon wrote to all the judges commanding them in the King's name to desist from further proceedings. Instead they continued with the hearing, after sending the King a letter drafted by Coke explaining that, under their oath, they were bound to disregard 'any letters' which came to them contrary to law. It was too much for James, who said he did not need to be taught the terms of the oath. The prerogative was being 'boldly dealt with' in Westminster Hall and he would no longer endure judicial meddling with it. When the judges had been called to the Privy Council in Whitehall he tore up their letter in front of them, putting on a show of divine wrath. The Lord Chancellor, Lord Ellesmere, ruled that to delay the Exchequer proceedings would have involved no breach of the oath. Asked point-blank whether they now conceded the principle, all the judges except Coke said that they did. Grudgingly Coke observed that when the situation arose he would do whatever was fit for a judge to do. It has been denied that he fell to his knees with the others, but in the circumstances he could scarcely have failed to make some sort of obeisance. The scene would have made a fascinating subject for a Court painter. Peers and bishops looked on without pity, for the pretensions of lawyers were often insufferable; and Bacon was there to gloat.

James was still not content with his revenge. Shortly afterwards he took his seat in the Star Chamber, put on his crown and reminded the legal profession at large of his divine powers. If pleaders became too bold in their ways and the judges permitted it, then he would have to punish both parties. Judges were not to stray from their own benches, invading other jurisdictions. He then specifically warned that there must be no more attempts to limit the powers of the Court of Chancery.

On the last issue, James had his way. John Chamberlain, that industrious letter-writer, thought that Coke's attempt to curb Chancery had done more harm than good, merely helping to confirm its 'exorbitant authority'. As a result 'suits become, as it were, immortal'. It was some indication of the public's dissatisfaction with Chancery that, about this time, an elderly suitor pulled out a pistol and shot a Master of Chancery in Lincoln's Inn, then tried to stab himself.

Meanwhile Bacon, with his eyes on the Lord Chancellorship, was still striving for the removal of the tiresome Coke. Various charges were trumped up against the Lord Chief Justice, but the only one worth answering was that he had shown 'indecent behaviour' towards the King. Coke was suspended from the Privy Council, ordered to stop riding circuit and insultingly told to go away and correct his Reports, which were said to be full of errors. As a parting shot Lord Suffolk complained that Coke had been allowing his coachman to drive bareheaded and asked him to do something about it. Shortly afterwards he was deprived of his chief justiceship. In the following year the triumphant Bacon was handed the Great Seal and rode to Westminster with two hundred horse, entertaining the company afterwards at a cost of £700.

The King had never seriously supposed Coke to be corrupt, nor had anyone else; but his aggressive behaviour, his constant spoiling for a fight, cost him some sympathy. There were times when he seemed ready to substitute a tyranny of judges for a tyranny of kings, or, as Bacon feared, to allow the Bench to become a third party of quarrelsome theorists infesting the paths of government. The Book of Common Law was not, after all, Holy Writ. It was a hodge-podge of judge-made freedoms and injustices. As yet there was no Parliament fit to undertake the task of safeguarding the nation's liberties. However, it was in that Parliament that Coke now continued the fight; and it was for his activities there that he was consigned to the Tower for eight months on a hopeless charge of treason, being freed in 1622.

Parliament had already expressed its displeasure at the King's attempts to rule by proclamation and to prescribe and award punishments. Now it became gripped by the idea that it was a court before which offenders might be hauled, notably false prophets and the like. Members showed that when it came to devising butcher-like penalties they were nowhere behind the peers, bishops and judges in the Star Chamber. In 1621, as if declaring war on wickedness, the Commons seized Edward Floyd, a recusant barrister, who had supposedly libelled the Princess Palatine. They imposed on him a fine of £1,000, ordered him to stand in three pillories and to be carried from place to place on an unsaddled horse sitting back to front and holding the tail in his hand. Reasonably enough, the King sent to inquire on what grounds the Commons had assumed a judicial function and which of their privileges was involved. Eventually the Commons handed their capture to the Lords, who instead of setting an example of magnanimity imposed far more grotesque penalties. Floyd was to be debarred from holding arms as a gentleman and was for ever to be held an infamous person, incapable of giving evidence in court. He was to be carried on a horse, in the manner prescribed by the Commons, around the pillories, in the course of which he was to be branded with a K (for knave) on his forehead and to be whipped at a cart's tail from the Fleet to Westminster. He was also to be fined £5,000 and imprisoned in Newgate for life. Much of the sentence was carried out. When being branded Floyd said he would give £1,000 to be hanged for murder in such a good cause.*

Such was the punishment for a libeller. For blasphemy, as we shall see, the Commons reserved additional torments.

Bacon's fall into dishonour belies the theory of Lord

State Trials.

Chancellor Audley that learning brings moral scruples. If the lives of great men remind us of anything, it is that genius and integrity do not necessarily coexist. To some extent Bacon was the victim of faction and envy. It can be argued that in accepting gifts he was only doing what others had done, and were doing; that he did not allow his judgment to be influenced; that he was ill and overworked and omitted to check whether gifts were from suitors or not; and that he was only trying to keep up the outward dignity of his position. But this was the man who, on attaining the law's highest office, had urged the judges, insultingly as it would now seem, to take care that 'your hands, and the hands of your hands (I mean those about you) be clean and uncorrupt from gifts; from meddling in titles, and from serving of turns, be they of great ones or small ones'. Never was there a more cynical exponent of 'Do as I say, don't do as I do.' And never did a high-minded philosopher behave more abjectly when his errors were unmasked.

It was in 1621 that Sir Robert Phelips informed Parliament that he wished to give some account of abuses in the courts of justice by Francis Lord Verulam, Viscount St Albans, Lord Chancellor of England, a man so blessed by Nature and art 'that I will say no more of him, being not able to say enough'. Soon the accusations and petitions against the Lord Chancellor began to multiply. The keeper of the King's conscience did not, at first, seem to be having trouble with his own conscience. John Chamberlain wondered whether he was dissembling or whether he just did not feel the disgrace that was overtaking him. To the Duke of Buckingham, who was responsible for his advancement and who hoped for good service in the Court of Chancery, the Lord Chancellor wrote saying, 'I know I have clean hands and a clean heart,' adding that 'greatness is the mark and accusation is the game'. At this stage he appeared to be looking to the King and Buckingham to lift the pressure from him. Both of them lived in a welter of financial dishonour – the King was selling titles for what the market would bear, and judges paid him for their appointments – and they had fellow feelings for their Lord Chancellor; indeed, the King cried for him.

The accusations were manifold. Among the more bare-faced was that of Christopher Aubrey, who complained that he had sent the Lord Chancellor £100 by way of a Member of Parlia-

ment to secure a favourable decision in an appeal, but that
the decision had been adverse to him. This, he thought, showed
dishonesty on the Lord Chancellor's part. The Member of
Parliament said that Aubrey had given him a box for the Lord
Chancellor but he did not know what was in it. Bacon had
hesitated, saying the gift was too much, but later said he was
willing to accept it as a present from the Member. Another
complainer, Edward Egerton, who had a suit before the courts,
said he had sent the Lord Chancellor a bag containing £400
as a recognition of past services, when he had been Bacon's
client, and to 'buy some hangings for the house'. The
Lord Chancellor demurred at the size of the gift but accepted
it on the understanding that it was for past services; though
he later wrote to Egerton thanking him and saying he had
'laid a tie on him to do him justice in all his rightful cause'.
Egerton seems to have been given a just decision, but was
dissatisfied with it. There was much more. The litigious Lady
Wharton claimed she had not got value for her £300 gift.
She had brought some of the money in a home-made purse
and the Lord Chancellor had gallantly exclaimed, 'What lord
could refuse a purse of so fair a lady's work?'

Bacon wrote self-pityingly to the King. 'When the book of
hearts shall be opened,' he said, 'I hope I shall not be found
to have the troubled fountain of a corrupt heart in a depraved
habit of taking rewards to pervert justice, howsoever I may be
frail and partake of the abuses of the times.' When the day
came he would not try to trick his innocency with 'cavillations
or voidances'. He offered to try to reform his ways. He rejoiced
to think, in the midst of his afflictions, that the greatness of
a magistrate was deemed to be no shelter for his crime. He
suggested that dismissal would be punishment enough. He listed
the names of distinguished peculators in the ancient world
who had been given a second chance. He asked for a cell in
which to retire to do the King service, suggesting that he might
write a helpful treatise on usury. Faced with a demand from
the unrelenting Lords for detailed explanations of the charges,
he no longer blamed the abuses of the times but said, 'I do
plainly and ingenuously confess that I am guilty of corruption;
and do renounce all defence and put myself upon the grace
and mercy of your Lordships.' By this time there were twenty-
eight charges against him, involving substantial gifts (sometimes

from parties on both sides of a suit) and sums to a total value of £11,000. It seemed that Bacon had also been careless in watching the hands of his hands, for some charges related to exactions by his staff. To the Lords he said, 'God's Holy Spirit be among you.' They responded by fining him £40,000, committing him to the Tower and banning him from approaching within twelve miles of Court; but he died pardoned and pensioned. He summed it all up by saying, 'I was the justest judge in England these fifty years; but it was the justest censure in Parliament that was these two hundred years.'

There was some slight consolation for Bacon in the thought that he had not paid the King to obtain his various advancements. The traffic in appointments was blatant. In 1616 Chamberlain wrote that Coke could have been Lord Chancellor if he had been willing to pay £10,000, instead of the smaller sum of 10,000 marks, when the opportunity arose; but he was thought to be unwilling to buy the King's favour too dear, since it was too uncertain and variable. Sir Henry Yelverton felt some guilt at having become Attorney-General without feeing the King, so on the first opportunity he rewarded his 'good master and worthy Prince' with £4,000 in cash; the good master put a grateful arm round Yelverton and said he needed money to buy new dishes. If Sir Julius Caesar, as is alleged, paid £15,000 to become Master of the Rolls he surely deserved his 'plum', for as judge of the Admiralty Court under Elizabeth he claimed to have worked nine years without receiving a penny and to have been £4,000 out of pocket. James Ley, later Earl of Marlborough, tried to buy the attorney-generalship when Bacon relinquished it, but his £10,000 was turned down. However, his marriage to Buckingham's niece is thought to have helped him later to become Lord Chief Justice of the King's Bench. The King did not necessarily sell to the highest bidder; he preferred a man who had both cash and loyalty to offer, with legal ability into the bargain. It is certain that a judge who had paid for the appointment had a strong inducement to stay of office and to take the line that was expected of him.

5

OFF WITH HIS EARS

In 1625 James I died, not before he had undergone the unusual experience of receiving communion at the hands of his Lord Keeper,* whom he had made Bishop of Lincoln. The new King left nobody in doubt that he, like his father, was answerable to God alone. A demand by Charles for forced loans led speedily to a clash with the Chief Justice of the King's Bench, Sir Randolph Crewe, who refused to sign a document confirming that such exactions were legal. The other judges demurred, but finally signed on explaining that they did so out of courtesy to the King, not because they believed him to be in the right. Crewe's stand earned him a tribute in Parliament some fourteen years later from Denzil Holles, who pointed out that the Judge had now lost some £26,000 as the price of preserving his integrity. 'He kept his innocency when others let theirs go; when himself and the Commonwealth were alike deserted; which raises his merit to a higher pitch. For to be honest when everybody else is honest, when honesty is in fashion, and is trump, as I might say, is nothing so meritorious; but to stand alone in the breach, to own honesty when others dare not do it, cannot be sufficiently applauded, nor sufficiently rewarded. And that did this good old man do . . .' This good old man who, sad to say, once left nine 'witches' for execution on evidence which even James I rejected, is best known for his stirring prologue in the Oxford peerage case: 'And yet time hath its revolutions; there must be a period and an end to all temporal things – an end of names, and dignities, and whatsoever is

*The Lord Keeper of the Great Seal had virtually the same authority as the Lord Chancellor and was usually promoted to that rank.

54

terrene, and why not of De Vere? For where is Bohun? Where is Mowbray? Where is Mortimer? Nay, what is more and most of all, where is Plantagenet? They are entombed in the urns and sepulchres of mortality. And yet let the name and dignity of De Vere stand so long as it pleaseth God.'

The judges were by now under threat from Parliament as well as from the King. In 1628 Sir William Jones, with other judges, was called before the Lords to answer for a decision. He informed them that he was responsible only to God and to his conscience, that he was *liber homo* and a believer in the principles of Magna Carta. 'I do not now mean to draw down God's wrath on my posterity and therefore I will neither advance the King's prerogative nor lessen the liberty of the subject, to the danger of either King or people.' Old Sir John Doddridge, known as the 'sleeping judge' from his habit of listening with closed eyes, told the Lords he might have one foot in the grave, but he still believed that 'the King holds to none but God'.

That year the King consulted his judges on a personal matter of some delicacy. The Duke of Buckingham, the favourite he inherited from his father, was assassinated by John Felton, a disgruntled Army officer. In the Privy Council the bishops who examined Felton were in favour of torture, in order to discover the names of possible accomplices, but Felton pointed out that he would have no control over what he said and might even incriminate the bishops. The Council then debated the legality of racking the suspect. For once the King decided not to use his prerogative and to refer the matter to the judges. They met at Serjeants' Inn and gave the unanimous view that no such punishment was known or allowed by the common law. Felton then created more difficulties by offering, after being sentenced to death, to have his offending right hand cut off. The court had no authority to make this order. Once again the King sent for the judges 'to intimate his desire that his hand might be cut off before execution,' but they said it would not be lawful.* It was true that a felon who threw a missile at a sitting judge could have his right hand severed before execution, but that was authorised under a special statute. So Felton had to be hanged whole.

* * *

State Trials.

All this time the Court of Star Chamber was beginning to attract an ever-mounting weight of odium. Coke had thought it the most honourable court in the Christian world, Parliament excepted; it was 'the court that doth keep all England in quiet'. To the Sovereign it was an instrument for swelling the revenue by huge fines. It was also becoming an engine for censorship, being concerned to maintain, not freedom of the press, but freedom from the press. At one end of the scale the Star Chamber was prepared to fine the City of London £70,000 for supposed neglect to develop lands granted to it at Londonderry (the penalty was later reduced to £12,000). In the middle of the scale it was capable of ordering a man to pay £12,000 for marrying his niece. At the lowest end of the scale it even contemplated proceeding against Charles' jester, Archie Andrews, who in a state of liquor made libellous observations about Laud (the Archbishop himself discouraged prosecution, at the risk of spreading a report that he had a sense of humour).

When the offence called for something stronger than a fine, noble minds applied themselves to devising ignoble punishments. A prudent executioner presumably took care to have branding irons in the shape of every letter of the alphabet, since the Star Chamber were always thinking of new initials, and combinations of initials, for burning on cheeks and foreheads: B for blasphemer, F for fraymaker, FA for false accuser, K for knave, SL for seditious libeller, SS for sower of sedition, and so on. If there was a degrading tradition to be followed, the Star Chamber could be relied upon to follow it. They did not overlook the custom of parading wrongdoers in Westminster Hall, while the courts were sitting. Thomas Lovelace, who had slandered a kinsman, was ordered to be carried back to front on an unsaddled horse round the four judgment seats before being pilloried and losing an ear. Since the commotion in Westminster Hall was always considerable, this additional contempt may have caused less inconvenience to pleaders than might be supposed. John Chamberlain tells how, in 1605, a judge in the Star Chamber dissented from a proposal to sit a man back to front on a horse, arguing that it would be better to specify an ass, for two reasons: it would cause more boys to gather round him and the slow pace of the ass would increase his ordeal. Lord Burghley made a point of devising penalties with an element of poetic justice, though they were

all too often impracticable. Lord Egerton sentenced a man
who assaulted his grandfather to be flogged in front of the old
man's portrait. The Court thought it a happy idea to order
a man who objected to pork on religious grounds to be
imprisoned and fed on nothing else. More admirable was Lord
Egerton's 'sentence' on an attorney who appeared in the
Court of Chancery with a brief 120 pages long. Observing
that sixteen pages would have been ample, Lord Egerton
ordered the man to make a hole in his brief, put his head
through it and walk round Westminster Hall as a disincentive to
long-windedness. The Lord Chancellor did not think it
necessary to mount him on an ass.

It was, however, the wanton mutilation of offenders which
brought immortal disgrace to the Star Chamber. A youth of
Merton College, Oxford, was sentenced in 1603 to be whipped
and to lose both ears for libelling the Vice-Chancellor of the
University; an offence which nowadays many would regard as
no offence at all. Among the worst punishments were those
imposed from 1630 onwards on various Puritan pamphleteers.
The judges who sat in the Star Chamber were as forward in
their vengeance as any of the bishops or courtiers. In the trial
of the Scotsman, Dr Alexander Leighton, who was accused of
publishing a scandalous book about kings, peers and prelates,
the two chief justices said that, given the opportunity, they
would not have scrupled to proceed against him for treason,
and that it was only by the King's great goodness and mercy
that Leighton was brought before the Star Chamber. Since he
could not be hanged, drawn and quartered, the prisoner was
ordered to be imprisoned for life, fined £10,000 and stripped
of his ministry in order that his person might be abused without
disrespect to God. His physical punishment involved being pilloried at Westminster, whipped and pilloried again, after which
one ear was to be cut off, his nose slit and the letters SS branded
on his forehead. Thence he was to be taken to the Fleet, to be
pilloried at Cheapside on a market day, whipped again and to
have his other ear cut off.* Much of this punishment was
carried out.

In 1634 Lord Chief Justice Richardson excelled himself at
the trial of William Prynne, a self-tormented bigot trained at
Lincoln's Inn, whose dreary *Histriomastix* was thought to asperse

State Trials.

the Court while professing to be an attack on stage players. When the time came for sentence the first to suggest appropriate penalties was Lord Cottington, Chancellor of the Exchequer, who proposed pillorying, severance of ears and other indignities, plus a fine of £5,000. When he suggested that the printer should stand in the pillory in St. Paul's Churchyard, the Archbishop of Canterbury objected that it was a consecrated place. 'I cry your Grace's mercy,' said the Chancellor, 'then let it be in Cheapside.' Lord Chief Justice Richardson, who followed, said that the rage for printing books was growing ever worse – 'every man . . . thinks he is nobody except he be in print'. What Prynne had published was 'a most scandalous, infamous libel' on a queen 'such . . . as this kingdom never enjoyed the like and I think the earth never had a better'. If he had Prynne before him in his own court he would 'go another way to work,' meaning, presumably, that he would have had him hanged, drawn and quartered. 'I protest unto your Lordships it maketh my heart so to swell, and my blood in my veins to boil, so cold as I am, to see this or any thing attempted which may endanger my gracious Sovereign,' said the Judge, adding, 'It is to me the greatest comfort in this world to behold his prosperity.' He pointed out that there was no statute authorising the pillory, but in the case of a 'high crime' it could be ordered at discretion. As for the Archbishop's objection about St Paul's Churchyard, had not heretical books been burned there? The Lord Chief Justice thought it especially desirable that the prisoner should be deprived of pen and paper in captivity, 'yet let him have some pretty prayer-book, to pray to God to forgive him his sins'.

The Earl of Dorset, proposing that the fine on Prynne be raised to £10,000, said, 'I will not set him at liberty, no more than a plagued man or a mad dog who, though he cannot bite, he may foam . . . He is fit to live in dens with such beasts of prey as wolves and tigers, like himself.' After discussing whether Prynne should be burned on the forehead or have his nose slit, the Earl said, 'I should be loath he should escape with his ears, for he may get a periwig, which he now so much inveighs against, and so hide them, or force his conscience to make use of his unlovely love-locks on both sides.'*

Prynne was duly mutilated, but not entirely to the taste of

*State Trials.

the Star Chamber. In 1637 he was back before the court along
with Dr John Bastwick and Henry Burton, accused of various
libels. When about to pronounce sentence Lord Chief Justice
Finch looked closely at Prynne and said, 'I thought Mr Prynne
had no ears, but methinks he hath ears.' The Lords then
joined in the scrutiny and to assist them the prisoner was
ordered to raise his hair. What they saw displeased them, for
the ears had not been cropped closely enough. When Prynne
observed that none of their Lordships would care to have ears
like his, one of them said, 'In good faith, he is somewhat saucy.'
The court took exception to Prynne's contention that the bishops
should not take part in the sentencing, on the grounds that 'our
adversaries should not be our judges'. The sentence was that he
should lose the rest of his ears and be branded on each cheek
with the letters SL. Similar sentences were imposed on the two
others. During their ordeal all showed great fortitude and were
cheered by the crowd. Bastwick's wife bore away his ears in a
handkerchief. When he came to Prynne the executioner took
brutal care to ensure that there should be no further criticism of
his handiwork. But the savagery of the act did not crush the
victim. 'The more I am beaten down,' he said, 'the more I am
lifted up.'

Bishops might sit in the Star Chamber but they were not
immune from its discipline. The former Lord Keeper, John
Williams, Bishop of Lincoln, appeared twice before the Court;
in 1635, for subordination of perjury, and in 1639, for possessing
letters which described Archbishop Laud as 'the little urchin'
and 'the little hocus-pocus'. The writer of the letters, Lambert
Osbaldeston, a master at Westminster School, was also charged.
Williams was ordered to pay £5,000 to the King and £3,000
to Laud; Osbaldeston to pay £5,000 to each. Lord Chief Justice
Finch had an additional punishment for Osbaldeston. 'That he
may be an example to his boys I would have him also to stand
in the pillory in Dean's Yard and one ear to be nailed in the
Palace and the other ear to be nailed in Dean's Yard.' The
Earl of Dorset, never at a loss for a vivid phrase, observed that
schoolmasters were the apes of tyranny.* While the Court was
concocting the sentence Osbaldeston quietly slipped away and
evaded the subsequent hue and cry. He found time to leave
on his desk a note saying, 'If the Archbishop enquire after me,

State Trials.

tell I am gone beyond Canterbury.' After this the Court's security arrangements were tightened up.

From time to time the judges had to abandon their courts to assist the peers in the task of casting out sinners in their midst. No fewer than eight judges, including the two Chief Justices and the Chief Baron of the Exchequer, were called upon in 1631 to hear charges against Lord Audley, Earl of Castlehaven, who was accused of rape and that crime *detestabile et abominandum, Anglice vocat buggery (inter Christianos non nominandum)*. The evidence disclosed a grievous state of domestic debauchery and the Earl was deemed unfit to live. He presented himself to the executioner with 'a very noble, manly and cheerful countenance'.* The eight judges then returned to their ordinary labours.

*Ibid.

6

THE FATEFUL QUESTION

The judges were first embroiled in the great ship money controversy in 1635 when they were called to the Star Chamber to hear an address by the Lord Keeper, Lord Coventry, on the eve of the summer assize. He informed them that the King had decided to build a greater fleet, which would be the responsibility not only of the maritime towns but of the whole country. So, in their charges at the assizes, the judges were to stress the zeal of His Majesty in preserving his honour, the honour of the country and the Dominion of the Sea. 'And you are to let them know how just it is . . . and with what alacrity and cheerfulness they ought and are bound in duty to contribute unto it.'

With as much alacrity and cheerfulness as they could muster, the judges assumed the role of revenue men, but the exhortations to the grand juries fell on stony ground. When the Lord Keeper next addressed the judges, eight months later, he voiced regret at the widespread opposition to the writs for ship money and said that an ignorant few were contemplating obstructive actions in the courts at Westminster. The King, much displeased, was anxious to test the legality of his writs by consulting his judges, who were 'sworn to give him faithful and true counsel in that which pertaineth to the law'. The question to which the King sought an answer was as follows:

'When the good and safety of the kingdom in general is concerned, and the whole kingdom is in danger: Whether may not the King, by writ under the Great Seal of England, command all the subjects of this kingdom, at their charge, to provide such number of ships with men, victuals and ammunition and for such time as he shall think fit, for the defence and safeguard of the kingdom from such danger and peril; and by law compel the doing thereof, because of refusal or refractoriness? And whether in such a case is not the King sole judge, both of the danger, and when and how the same is to be prevented and avoided?'

Perhaps the judges were overwhelmed by the royal condescension in seeking their views, or by their affection for the Sovereign, or by the thought of the money invested in their appointments. Perhaps they honestly believed the country to be in danger. Whatever the reason, they gave the King the answer he wanted. Two of them, Mr Justice Hutton and Mr Justice Croke, had their doubts, but they signed in the interests of unanimity. The Lord Keeper then said the decision was one which ought to be published to the world, not 'kept in a corner'. He added : 'You have great cause to declare it with joy and you can hardly do it with honour enough to the King, that in so high a point of sovereignty he hath been pleased to descend and to communicate with you, his judges; which sheweth that justice and sovereignty in His Majesty do kiss each other.' Lord Coventry was a better courtier than a lawyer.

If the judges were unaware of having disposed of a fundamental liberty, there were voices aplenty in the country to tell them; though not in Parliament, since the King had dispensed with its services. Those who had been ready to pay ship money of their own free will rebelled at the idea of giving the King power to take as much money as he wanted whenever he wanted. A temporary tax, it was widely suspected, would soon become a permanent one. Some citizens may have recalled that when Elizabeth asked London for fifteen ships and five thousand men, the City had immediately offered her thirty ships and ten thousand men; but Elizabeth was Elizabeth and the country had been under direct threat from Spain.

In 1638 came the case against John Hampden, gentleman, in the Exchequer Court. Hampden refused to pay his levy. The judges had virtually disqualified themselves from hearing any action involving ship money, but they were the only judges the country had. The barons of the Exchequer had no wish to take a decision on their own. Over a long period, and often at great length, the judges gave their individual decisions. Lord Chief Justice Finch said his brothers held a great variety of opinions, 'a thing usual and frequent in all great cases and consultations', which argued 'a candour and clearness in those between whom any suspicion of combination and conspiracy would be most odious'. All of them were agreed – somewhat belatedly, it would seem – that the issue was 'the greatest case that ever came in any of our memories or the memory of any man'. The Lord Chief Justice voted for the King, as did six others, though two of them, while upholding the royal right to levy the tax, decided in favour of Hampden because of supposed technical flaws in the writ. Two judges were outspoken against the King, the same two who had earlier entertained doubts. Sir Richard Hutton, of the Common Pleas, said 'the subjects of England are free men, not slaves, free men, not villeins'. He was a man whom Charles had described as 'the honest judge'.

It was by no means the clear-cut victory Charles had hoped. One of his loyal subjects, a High Churchman called Thomas Harrison, showed his sympathy towards the King by entering the Court of Common Pleas where Mr Justice Hutton was sitting and loudly accusing him of high treason. This attempt to uphold the King's Majesty was, of course, an insult to the King's Majesty and Harrison was fined £5,000 in the Star Chamber. Fantastically, Mr Justice Hutton then brought a civil action against the offender, who was ordered to pay damages of £10,000.

The country cared nothing for the decision in the Exchequer Court. In some areas sheriffs refused to try to collect ship money and magnates declined to put pressure on their tenants. Parliament, at long last recalled, began to stoke up the indignation. 'Those who should have been as dogs to defend the sheep have been as wolves to worry them,' said Lord Falkland in the Commons, in 1640. The judges had delivered an opinion and judgment in an extra-judicial manner on something beyond their cognisance, 'they being judges and neither philosophers nor politicians'. Where was the mighty and imminent danger to the realm? The only threat lay in a few contemptible pirates. Lord Falkland did not shrink from suggesting that the judges had been corrupted by the King. Edward Hyde, the future Earl of Clarendon, lamented that 'men who had lost their innocence could not preserve their courage'. They had fallen into 'a tame easy trance of flattery and servitude' which had wrought 'a fatal declension in their understandings'. A Member called Bagshaw spoke of judges who made the laws speak loudly or softly as they themselves were tuned for it, who contracted their power when they ought to have extended it. At its harshest, the Parliamentary case against the judges was that they had destroyed a liberty which not even bribes, force of arms or treasonable conspiracies could have undermined.

The chief object of scorn was the Lord Keeper, as Finch had now become, and a move to impeach him was soon under way. In 1640 he stood at the bar of the Commons where he had once been Speaker, declining a chair and a stool on which to lay his purse. He regretted being torn 'between the displeasure of a gracious King and the ill opinion of an honourable assembly', but insisted that the judges had been bound by their oaths to return their opinions. They had never had the least intention to subvert the common law. His 'sweet tongue' did not beguile Alexander Rigby, who demanded that the Judge should pay with his life. 'Hath not this kingdom seen (seen, say I?) nay felt and smarted under the cruelty of this man's justice?' All the courts could bear witness to it; the poor were hanged for theft of hog or sheep or even a penny. 'Now shall not some of them be hanged that have robbed us of all propriety and sheared at once all our sheep and all we have away, and would have made us indeed poor Belisarios to have begged for halfpennies when they would not have left us one penny that we could have called our own?'

On the following morning Lord Keeper Finch rose early, disguised himself and slipped away to Holland. From there he later wrote to the Lord Chamberlain, mentioning his poor circumstances, expressing the hope that wisdom would wipe away all tears from his eyes and asking God to bless Parliament. Meanwhile, his impeachment went on. His enemies were not content with censuring him for his role over ship money; they unearthed other malpractices he was supposed to have committed. In such bad odour were the judges that anyone with a grievance against the Bench hastened to bring it to the notice of Parliament. The first item on the impeachment charged that Finch 'traitorously and wickedly' tried to subvert the laws and to introduce an arbitrary, tyrannical government. Under other headings he was accused of unlawfully enlarging a forest in Essex, manipulating jurors with 'menacing, wicked speeches', forcing Hutton and Croke to sign the original opinion against their will, oppressing executors and labouring 'by false and

A judge of the period of
Henry VII

The Court of King's Bench at
the time of Henry VI. The
prisoners are chained at the bar:
the jurors on the left

A judge rides out of Colchester after
the trial of Abbot Thomas Beche,
who is being executed in the distance,
1539

Charles I faces the 'Lord President of the High Court'

Sir William Scroggs

malicious slanders . . . to incense His Majesty against Parliaments'. Nor did the Commons spare the other judges who had supported the levying of ship money. All six were bound over in the sum of £10,000 each to answer charges in Parliament. Of these, Sir Robert Berkeley was the first to be arrested. By command of the Commons, Black Rod entered the King's Bench when the court was sitting and removed Berkeley from the Bench, thus causing 'great terror to the rest of the brethren'. This judge had gone out of his way to uphold the royal prerogative. He had pronounced *Rex* to be *lex* and had enunciated the proposition that 'many things which might not be done by rule of law might be done by the rule of government'. For good measure he was further accused of giving wrong decisions on the rating of corn, denying justice to soap-makers and reviling a grand jury in a case which involved the positioning of an altar table, 'to the great grief and trouble of their consciences'. William Pierrepoint discoursed on the Judge's fatal ambition. Ambition, he said, was worse than bribery, for even a bribed judge might pronounce a just decision.

Sir Robert Berkeley spent many unhappy months in prison. He must have been as surprised as anybody when, in 1641, Parliament praised his modesty and humility in adversity and invited him to sit in court during the Michaelmas term, since there was a shortage of judges. This did not mean that his punishment was to be remitted. In due time he was tried and fined £20,000, deprived of his office and ordered to be detained in the Tower during the Lords' pleasure. He was excused payment of half the fine. During the Civil War his property was plundered by both sides.

Parliament at last had the ascendancy. It wound up the Court of Star Chamber and the Court of High Commission. It ruled that the ship money writs were illegal and ordered the judges to announce the fact on assize. It did not, however abandon the royal practice of consulting the judges on possible prosecutions. In 1641 the Lords called on them to give a preliminary opinion on whether the King's First Deputy in Ireland, the Earl of Strafford, was guilty of treason; and this the judges did, in scandalous prejudgment of the issue. The lions under the throne were becoming everybody's jackals.

In 1642 the Civil War began.

*　　*　　*

C

If the judges expected freedom from oppression under Cromwell, they were soon disabused. At the Protector's whim they were dismissed, suspended and scolded; yet a few retained some measure of independence. Sir Matthew Hale on circuit found that Cromwell had been selecting a jury and refused to try the case. When Cromwell said he was 'not fit to be a judge', Hale agreed that it was very true. William Lenthall, ex-Speaker and Master of the Rolls, objected to one of the Protector's Chancery reforms and said he would be hanged in front of the Rolls gate before he would accept it. When he saw two of his brethren dismissed for making the same objection, he accepted it. One judge unvexed by scruples was John Wilde, who seems to have received special Parliamentary grants for his zeal in hanging royalists.

A martyr's crown narrowly eluded Judge Jenkins, a bold, hot-tempered Welshman whose royalist passions led him to indict several eminent Parliamentarians for high treason. He also drew a rapier against Parliament. Captured at Hereford, he was sent to the Tower and afterwards to Newgate. In 1647 he was impeached and, from the Bar of the Commons, where he refused to kneel, he voiced 'divers reproachful words such as . . . were never offered in the face of Parliament and to which there was loud and frequent protest'. The House was the House of Rimmon, said the Judge. It was a den of thieves. He would eat liquorice and gingerbread to strengthen his voice and proclaim their wickedness from the gallows, where he would stand with the Bible and Bracton suspended from his person. He would read to the mob Romans xiii, 1–2 which proclaimed that the powers that be were ordained of God and that those who resisted them would receive damnation. Though much offended, Parliament was content to fine him £1,000 and order him into perpetual custody. Some time later the Commons sent a deputation to remind him that he had a wife and nine children and to say that if he would accept their authority they would remove the sequestration from his estate and give him a pension of £1,000. To this the Judge in a great rage said, 'Had my wife and children petitioned you in this matter I should have looked on her as a whore and them as bastards.'* Eventually he was restored to his estate, where he became a patron of Welsh bards.

In 1649 the King himself was arraigned in Westminster Hall

*W. H. Terry: *Judge Jenkins.*

before a self-created High Court of Justice. Lawyers viewed the proceedings askance. There was some difficulty in finding a reputable judge willing to order the extinction of his Sovereign. Like many better men, John Bradshaw, a former Chief Justice of Chester and a judge in Wales, begged to be excused; but under pressure he accepted the distasteful task, as a good republican. As a reward, he was allowed to occupy the Deanery at Westminster. Bradshaw may well have been the only judge to enter Westminster Hall in a bullet-proof hat. He sat on a chair of red velvet and behaved somewhat pettily for one whose title was Lord President of the High Court. When the King disputed 'the fundamental power that rests with Parliament', Bradshaw replied, 'If this be all that you will say, then, gentlemen, you that brought the prisoner hither take charge of him back again.' The King persisted that he would require more information and Bradshaw snubbed him with, 'Sir, it is not for prisoners to require.' Later the King was told, 'You appear as a delinquent' and the exchanges ended with 'Serjeant, take away the prisoner.'

In the *State Trials* is a copy of the speech the prosecution would have made if the King had pleaded. It began, 'Charles Stuart, whom God in his wrath gave to be a King to this nation,' and listed his insults to the judiciary. The syntax is not of the best : '. . . that if so the judges should not declare the law to be as he would have it, he might with a wet finger remove them, and put in such as would not only say but swear if need be, that the law was as the King would have it. For, when a man shall give five or ten thousand pounds for a judge's place, during the King's pleasure, and he shall the next day send to him to know his opinion of a difference in law between the King and subject; and it shall be intimated to him, That if he do not deliver his opinion for the King he is likely to be removed out of his place the next day; which, if so, he knows not how to live, but must rot in a prison for the money which he borrowed to buy his place . . .'

Parliament had not abandoned its pretensions to act as a judicial tribunal. In 1656 the Commons were driven to insensate anger by the behaviour of the fanatic Quaker, James Nayler, self-styled Son of God. For seven days they debated whether he should die and, if not, how best to mangle him. A present-day Speaker has put their deliberations on record.* There was

*Horace King: *State Crimes.*

general agreement that the impostor's tongue should be bored through ('an ordinary punishment for swearing'). Major Beake wanted to cut out the whole tongue, to sever Nayler's right hand and then 'turn him beyond the seas'. To this Colonel Cooper objected, 'If you cut off his right hand he may write with his left.' Other proposals were for branding Nayler with a B, slitting his lips, hacking off his long hair, standing him in the pillory and whipping him from Westminster to the Old Exchange. Suggested places for exile ranged from the Isle of Dogs to Jamaica. The only Member with judicial qualifications, referred to as Judge Smith, thought Nayler could well be stoned to death. This was the Commonwealth Parliament, which now prided itself on having replaced the King as the fountain of justice.

However, the fate of a man who talked too much was mild compared with that of a man who failed to talk at all. In 1659 Lord Chief Justice Glynne ordered Major Strangeways, charged with murdering his brother-in-law, to undergo *peine forte et dure,* the penalty for refusing to plead. The direction, in accordance with rules laid down by Henry IV's judges, was that the offender 'be put into a mean house, stopped from any light, and that he be laid upon his back with his body bare; that his arms shall be stretched forth with a cord . . . and in like manner shall his legs be used; and that upon his body shall be laid as much iron and stone as he can bear, and more; and the first day shall he have three morsels of barley bread, and the next day shall he drink thrice of the water in the next channel to the prison door, but no spring or fountain water; and this shall be his punishment till he die'. In the press yard of Newgate the weights were laid on Major Strangeways by his friends, who then added their own weight 'to disburden him of his pain'.* He died within eight or ten minutes.

Those who deny that torture was authorised by the common law overlook *peine forte et dure,* which was still being applied at the Old Bailey in the days of Pope; though it was customary to use an unofficial whipcord torture on the thumbs in the hope that this would provoke a plea and save the ultimate barbarity. How Lord Chief Justice Glynne received the news that his prisoner was no longer capable of pleading we do not know. An earlier Chief Justice, Sir John Fortescue, had speculated on

*Charles Knight: *London.*

how the judges of France salved their consciences in similar circumstances. 'Perhaps the judge will say, I have not done anything of myself in inflicting these tortures, which are not by way of punishment but trial; but how does it differ whether he does it himself, while he is present on the Bench and, with reiterated commands, aggravates the nature of the crime and encourages the officer in the execution of his office? It is only the master of the ship who brings her into port, though, in pursuance of his orders, others apply the steerage; I see not how it is possible for the wound, which such a judge must give his own conscience, ever to close up or be healed; as long at least as his memory serves him to reflect upon the bitter tortures so unjustly and unhumanly inflicted on the innocent.'*

In 1660 Charles II was King and the body of John Bradshaw was dug up, along with those of Cromwell, Ireton and Pride, for official humiliation. The corpses were drawn on hurdles to Tyburn, hanged there and then beheaded; after which the trunks were buried below the gallows and the heads exposed on Westminster Hall. It was Parliament's idea. Had Bradshaw been alive, he would have gone down to history as the first judge to be hanged, drawn and quartered, for that was the fate of the other regicides. Or rather, of certain selected regicides; for among those who sat in judgment were many who had helped to destroy the King.

---

*A. Amos (ed.): *De Laudibus Legum Angliae*.

7

ROGUE JUDGES? (1) SCROGGS

'The Stuart taste in judges as in personal friends was peculiar and the apologist of Jeffreys needs consummate literary skill,' warns the historian David Ogg.* So, perhaps, does the apologist of Jeffreys' much-execrated contemporary, Lord Chief Justice Scroggs. For centuries these two men have stood side by side in the judicial pillory and it is not easy to discern the true features under the garbage. Jeffreys has been reviled for causing the guilty to be hacked to pieces in unseemly numbers, Scroggs for 'hounding' the innocent to the gallows on the word of Titus Oates. In the latter task Scroggs frequently had the moral support of Jeffreys, sitting on the same bench; from which eminence both men, as good Anglicans, deplored the papist custom of canonising murderers.

For the judges the Restoration brought in no era of liberty. It was soon obvious that they, like their predecessors under the early Stuarts, were to retain their posts only during the royal pleasure; also that, the more they showed loyalty to the Throne the more they would be mauled by Parliament. The reigns of Charles II and James II were to be notable for the number of judges dismissed or downgraded, not only for what they did or did not do, but for what they might or might not do, or because they could not get on with favourites or were blocking the path of favourites. For the judges it was the old problem which faces the collaborator : whether to save one's honour and go, or stay on and prevent the appointment of a worse man. As the pressure mounted, Westminster Hall saw the unfamiliar sight of dismissed judges returning to the Bar and pleading in front of

*England in the Reign of Charles II.

the less fastidious, and occasionally more fastidious, judges who had replaced them. Sir Francis Pemberton, not quite the whitest of martyrs, was dislodged from the Bench three times and ended up in Newgate after the Revolution, but in the intervals his services were available to clients. Both monarchs continued to exercise the right to ask the judges for their advice on current problems. Charles even questioned them on whether he was entitled to shut down coffee-houses as nests of sedition.

Sir William Scroggs came to the chief justiceship of the King's Bench just before the Popish Plot plunged the nation into a malign dementia. The prime plotter was Rutland's least-loved son, Titus Oates, a perjurer of stunning depravity who helped to swear away the lives of some thirty-five people, mostly innocent. Sent down in disgrace from two Cambridge colleges, he was welcomed into the Church of England and became chaplain to the Protestant members of the Duke of Norfolk's household. Here he made contacts with Roman Catholics and infiltrated their establishments on the Continent, being expelled from at least one for homosexual offences. By 1678, with the aid of like-minded rogues, and in the hopes of gain, he had concocted a circumstantial story about a Jesuit plot to seize power in Britain. Nurtured by the Earl of Shaftesbury ('Achitophel') and groups of frustrated Whigs, the Plot was sustained by months of solid perjury. It had as its immediate object the whipping up of intolerance towards Roman Catholics and the strangulation of any hopes the Duke of York might entertain of becoming James II. Dryden penned the perfect summary :

> .. that Plot, the nation's curse,
> Bad in itself, but represented worse,
> Raised in extremes, and in extremes decried,
> With oaths affirmed, with dying vows denied.
> Not weighed or winnowed by the multitude,
> But swallowed in the mass, unchewed and crude.
> Some truth there was, but dashed and brewed with lies
> To please the fools and puzzle all the wise . . .*

The King swallowed few, if any, of the lies, but he had no wish to court trouble by informing his subjects that they were deluded bigots. So the mob howled for judicial murders and got them.

*Absalom and Achitophel.

Scroggs was no grave and learned figure. Rather was he a voluptuary and associate of rakes, but in those days it was difficult not to be. If he was the son of a one-eyed butcher, as was said, at least that one-eyed butcher was able to send him to Oriel and Pembroke. As a serjeant he was arrested on a King's Bench warrant for assault and battery and impudently tried to plead the protection of his order; but the austere Sir Matthew Hale would have none of it. Scroggs was bold, handsome, witty and what would now be called articulate. More important than this, he was a strong King's man. When he became a justice of the Common Pleas in 1676 he went out of his way to proclaim his loyalty; and by 1678 he was Lord Chief Justice of the King's Bench. In that capacity he was called to the House of Commons to listen to the interrogation of Titus Oates, whose inventions he seems to have swallowed whole; or perhaps he found it convenient to appear to swallow them. He assured the Speaker that, where the honour of his King and country were concerned, he feared no man.

The accusations of Oates and his confederates now seem preposterous to a degree, but the Gunpowder Plot had seemed preposterous too. Those who hatched the lies knew that the nation was in a mood to credit any ill of papists. Not only the illiterate but the educated believed that the country was in danger of invasion by a Jesuit-led army, backed by France and Spain, and that the King was to be shot by pistol-carrying priests armed with silver bullets, failing which he would be poisoned by the Queen's Physician, Sir George Wakeman. In our own time adepts of 'black' political warfare spread some hilarious lies in Hitler's Germany, with fair success. The Popish Plot was an act of political warfare in peacetime, malevolently designed to 'scratch the itch of the age' (a phrase of Jeffreys). Initial excitement in London turned to panic when Sir Edmundbury Godfrey, a justice of the peace for Westminster, before whom Titus Oates had initially sworn his statements, was found dead in a ditch with a sword thrust clean through him. It is still not clear by whom he was killed, or why, but he was known to have been in a highly agitated state before his death and the mob were ready to believe that it had been done for a dark Jesuitical purpose. In this atmosphere of hysteria, before juries packed by the Whigs with papist-haters, the first men accused by Oates were brought to trial.

It is a rare judge who can remain objective and unemotional at a time of supposed national peril. Scroggs may well have felt that any scepticism on his part would have betokened disloyalty to the King; that any civility towards Roman Catholics would have shown a secret leaning towards Rome. But zeal for his King and country led him to usurp the role of prosecutor, to indulge in bitter abuse of prisoners and to sum up disgracefully.

The trials were conducted mainly in the King's Bench or at the Old Bailey. Most of England's twelve judges took part in them and many future judges appeared as prosecutors, but Scroggs almost alone has been blamed for what happened. When he took his seat at the Old Bailey the supporting judges included Sir George Jeffreys, who was Recorder of London; and when Scroggs sat in the King's Bench Jeffreys was often in the prosecuting team. One of the first to be indicted for high treason, on the evidence of Oates, was Edward Coleman, the Duchess of York's secretary, who had engaged in rash correspondence with Roman Catholics abroad. The Lord Chief Justice told him he knew of only two things which could make a man a Roman Catholic: personal interest and gross ignorance. 'No man of understanding, but for by-ends, would have left his religion to be a papist. And for you, Mr Coleman, who are a man of reason and subtility, I must tell you . . . that it could not be conscience, I cannot think it to be conscience. Your pension was your conscience, your secretary's place your bait.' Speaking of priests in general, he said: 'I could never meet with any here, that had other learning or ability but artificial, only to delude weak women and weaker men. They have indeed ways of conversion and conviction, by enlightening our understanding with a faggot and by the power and irresistible argument of a dagger.'*

The Lord Chief Justice told the jury that he was content to wait a while for their verdict, otherwise they would have to stay together until morning; but Mr Justice Wild saw proper to enlarge on this, saying, 'We do not speak to you to make more haste or less, but to take a full consultation of your own time. There is the death of a man at stake and make not too much haste.' After not too much haste the jury found Coleman guilty. The Lord Chief Justice continued to mock the prisoner's faith, playing on the words attrition and contrition, and then

State Trials: the principal authority for this chapter.

said, 'You may assure yourself there are but a few moments
between you and a vast eternity where will be no dallying, no
arts to be used . . .' In urging Coleman to abandon all hopes of
a reprieve, Scroggs appeared to tread on the royal prerogative.
The King, he said, was 'full of mercy almost to a fault,' yet if
he should incline to clemency, 'I verily believe both Houses
would interpose between that and you.' After being sentenced
to be hanged, drawn and quartered, Coleman began, 'My Lord,
I humbly thank your Lordship . . .' and reasserted his innocence.
Scroggs said, 'I am sorry, Mr Coleman, that I have not charity
enough to believe the words of a dying man.' He also had some
difficulty in finding charity enough to allow the prisoner to see
his wife, fearing that there might be some exchange of papers –
'I do not know what arts the priests have and what tricks they
use.'

As batches of priests and supposed plotters were brought
before him, the Lord Chief Justice intensified his virulence
against popery, though he said little which had not been said
with equal venom by Elizabeth's judges and attorneys-general.
At the Old Bailey he assured William Ireland, Thomas Pickering
and John Grove that he had no wish to asperse priests. 'If they
had not murdered kings, I would not say they would have done
ours. But when it hath been their practice so to do; when they
have debased men's understanding, overturned all morals and
destroyed all divinity, what shall I say of them? When their
humility is such that they tread upon the necks of emperors;
their charity such as to kill princes; and their vow of poverty
such as to covet kingdoms, what shall I judge of them?' Then
came the phrase he had been saving up: 'They eat their God,
they kill their King and saint the murderer.'

Finally, and as it would seem reluctantly, the Judge turned
to the jury and said, 'The matter is as plain and notorious as
can be . . . Let prudence and conscience direct your verdict
and you will be too hard for their art and cunning.' As instructed, the jury returned a verdict of guilty. It was the function
of Jeffreys, as Recorder, to pass sentence. 'I speak to you, gentlemen, not vauntingly,' he said, 'for it is against my nature to
insult upon persons in your sad condition.' They were about to
enter a vast eternity in which 'masses will not signify so many
groats, not one farthing'. Not all Roman Catholics, he agreed,
supported the principles of murdering kings and subverting

governments. 'There are many honest gentlemen in England, I dare say, of that communion, whom none of the most impudent Jesuits durst undertake to tempt into such designs.' He reminded the three men that in preparing for execution they would have the assistance of Protestant divines.

When Pickering said he would take his oath that he was never in the company of the witness William Bedloe, the Lord Chief Justice said, 'I make no question but you will, and have a dispensation for it when you have done.' Ireland pleaded that his relations had been plundered for siding with the King, to which Scroggs said, 'No, I will tell you why it was; it was for being papists and you ran to the King for shelter.'

Jeffreys on the whole showed a decent reticence towards Oates' victims, but at the trial of Richard Langhorn he felt driven to say: 'What a strange sort of religion is that, whose doctrine seems to allow them to be the greatest saints in another world that can be the most impudent sinners in this! Murder and the blackest crimes here are the best means among you to get a man canonised a saint hereafter.'

So far Scroggs had expressed no outward doubts about the evidence. In the Pickering trial he said that nothing could be plainer than the existence of a plot, and a villainous one. To the jury who tried Langhorn he said, 'I must tell you that the Plot is proved as plain as day and that by Oates; and farther, Oates' testimony is confirmed by that which can never be answered.' In sentencing Robert Green, Henry Berry and Lawrence Hill for the murder of Sir Edmundbury Godfrey (they were 'the Pope's bravos' come to murder 'for the honour of his Holiness') he commended the jury's verdict of guilty and said, 'If it were the last word I were to speak in this world I should have pronounced them guilty.'

What caused a belated scepticism to break out in the Lord Chief Justice is not wholly clear. Roger North has an unconvincing explanation. He says that Scroggs was returning from Windsor in a coach with Chief Justice North of the Common Pleas and asked him whether it was true that Shaftesbury really had so much power with the Sovereign. The reply was, 'No, my Lord, no more than your footman hath with you.'* It is hard to believe that Scroggs was such a political innocent as this suggests. Significantly, the turn-round by Scroggs occurred

*Life of Francis North.

in the trial of Sir George Wakeman, the Queen's Physician, who was said to have refused £10,000 to poison the King and to have held out for £15,000. This was the plotters' highest audacity so far. They had brought down the Queen's secretary and if they could topple her physician they were certain to strike even closer to the Throne. Charles was much exercised at the danger and it seems more than probable that he hinted to the judges that the time had come for the Plot to be discredited. He is known to have hated signing the death warrants. According to Sir Arthur Bryant, he had felt that the only way to keep the peace was to allow the laws to take their course. 'Let the blood lie on them that condemn them,' he said, 'for God knows I sign with tears in my eyes.'* By this time Scroggs and his fellow judges may have acquired sufficient distaste for Oates and his associates to look for some excuse for halting the persecution. Whatever the reason, the result of the Wakeman trial was a sharp setback to the conspiracy.

As before, the Lord Chief Justice did much of the questioning. 'Dr' Oates, as he was addressed in court, was so shaken by his interrogation that he asked to leave on the grounds that he was not well, but was ordered to stay where he was. Jeffreys, as Recorder, said, 'If you desire to have any refreshment, you shall have it got for you.' In his evidence Oates was foolish enough to sneer at the Privy Council, of whom he said, 'To speak the truth, they were such a council as would commit nobody.' Jeffreys commented, 'That was not well said,' and Sir George Wakeman intervened with, 'He reflects on the King and all the Council.'

When he summed up the Lord Chief Justice did not deny the existence of a papist conspiracy, but said, 'Let us not be so amazed and frighted with the noise of Plots as to take away any man's life without any reasonable evidence . . . These men's bloods are at stake and your souls and mine and our oaths and consciences are at stake; and therefore never care what the world says, follow your conscience.' Bedloe interrupted with, 'My Lord, my evidence is not right summed up,' to which Scroggs said, 'I know not by what authority this man speaks.' The jury, though presumably a packed one as before, seems to have decided to follow its conscience, for it acquitted. Oates and Bedloe retired in dudgeon, complaining that their honour had been slighted.

*King Charles II.

For Scroggs the decision to cast doubt on the evidence must have required a degree of courage. He knew both sides would assail him and they did. The mob threw a half-hanged dog in his coach. On the day after the acquittal the Portuguese Ambassador, from whose country the Queen came, called on the Lord Chief Justice to thank him for his conduct of the trial, thus starting a rumour that the Bench had accepted a bag of Portuguese gold. In the Privy Council Shaftesbury complained of Scroggs' treachery, but the King appears to have upheld his loyal judge, saying to him, 'They have used me worse and I am resolved we stand and fall together.' Pamphleteers, using bile for ink, were calling Scroggs 'Mouth' and reminding him of the fate of Tresilian and Alfred's forty-four judges. In the King's Bench the incensed Lord Chief Justice, fining Richard Radley £200 for printing scandalous words about the Bench, issued a public warning. It was impossible, he said, that the courts of justice should be awed by vulgar noise or that judges and juries 'should manage themselves so as best to comply with the humour of the times'. The people ought to be pleased with public justice and not justice seek to please the public. 'Justice should flow like a mighty stream; and if the rabble like an unruly wind blow against it, they may make it rough, but the stream will keep its course.' Scroggs said he was neither afraid nor ashamed to mention the Wakeman trial. 'Let us pursue the discovery of the Plot, in God's name,' he said; but we should not overdo our zeal or 'stretch anything beyond what it would bear.'

Another of the tribe who, as Scroggs put it, 'write to eat and lie for bread', called Henry Carr, was prosecuted at Guildhall for seditious libel in a rabble-rousing sheet called *A Weekly Packet of Advice From Rome*. Jeffreys, who prosecuted before Scroggs, boldly observed that much mischief had been done under the guise of saving the nation from popery. Scroggs proclaimed that there was no such thing as freedom of the press and undoubtedly believed it. This prosecution inflamed the enemies of both judges and they did not forget it.

The Plot continued to claim lives and it was obvious that the mighty stream of justice was still off course. However, Oates and Bedloe found it intolerable that perjury had ceased to pay automatic dividends. Possibly Oates feared for the withdrawal of the pension a grateful nation had awarded him. To his discomfiture Oxford University had declined to award him an expected degree of Doctor of Divinity. It was necessary to counter-attack. Between them, Oates and Bedloe scraped up thirteen accusations against the Lord Chief Justice. They alleged that 'in contempt of the King' he set at liberty persons charged with high treason, without sending them for trial; that he 'did browbeat and curb Dr Titus Oates and Mr William Bedloe, two of the principal witnesses for the King'; that he took upon himself to oppress Henry Carr, printer of *The Packet Of Advice From Rome;* that 'he was very much addicted to swearing and cursing in his common discourse, and a drinker to excess, to the great disparagement of the dignity and gravity of his place'; that he refused to issue warrants for the arrest of priests; that he announced at Monmouth Assizes his belief that Langhorn, whom he condemned, died wrongfully; that he did 'make merchandise' of the trials of priests in Staffordshire; and that before Wakeman's trial he struck a bargain with two booksellers for permission to print a report, at a fee of 150 guineas, plus 100 guineas if the trials lasted more than a day.

In the Privy Council, with the King present, Scroggs repelled the charges with contumely. He said he thought he was entitled to express doubt on the evidence of Oates and Bedloe without being accused of a misdemeanour. The allegation of swearing was 'an insolent scandal'. His statement at Monmouth was prompted by a discovery of a discrepancy in Bedloe's evidence which had not previously come to light. His publishing arrangements were 'a mere contract with other men' and nothing to do with anybody else. The King and Council were reasonably satisfied and Scroggs was given leave to proceed against his accusers, for what that was worth. If a news writer is correct, Oates was present at the Council meeting. When the question of drinking came up Scroggs agreed he had been at the Lord Mayor's and had drunk the health of the Duke of York, 'which he supposed might be in Mr Oates' judgment a cup too much, to which Mr Oates did not make any reply'.* It seems to have been a not-too-inquisitorial occasion.

What finally led to the impeachment of Scroggs was his action, no doubt royally inspired, in blocking a daring attempt by Shaftesbury to indict the Duke of York as a papist recusant, for refusing to attend divine worship. This the Lord Chief Justice

*Calendar of State Papers (Domestic).

did by suddenly discharging the Middlesex grand jury before it
could make the necessary presentment. It was too much for the
Whigs. Like Oates and Bedloe, they began to scrape up all the
grievances against Scroggs they could find; they also decided
that Sir Thomas Jones, who had shared the Bench at Middlesex
with Scroggs, must be removed too. In Parliament Sir Francis
Winnington said, 'I think we are come to old times again when
the judges pretended they had a rule of government as well as a
rule of law. If they did never read Magna Carta I think they are
not fit for judges; if they had read Magna Carta and do thus
so contrary they deserve a severe chastisement . . . If the judges
instead of acting by law shall be actuated by their own ambition, and endeavour to get promotion rather by worshipping
the rising sun than by doing justice, this nation will soon be
reduced to a miserable condition.' One Member remarked that
in former times judges had been hanged for less, but mentioned
no names. Another thought that the judges were guilty of
crimes against Nature, the King and posterity, and that such
proceedings would be cursed by children unborn. The considered view of the Commons was that the discharge of the
grand jury was arbitrary, illegal, destructive of public justice,
a manifest violation of the oath and an attempt to subvert the
fundamental laws of the kingdom. Which is a measure of the
Whigs' fury at being baulked by an adversary even more high-
handed than themselves. While gathering evidence against
Scroggs and Jones they also decided to impeach Mr Baron
Weston, who in a charge to the Kingston grand jury was held
to have scandalised the Reformation.

When the Articles of Impeachment were published it was
clear that though others might have lost faith in the great
conspiracy Parliament had not. It was alleged that the Lord
Chief Justice, well aware that there had been 'a horrid and
abominable plot contrived and carried on by the papists', had
scandalised several of the witnesses who had proved treasons.
'As much as in him lay' he had traitorously and wickedly
stifled discussion of the Plot and encouraged the conspirators to
proceed to the great and apparent danger of His Majesty's
sacred life. Borrowing from Oates, the Articles then complained
that a judge who should have been of 'sober, grave and virtuous
conversation' had by his 'frequent and notorious excesses and
debaucheries and his profane and atheistical desires' daily

affronted Almighty God, dishonoured His Majesty, given countenance to the encouragement of all manner of vice and wickedness and brought the highest scandal on public justice. In case
the point had not been sufficiently made, the Articles ended by
saying, 'all which words, opinions and actions of the said Sir
William Scroggs were by him spoken and done traitorously,
wickedly, falsely and maliciously to alienate the hearts of the
King's subjects from His Majesty'.

It was clear that in the matter of framing accusations Oates
and Bedloe lagged behind the Whigs in Parliament. However,
motions in the House of Lords to suspend the Lord Chief Justice
were defeated. Twice he was saved from further trouble by
dissolutions of Parliament. Then in 1681 the King, convinced
that nothing was to be gained by keeping a much-hated judge
on the Bench, removed him. As compensation for his loyalty he
was paid a pension of £1,500 and his son was made a King's
counsel. The pamphleteers gave him little rest. *The Bellowings
of a Wild Bull, or Scroggs' Roaring Lamentations For Being
Impeached For High Treason* is a fair sample. 'What a damned
Fool was I that I had not run away in time! Could I not have
had the wit of Wakeman, put my 10,000 Bags of Guineys under
my Arm and trooped off to drink the waters of Burboon?* A
dull Beast! to stay thus to be Nooz'd . . . Was it for this I
perverted justice, did things contrary both to the law of God
and Man? . . . A Plague of my Starrs, that ever I should be
born in a time of Printing! By Wakeman's soul I hope he's
frying in Hell that first invented that Heretick Art! I thought to
have sent all those mangy Booksellers, Printers etc. to the Devil
by wholesale and to have set up an Inquisition against Printing
. . .' It was not only the judges of the King's Bench who regretted
the invention of the Heretick Art. The dawn of political
journalism raised no enthusiasm in the breasts of grave, God-
fearing men.

The behaviour of the judges in the Popish Plot has been
called 'possibly the most humiliating episode in the entire history
of the English judiciary'.† It has been said that 'the obloquy
which is attached to the name of Scroggs is a warning to every
man to avoid obsequiousness to those from whom favour flows'.‡

*Bourbon.
†G. W. Keeton: *Lord Chancellor Jeffreys and the Stuart Cause.*
‡Edward Foss: *A Biographical Dictionary of Judges.*

The *Dictionary of National Biography* calls Scroggs 'undoubtedly one of the worst judges that ever disgraced the English Bench'. Lord Campbell regrets that he did not end up on the scaffold. Since he was Lord Chief Justice of England Scroggs must shoulder most of such blame as can be made to stick; but the trials took place over a period of many months and if his brethren of Bench and Bar had entertained grave doubts about the evidence put before them they could have made their objections known. There is no evidence that they did so, or that Scroggs was the type of lord chief justice who overbore his fellows. Were they all, in truth, cowed by the popular frenzy? Roger North says that his brother, the Lord Keeper, supported the view of those judges who thought it better to 'let the vessel drive which they could not stop and reserve themselves for fairer opportunities when such might happen for them to do something good without pretending to move mountains'.* Is it naive to suppose that, initially, the judges saw no reason to disbelieve the evidence? Long after the Wakeman acquittal the peers were ready to accept Oates' story that the Pope had nominated Viscount Stafford as paymaster-general of his liberating army; and on the strength of this lie Stafford was beheaded on Tower Hill, after a trial presided over by the Lord Chancellor (Lord Finch, later Earl of Nottingham) in the role of Lord High Steward. Even Stafford's kinsmen, for the most part, voted him guilty. This occasion, for all its pomp and majesty, was a greater atrocity than any of the early trials presided over by Scroggs. The Lord High Steward informed the prisoner that he faced the highest court in the Christian world, adding, 'Here you may be sure no false weights or measures will ever, or can be, found.' In the prosecuting team Serjeant Maynard, a future judge, complained of efforts to discredit the Plot. Sir William Jones, another prosecutor, said in defence of Oates: 'A man who is not of a deep judgment could never have contrived and invented a narrative consisting of so many particulars, and they so coherent, if they were false. And if his narrative be not true he must be endued with more subtlety and wicked policy than upon trial we can find in him.' With a grand gesture the Lord High Steward himself threw a false weight into the scales. After saying that the Plot was 'now apparent beyond all possibility of doubting,' he asked, 'Does any man now begin

Life of Francis North.

to doubt how London came to be burnt?' So Stafford went to the block knowing that he was helping to expiate the Great Fire.

Five years later, summing up at the trial of Titus Oates for perjury, Jeffreys as Lord Chief Justice deplored how the Plot had been manipulated for political ends by those who had not shrunk from corrupting the ways of justice. Was he aware at the time of being manipulated? Was he one of those who were prepared, however reluctantly, to let the vessel drive? He never gave the impression of being carried away with excitement, as Scroggs and others did. Among those others was Sir William Jones, whom Roger North quotes as saying that 'the greatest load of all that sat upon and oppressed his spirits was his undue fervour in prosecuting men to death for high treason upon the foot of Oates' plot'.

Oates was convicted of perjury after a trial impeccably conducted by Jeffreys. Although his blood guilt was prodigious he had apparently committed no capital offence, comparable with stealing a sheep. He was fined, whipped, pilloried and sentenced to life imprisonment, with outings each year to stand in five specified pillories. The whippings by Jack Ketch nearly killed him. Released in 1688, he whined for a pension and was given one of £5.

8

ROGUE JUDGES? (2) JEFFREYS

Some of the lions under the throne of Charles II were spiritless beasts with a touch of mange. The most faithful and the most audacious was Jeffreys, who was little more than an overgrown cub when his master began to pick out tit-bits for him. If it is true, and it seems unlikely, that the King once described him as having 'no learning, no sense, no manners and more impudence than ten carted street-walkers' he seems to have altered his opinion rapidly.

As it happens, a supposed talent for exchanging impudence with carted street-walkers forms the basis of one of the popular complaints against Jeffreys. As Recorder of London in his early thirties it fell to him to order prostitutes to be scourged at the cart's tail ('let them be well heated' he directed, one cold morning). Macaulay has it that the daily bandying of insults with sluts and ruffians at the Old Bailey served to coarsen Jeffreys' behaviour, though the Old Bailey has no especial reputation for debauching the judiciary. It was not for flogging women, which was a routine punishment at that court, that he was forced to resign from the recordership, but for frustrating City petitions to Parliament. Charles amusedly noted that the young judge was not 'Parliament-proof', but he was determined to save him from the Whigs. In 1683, after a spell as Chief Justice of Chester, Jeffreys became Lord Chief Justice of the King's Bench, when not yet forty. In this role, John Evelyn notes, he administered 'severe justice among the obnoxious in Westminster Hall'. The obnoxious included 'factious snivelling Presbyterians' whom Jeffreys sharply discouraged from making a conventicle of the King's Bench. He

would brook no 'sauciness from prickeared fellows' whether they
were prisoners or counsel. 'I observe you are in all these dirty
causes,' he said to a counsel called Wallop, 'and were it not for
you gentlemen of the long robe who should have more wit and
honesty than to support and hold up these factious knaves by
the chin we should not be at the pass we are at.' More than
once, as the *State Trials* show, he warned jurors to report to
him if counsel attempted to whisper to them, which shows the
relaxed state of court discipline in those days. The probability
is that rough justice was more likely to be done under a strong
and censorious judge than under a mild and tolerant one. A
typical harangue by Jeffreys, or attributed to him, was the
following, addressed to Richard Baxter, a preacher accused of
seditious libel : 'Richard, Richard, dost thou think we will hear
thee poison the court? Richard, thou art an old fellow, an old
knave; thou hast written books enough to load a cart; every
one is full of sedition (I might say treason) as an egg is full of
meat; hadst thou been whipped out of thy writing trade forty
years ago it had been happy. Thou pretendest to be a preacher
of the Gospel of peace and thou hast one foot in the grave; it is
time for thee to begin to think what account thou intendest to
give; but leave thee to thyself and I see thou will go on as thou
hast begun; but by the Grace of God I will look after thee . . .'
Jeffreys looked after him with a £500 fine. It sounds highly
illiberal but Jeffreys was enforcing the law of the land and even
Macaulay concedes that the sentence was a light one for the
times. But for Jeffreys' subsequent notoriety this harangue would
have received little attention. The Judge must be accounted
lucky that history has not obliterated his protest, voiced at the
trial of Thomas Rosewell in 1684, that a man accused of a
'twopenny trespass' could be represented by counsel, when a
man accused of felony or treason – 'when life, estate, honour and
all are concerned' – had to defend himself unaided.

Although Jeffreys, like Scroggs, was much accused of public
and private drunkenness, he always got through his work with
dispatch. Evelyn was pained to see him and other judges
'exceeding merrie' at a wedding only a day or two after the
death of Algernon Sidney, at whose trial Jeffreys had presided;
but executions did not normally plunge the administration into
mourning. On circuit Jeffreys was a popular figure with the
gentry, and even when, on the King's behalf, he demanded the

surrender of city charters he rarely antagonised the authorities, well though they knew that the King was trying to trim their powers. On the Humber Jeffreys was even received with salutes of guns as well as the usual church bells.

When Charles died, in 1685, James lost little time in raising the Lord Chief Justice to the peerage as Baron Jeffreys of Wem, a most unusual honour for the rank. The Lord Chancellorship was almost within Jeffreys' grasp, for Lord Guilford (formerly Chief Justice North) was dying, though he had no intention of yielding up the Great Seal while breath survived. Suddenly came the Monmouth Rebellion, speedily stamped out at Sedgemoor; and to Jeffreys, by virtue of his office, fell the task of carrying out the new King's vengeance in the West.

Today the most charitable evaluation of Jeffreys' performance on the Western Circuit goes like this: he was a loyal King's man who was given a vile task of retribution to perform and did it with no noticeable flinching or even gloating; his name was blackened by scurrilous Whig pamphleteers from the camp of Titus Oates, so much so that even the Tories gave up hope of trying to clear him; he is no more to be blamed for the Bloody Assizes than Jack Ketch, the hangman; he has borne censure which should have been heaped on James II, who could have ordered clemency had he wished and was treacherous enough to have disowned Jeffreys publicly if he thought retribution had gone too far. Yet scorn for lying Whigs has not driven anyone to pretend that the scenes on the Western Circuit were anything but bestial, even by the standards of Ivan the Terrible.

The Duke of Monmouth landed at Lyme, issued a declaration full of falsehoods, rallied some thousands of deluded nonconformists to his banner, crowned himself in the market-place at Taunton and was routed by the King's troops. Had his treason prospered, none would have dared call it treason; but it failed to prosper, and treason it was. The penalty for this offence was hanging, drawing and quartering, a fate for which an alarming total of James' subjects had qualified themselves.

It now seems very doubtful whether Jeffreys was given the temporary rank of a general, entitling him to 'command' all forces of law and order in the West. The fact that the King talked about Jeffreys' 'campaign' has little significance. Already the military were out there, mopping up; the threat was over. Jeffreys was sent on circuit at the head of a Special Commission

of Oyer and Terminer and General Gaol Delivery. With him
were four other judges: Sir William Montague, Lord Chief
Baron; Sir Cresswell Levincz, of the Common Pleas; Sir Francis
Withens, of the King's Bench; and Sir Robert Wright, of the
Exchequer. Thus, all the common law courts were represented
on the Commission; a useful reminder that, whatever the
specialised jurisdictions of the judges, all of them were ready to
leave their benches at any time to hang the King's enemies.
Certainly it was unusual to have four judges on a commission,
but an unusual amount of work awaited them. At Taunton the
grand jury had 1,811 persons to present, at Exeter 488 and at
Dorchester 312; a total of 2,611.

Jeffreys had been undergoing treatment for the stone at
Tunbridge Wells and the journey west could only have worsened
his condition. Whether drink was the cause of the stone or a
means of relief from it has inspired some speculation. On their
way westward the judges were entertained with prodigality at
Farnham by the Bishop of Winchester, who had sent his carriage
horses to drag the King's guns at Sedgemoor. The first prisoner
for trial, in Winchester Castle, was a widow of one of Cromwell's judges, 'Dame' Alice Lyle, popular with both Whigs and
Tories as a Lady Bountiful. She had sheltered two rebels in her
home, 'a venial and amiable transgression', according to
Macaulay, who presumably would have done the same. At the
outset Jeffreys assured the prisoner that though they came as
judges with authority from the King, 'yet we are accountable
not only to him but to the King of Kings, the Great Judge of
Heaven and Earth'. The trial is notable for its ferocious exposure by Jeffreys of James Dunne, a baker, who was lying in
an effort to save a life. If the *State Trials* are to be believed
(and this account has probably been touched up) Jeffreys did
almost all the questioning, counsel making only an occasional
contribution. The Judge began by reminding Dunne that if he
deviated from the truth 'the God of Heaven may justly strike
thee into eternal flames and make thee drop into the bottomless
lake of fire and brimstone'. A few moments later he was saying
he would not trust Dunne with twopence. Questions rained on
the witness, who was addressed as 'Sirrah', 'blockhead' and 'vile
wretch'. Constantly Jeffreys called on Heaven to witness the
impossibility of getting the truth out of a lying Protestant knave.
'Jesus God! There is no sort of conversation, nor human society,

to be kept with such people as these are who have no religion
but only in pretence and no way to uphold themselves but by
countenancing lying and villainy . . . A Turk is a saint to such
a fellow as this, nay a pagan would be ashamed to be thought
to have no more truth in him. O blessed Jesus, what an age do
we live in, and what a generation of vipers do we live among . . .
Hold the candle to him that we may see his brazen face . . .'
Towards the end of the interrogation Dunne, instead of answering, 'stood and mused' or 'stood a good while and made no
answer'.

Alice Lyle was sentenced to be burned, since that was the
penalty for a female traitor (it was held to be more decent than
dismemberment, which in any event called for outrages an-
atomically impossible on a woman). She was allowed to appeal
to the King, who changed the sentence to one of beheading.
Dame Alice met her fate with serene courage, according to
Macaulay; one of the gallant pamphleteers said she was 'old and
dozey and died without much concern'.

At this trial Jeffreys announced that the King had given
him authority to order delays in execution, but where he found
obstinacy or impenitence he could order executions at whatever
speed he thought best. Here, to be sure, the defender of Jeffreys
(and James II) needs consummate literary skill. Henceforth a plea
of not guilty was construed as a display of obstinacy. What
judge would wish to preside over 2,611 trials?

The judges rode on to Dorchester, which awaited them in
panic. Here the Lord Chief Justice is supposed to have smiled at
a reference to mercy in the Assize sermon; Macaulay's version
is that his features were 'distorted by an ominous grin'. Most
of the prisoners who lay there were induced to plead guilty on
the assurance that this was the only way to clemency. If so,
they were fatally deluded. It is said that Jeffreys and his
brother judges held out this promise, though Muddiman's
account of the Assizes puts the blame firmly on the prosecutor,
Henry Pollexfen, who became a judge under William III.* At
Dorchester those who defied the court by pleading not guilty
were executed summarily on conviction, as if to ensure that no
reprieve should reach them. In one respect all the condemned
rebels were fortunate. Although the sentence called for dismemberment when alive, they were not cut down until they were

*J. G. Muddiman: *The Bloody Assizes.*

dead. According to Muddiman, Jack Ketch and his assistant, a professional butcher called Pascha Rose, were ordered to quarter twenty-nine prisoners in a day but refused, presumably on the grounds that it was humanly, or even inhumanly, impossible. As it was they were able to quarter thirteen of them. The suggestion that the military assisted in these barbarities can be discounted; the troops of those days may have been brutal and licentious, but they had neither the taste nor the aptitude for dismembering the dead. In all some seventy-four rebels were executed in Dorset, mostly in batches where it was thought the spectacle would do most good. The scene was one of Grand Guignol magnified and multiplied. It had been the responsibility of the sheriffs to prepare spears and poles on which to transfix heads, cauldrons of tar for boiling the limbs, salt at the rate of half a bushel to each traitor and enough faggots for burning the bowels.* These preparations did not pass unnoticed by the families whose menfolk were in gaol. Meanwhile the Lord Chief Justice, as his correspondence with the Earl of Sunderland ('my dearest, dearest Lord') reveals, was suffering intense pain from the stone.

The judges moved on, by way of Exeter, to Taunton, where panic had given way to terror. In this county nearly a hundred rebels were executed and the same infernal scenes were staged. The more pardonable exaggerations by the pamphleteers were those in which they referred to 'trees laden almost as thick with quarters as with leaves' and 'the houses and stables covered as close with heads as at other times frequently in that country with crows and ravens'.† There were few families which did not see heads or haunches of their neighbours hung in the stinking air. Some of these horrors the five judges must have viewed, but much of the butchery occurred after they had passed on.

The Commission ended its duties at Wells. Although the West Country had been 'converted into a vast anatomical museum',‡ a great number of rebels escaped dissection, either by collusion of gaolers, bribery or other tricks and devices. A number succumbed to an epidemic, variously described as smallpox and gaol fever, in the prisons. The total number executed has been the subject of much earnest inquiry; it was probably much nearer two hundred than three hundred. Some

*Ibid.
†Ibid.
‡Ibid.

847 persons were ordered to be transported to the American plantations, but of these a number escaped. The traffic in transportation was an unusually cynical one, in that rights to make profits out of prisoners were bestowed on courtiers, maids of honour and friends of the King. Even while the trials were in progress the Earl of Sunderland was transmitting the King's wishes to Jeffreys. 'Of such persons as you shall think qualified for transportation His Majesty intends Sir Philip Howard should have 200, Sir Richard White 200 . . .' began one letter, which asked for a thousand prisoners all told. It also had a postscript: 'The Queen has asked a hundred more of the rebels . . .' For once Jeffreys queried a royal order. He pointed out that the prisoners were worth from £10 to £15 a head on the market and that 'if Your Majesty orders them as you have designed persons that have not suffered in your service will run away with the booty'.* Whether as a result of this protest or not, the King put a large personal profit in Jeffreys' way. Edmund Prideaux, of Ford Abbey, an offender of some standing, was 'given' by the King to Jeffreys, who was invited to treat with him for a sum of money in return for which the King would grant a pardon. Prideaux, cornered, settled his account for £14,500. With the aid of this sum Jeffreys bought an estate which his enemies called Aceldama, after the Biblical field of blood. The Prideaux transaction now seems flagitious in the extreme and even in those days it was not highly regarded. Many stories circulated about trafficking in pardons and it is not hard to see how they were inspired. Jeffreys is even accused of having tossed a pardon to his 'jester' during a carouse at Taunton, with an invitation to sell it for what it would fetch.†

Yet even the Bloody Assizes had one bright episode. At Bristol, which Jeffreys described as 'this most factious town . . . worse than Taunton', the Mayor and aldermen had been making fat profits out of trading in criminals, whom they dispatched to the colonies. Not content with snatching convicts from the assizes they had taken to drafting petty offenders from their own court-house; nor had they baulked at shipping children. According to Roger North, Jeffreys was delighted with such an opportunity of ranting. He abused the Mayor, Sir William Hayman, with 'all the ill names that scolding eloquence could

*Calendar of State Papers (Domestic).
†Chambers' Book of Days.

supply', and made him leave the Bench and stand at the bar as a common rogue, bawling at him when he hesitated. 'Thus the citizens saw their scarlet chief magistrate at the bar, to their infinite terror and amazement'* In his own report Jeffreys says he sent his tipstaff to arrest others equally concerned in the civic villainy. 'I will pawn my life and health that Taunton and Bristol and the County of Somerset too shall know their duty before I leave them,' he wrote.† In the following year the Mayor and his leading accomplices were heavily fined.

Jeffreys' profit on the circuit was not confined to the £14,500 wrung from a treacherous landowner. He returned to be made Lord Chancellor and to be warmly thanked, along with the other four judges, by the King at Windsor. None ostracised him. He was fêted at his old university, Cambridge, where a senior fellow composed a laureate-style panegyric regretting that London had once rejected him, as the Jews had rejected Christ.‡ Great Jeffreys, said the bard, had wielded a flaming sword, but nothing was said about a butcher's cleaver. John Evelyn dined with the new Lord Chancellor and was treated with 'great respect'. Jeffreys, said the diarist, was of 'an assured and undaunted spirit' and had 'served the Court interest upon all the hardiest occasions', though 'of nature cruel'. At the time Evelyn had a suit before the Court of Chancery and he was gratified by the way the Lord Chancellor berated his opponent's smooth-tongued solicitor. 'Blessed be God for his great goodness to me this day,' says the diarist. In 1686 Evelyn was once more scandalised by Jeffreys' social behaviour. He dined with the Lord Chancellor and a number of serjeants who boasted of how long they had detained their clients in tedious processes, like so many highway thieves gloating over all the purses they had taken. 'This they made but a jest of,' says the diarist, 'but God is not mocked.§

To the surprise of some, Jeffreys proved to be a strong and dignified Lord Chancellor, sound in judgment. Moreover, he was a very hard worker. The Court of Chancery had been

*Life of Francis North.
†*Calendar of State Papers (Domestic).*
‡Reproduced in G. W. Keeton's *Lord Chancellor Jeffreys and the Stuart Cause.*
§E. S. de Beer (ed.): *The Diary of John Evelyn.*

recently satirised in Samuel Butler's *Hudibras,* which told of
the disastrous lure it held for the litigious :

> When fools fall out, for ev'ry flaw
> They run horn-mad to go to law;
> A hedge awry, a wrong-placed gate
> Will serve to spend a whole estate . . .

Roger North refers to the 'prodigious injustices and iniquitable
torment inflicted upon suitors by vexatious and false adversaries
associated with the knavish confederating officers and other
chicaneurs that belong to the court'. Half a dozen of these
chicaneurs had come close to ruining Lord Keeper Guilford, who
accepted a gift of £1,000 from them as a mark of respect, when
it was obviously tendered in the hope that he would overlook
their mischiefs.* Jeffreys conducted a purge of such Chancery
riffraff when he took over the Great Seal. He tried hard to cut
down the garrulity of barristers, all labouring and relabouring
the same points, to the financial detriment of the suitors—

> . . . while their purses can dispute
> There's no end of th'immortal suit.

When James had a willing horse he did not hesitate to
increase its burden. The new Lord Chancellor was induced in
1686 to join the bishops on a Commission for Ecclesiastical
Causes, which was the old Court of High Commission under
a new name. Though it had power to harry adulterers and
fornicators, its real function was to put pressure on official
bodies, notably the universities, to admit Roman Catholics. It
was this body which made a famous visit to Magdalen College
to bully the dons, a task in which Sir Robert Wright, a veteran
of the Bloody Assizes, assisted. Not surprisingly for a strong
Anglican, Jeffreys did not have his heart in the job. He
probably had many secret reservations when he accepted it.

Meanwhile James was coercing the rest of the judges, re-
moving them when they denied his power to dispense with, or
to suspend, the laws against Roman Catholics. He also demanded
the right to operate martial law in peace-time. When Lord Chief
Justice Herbert refused to order the execution of an Army
Life of Francis North.

deserter, the King transferred him to the Common Pleas and replaced him with Sir Robert Wright, who obediently ordered the soldier to be hanged. Soon afterwards, as an extravagant demonstration of loyalty, Wright fined the Earl of Devonshire £30,000 for an assault committed in the King's ante-chamber, an offence which he thought was 'next door to pulling the King out of his throne'. The process of royal intimidation was summed up in the exchanges which marked James's dismissal of Sir Thomas Jones from the chief justiceship of the Common Pleas. 'I will have twelve judges of my opinion,' said the King. To this the Chief Justice replied that he might get twelve judges but he would not get twelve lawyers. The kind of judge he got was the arrogant ignoramus, Mr Justice Allybone, who, in the hour when the heavens were falling, informed a grand jury at Croydon that the verdict on the Seven Bishops was a gross error and that their petition to the King had been tantamount to treason.

When the hour of reckoning came James demanded the Great Seal from Jeffreys, dropped it in the Thames, sailed down river and caught a ship to France, leaving his loyal Lord Chancellor to make his own arrangements. Disguised as a sailor, the Lord of Aceldama hid in a vessel off Wapping, whence he hoped to follow his master; but on a trip ashore to a tavern he was recognised by a scrivener who had seen him in the Court of Chancery. Pelted by the mob, he was rescued and carried before the Lord Mayor, who swooned with excitement. In the Tower Jeffreys is reported to have said that the Western Circuit had not been bloody enough for the King. The King, for his part, was saying in exile that Jeffreys had exceeded his instructions, though there is no record of his having said it at the time. The two were in constant communication throughout the Assizes.

Ill-health overtook Jeffreys in the Tower, where he died in 1689. Four years earlier, if the dying Lord Guilford could have been persuaded to yield up the Great Seal, or if he had expired a week earlier, another judge might have been saddled with the Bloody Assizes. Conceivably, a strong-minded judge with a humanitarian streak (had one existed) could have tempered the policy of retribution or attempted to confine it to the ring-leaders. At the time, some two hundred deaths exacted from a total of 2,600 guilty men did not seem excessive to anyone outside the West Country. The hatred which Jeffreys attracted in his day was inspired more by the zeal with which he put his abilities at the disposal of royal absolutism; and on his head were piled the coals which await those who remain faithful to the unsuccessful side.

Royal absolutism was now over. The Glorious Revolution which put William of Orange on the throne heralded a new deal for the judges.

9

RIDING THE CIRCUIT

The Bloody Assizes reveal the judicial circuit at its most horrendous. In normal times, although the sheriff's trumpets and the church bells might sound a *nunc dimittis* for the odd wretch who lay on straw in gaol, the judges' arrival brought some cheer to hotel-keepers, landlords and all who were clever enough to squeeze money out of attorneys. Litigious inhabitants also welcomed the assize, for in a court set aside for civil actions, such quarrels as the local justices could not resolve were thrashed out before a judge of experience and authority, immune from local influences.

Before the judges set out on circuit the Lord Chancellor would call them together and remind them of their duties. 'Circuits are for the service of the King and the good of the people,' said Lord Keeper Coventry, on the eve of the summer assize of 1635. 'In the Term the people follow [the King] and seek for justice; but in the circuit justice . . . followeth the subjects home to their own doors.' To the judges this can hardly have been news. The Lord Keeper's first caution was 'to look to the corruption of the sheriffs and their deputies'. Next, they were to be on their guard against 'the bearing and siding of men of countenance and power in their county' and deal in severe and exemplary fashion with any attempts to overbear justice. 'I shall commend unto you,' he continued, 'the presenting and convicting of recusants; for as it concerneth religion so it hath relation to His Majesty's profits, which are two great motives, to which you may add a third, because the King hath many years since assigned these forfeitures to public defence. In the

94

next place I do require you that you make a strict inquiry after depopulations and enclosures; a crime of a crying nature that barreth God of his honour and the King of his subjects; churches and houses go down together.' Thanks to high oppression people were 'eaten up like bread to satisfy the greedy desires of a few'. Next, the judges were to look to the rectifying and repairing of ale-houses and tippling-houses, 'one of the greatest pests of the kingdom'; and they were to attend (or see that the justices of the peace attended) to such matters as the punishment of vagabonds and the binding of apprentices. After all this came the Lord Keeper's instruction, noted in an earlier chapter, to encourage the people to pay their ship money cheerfully. Officially the judges might constitute a Commission of Oyer and Terminer and General Gaol Delivery, but the shadow of the old Eyre inquisition still hung over the assize. Year in, year out the judges had to be reminded that the harrying of recusants was not bringing in as much money as it should. As circuit followed circuit, a judge would find himself inveighing against nearly everything that vexed the Government, not only tax-dodging but profaning the Sabbath, fornication and pulling the wool from living sheep.

Some circuits were more popular than others. The Western enjoyed a good deal of prestige; judges received generous hospitality from the nobility and gentry and the more able-bodied ones might even be invited to hunt the deer in Devon. In 1634 Lord Chief Justice Richardson in a charge to a grand jury on this circuit made some unfortunate remarks about behaviour at wakes and church ales. A report was carried back to Archbishop Laud, who regarded the Judge's remarks as an infringement of ecclesiastical rights and complained to the Privy Council. The result was that Richardson found himself on the Essex Circuit, which enjoyed little prestige and was unrenowned for its hospitality.

The judges' progress was not yet free of the perils which beset it centuries earlier in Sherwood Forest. John Clavell's *Recantation of an Ill-Led Life,* published in 1634, has this warning for Bench and Bar :

There needs no cunning Settor to betray
To his companions when, nor yet, which way
You are to ride, nor heed the Theeves be told

What store of Coyne you carry; they all hold
You to be rich and certaine prize; beside
They know when from, when to, the Terme you ride.*

Sir William Morton, a King's Bench judge, set himself up as
an especial terror to highwaymen. When Claude Duval was
taken, in 1669, and ladies of high rank began to intercede for
him, the Judge is said to have threatened to resign if the
highwayman's life was spared. Whether this influenced the King
is open to much doubt. When the body was laid out in a tavern
in St Giles, Morton gave orders that the crowds should be
dispersed.

It was the sheriff's function to ensure the judges' safety. At
the boundary of each county he would wait with his retainers,
many of them armed with javelins and halberds, along with
a company of gentlefolk who regarded it as a privilege to escort
the King's representatives. In the turbulent north of England
the escort was no mere formality. Roger North, who accom-
panied Chief Justice North on his journeys, observed that the
tenants of certain manors would not move an inch beyond their
allotted boundary 'to save the souls of them'. They were 'a
comical sort of people', long-bearded, riding upon under-sized
horses, with broadswords and legs almost touching the ground.
All came up and talked cheek by jowl with the Judge, who was
well pleased with their discourses, since they were antiquarians
on their own ground.

The Northumberland sheriff gave the judges a dagger, a
pen-knife and knife and fork. In later generations the dagger
became a symbolic gift. On the Border conditions were such
that farmers built their houses of stone with square towers
and an overhanging battlement under which the cattle were
herded at night. If rustlers came the family bombarded them
with stones and scalding water from the roof. Rough and speedy
justice was done by a permanent Border Commission, which
had an equal number of Scots and English on it. At Newcastle
Chief Justice North tried a notorious character, Mungo Noble,
on charges of theft, but 'his Lordship was so much a south
country judge as not to think them well proved'. This caused
some local indignation. When the Judge discussed the evidence
and its defects a Border Commissioner said, 'My laird, send him

*Quoted in William Irving's *John Gay's London*.

ord Chancellor Jeffreys
erved the Court interest
a all the hardiest
ccasions'

ord Chancellor Jeffreys,
ring to escape in disguise,
caught by the mob at
apping

The Judges of the Common Pleas as seen by Hogarth, 1720

A State Trial in Westminster Hall:
the accused is the Duchess of Kingston,
charged with bigamy, 1776

to huzz and yees neer see him mere.' The area was also infested
by thugs called Bedlamers, one of whom, accused of killing a
member of his own fraternity, went dumb and had to be
threatened with *peine forte et dure*.

As part of the county's hospitality, the judges were invited to
visit coal mines, salt works and other sights foreshadowing the
Industrial Revolution. The Chief Justice listened to the sad
tales of colliery owners who had sunk laborious shafts without
profit; and with greater pleasure to Sir Ralph Delaval, who had
built a prosperous port at Seaton Delaval. The judicial party
went to Tynemouth aboard a civic barge, with 'four or five
drone bagpipe' in the prow and trumpeters astern; after which
they picknicked on an isle and listened to Scots anecdotes.

On the Western Circuit Chief Justice North was on especially
good terms with the gentry who – or so his brother says –
regarded him as 'the darling of the West'. The Cornishmen,
he found, were 'very fierce and contentious and strongly given
to indict one another'. The Judge was very much a King's man
and, in cases where popular sentiment was concerned, 'had to
tread upon eggs'. He had an uncomfortable experience when
he accepted the wrong kind of hospitality on the way to Exeter.
His host did not see fit to engage a parish minister for the
service before supper, but himself stood behind a table in the
hall, read a chapter of the Bible and then gave a long-winded
prayer in the Presbyterian manner. The judges took it ill but
did not think fit to rebuke the man in his own house. Next day
the wags had it that the judges had attended a conventicle and
were to be presented by the grand jury. Hospitality had worse
perils than this, however. Before he became a judge North rode
on the circuit to Colchester, where 'a scurvy downfall had
well nigh cost him his life'. They were entertained by Sir John
Shaw, 'one of the greatest kill-cows at drinking in the nation',
whose object seemed to be to get the whole circuit intoxicated.
When the time came to move on, some dropped but others
proceeded. North's horse with its comatose rider stopped to drink
in a pond, where the rider was saved from slithering in by a
tipsy clerk. He was put to bed and did not wake up until next
day, when he found himself in a strange cottage, far in the rear
of harder heads.

The Western Circuit had a long-standing reputation for
generosity towards the judges, who were plied with venison,

peacocks, sturgeon, turbot, wine, sugar loaves and much else. Occasionally a judge like Lord Chief Baron Hale would decline such hospitality. He was said to be so honest that if he received a false coin he would not pass it on to somebody else. Once on the Western Circuit, Hale was called on to hear an action in which the plaintiff was a country gentleman whose family had long been in the habit of sending buck to the judges. This dialogue occurred:

Lord Chief Baron: Is this plaintiff the gentleman of the same name who hath sent me venison?

Judge's servant: Yes, please you, my Lord.

LCB: Stop a bit then. Do not yet swear the jury. I cannot allow the trial to go on until I have paid him for his buck.

Plaintiff: I would have your Lordship to know that neither myself nor my forefathers have ever sold venison and I have done nothing for your Lordship which we have not done for every judge that has come this circuit for centuries bygone.

LCB: That is nothing to me. The Holy Scriptures say, 'A gift perverteth the ways of judgment'. I will not suffer the trial to go on till the venison is paid for. Let the butler count down the full value thereof.

Plaintiff: I will not disgrace myself and my ancestors by becoming a venison butcher. From the needless dread of selling justice your Lordship delays it. I withdraw my record.*

At Aylesbury Hale took violent offence when a knight who was the prosecutor in a case before the court sent him two sugar loaves. Pocketing the written evidence, he said, 'I will relate the foulness of the business as I find occasion.' But, as Roger North tells, his very determination not to be bribed laid him open to trickery. A courtier who had a cause to be tried before him got someone to call on the Judge as from the King, to speak in favour of his adversary, and won the desired judgment, for the Judge 'could not think any person to be in the right that came so unduly recommended'.

Not all judges were equally welcome on circuit. Mr Justice Allybone, one of James II's least happy appointments, complained to the grand jury at Lancaster that only three members of the gentry had turned out to welcome the official party. He was a militant Roman Catholic and it was observed that when his fellow judges attended the assize service in the parish church,

*F. C. Moncreiffe: *Wit and Wisdom of Bench and Bar*.

Allybone went to mass in a school house. Those who could over-look his religion could not overlook his arrogance on the Bench. The gentry would show themselves equally wary of a judge who appeared to lean to the popular party. Such a man might display insufficient indignation when shown copies of seditious news-sheets which were polluting their district; but a prerogative judge like Chief Justice North would share their anger and promise to use his influence in Whitehall. There were also judges whose appearance and habits did nothing to endear them. Sir Nicholas Hyde, noted for his meanness, was said to have ridden the circuits on horseback in a white-blue cloak looking 'more like a clothier or a woolman than a Lord Chief Justice'. The circuits seem to have been spared a visit by Lord Chief Justice Saunders who, had he not died in 1683 soon after his appoint-ment, might have presided over the Bloody Assizes. Roger North has painted Saunders as a reeking Silenus whose 'foetid mass . . . offended his neighbours in the Bar to the sharpest degree'. The corruption of his body was due to 'continual sottishness', yet when those near him complained of the stench 'he ever converted the complaint into content and laughing with the abundance of his wit'. One example of his wit was his assertion that 'none could say he wanted issue of his body, for he had nine in his back'. North allows that he was incorruptible, generous, loyal to his friends and was regarded by some as a model of rectitude in a vicious age. He seems to have been a family man, his home being 'a tailor's house in Butcher Row, called his lodging, and the man's wife was his nurse, or worse'.

Occasionally juries, no less than judges, found themselves riding the circuit. The practice of carting refractory jurors had been indulged since Plantagenet times and it was thought a particularly suitable discipline for Irish juries. If the twelve good men failed to reach a verdict, or reached an unsuitable verdict, or showed an unhelpful attitude to the court, they were loaded into an open waggon which then departed, with suitable escort, to the county boundary, where they were turned out and left to walk perhaps twenty or thirty miles home. The primitive state of the roads made the outward trip no less arduous than the homeward one. If the procedure sounds grossly high-handed, it should be remembered that not every jury was animated by the purest principles of justice. Mr Justice Harvey on circuit is said to have fined the members of a jury £10 each after they had

given perverse verdicts in four different criminal trials. For brow-
beating juries and deriding Magna Carta, which he referred to
as Magna Farta, Mr Justice Kelynge in 1667 earned the displeasure of Parliament, but displeasure was all he earned.
Friction between judge and jury sometimes had peculiar consequences. When Mr Justice Doddridge commented adversely on
the quality of jurors at Huntingdon, the sheriff empanelled a
new body of men, to whom he gave high-sounding fictitious
names, like Mamilian, Prince of Tozland and Henry, Prince of
Godmanchester. The Judge seems not to have noticed anything
amiss. In Cumberland Chief Justice North observed that the
local gentry were taking their own steps to correct what they
deemed to be wrongful verdicts; they had started to serve on the
common juries themselves, thus presenting the unusual spectacle
of 'pantaloons and shoulder-knots crowding among the common
clowns'.

Easily the worst collision between judge and jury occurred
at London's own assizes, at the Old Bailey, in 1670, during the
trial of William Penn, the founder of Pennsylvania, and his
fellow Quaker, William Mead. The affair is commemorated
by a panel at the Old Bailey. If the events really happened
according to the account in *The People's Ancient And Just
Liberties Asserted In The Trial Of William Penn And William
Mead* (1670) it was a more flagrant example of intimidation
than occurred in the Throckmorton trial. The two men had been
addressing a meeting in Gracechurch Street and were charged
with causing an unlawful and tumultuous assembly. As a rule
Quakers refused to doff their hats in court, but Penn and Mead
presented themselves bare-headed. At this the Lord Mayor, Sir
Samuel Starling, possibly feeling that the court was to be
deprived of its sport, cried to an usher, 'Sirrah! Who bid you
put off their hats? Put on their hats again.' When this was done,
the Recorder, Thomas Howel, admonished Penn with 'Do you
not know it is the King's court? Why do you not pull off your
hat then?' Penn replied, 'Because I did not believe that to be
any respect.' The Recorder then fined each forty marks for
contempt, brushing aside Penn's objection that the hats had been
placed on their heads for this purpose. Asked to plead, Penn
demanded to know under which law they were indicted and was
told by the Recorder, 'You must not think I am able to run up
so many years and over so many adjudged cases, which we call

common law, to answer your curiosity.' Penn observed that 'if
the common law be so hard to understand it's far from being
very common', and was called a saucy and pestilent fellow; and
when Mead quoted in Latin the Lord Mayor said, 'You deserve
to have your tongue cut out.' Soon the wrath of the Bench was
switched to the jury, which refused to convict. The Recorder
warned one juror, 'I shall set a mark on you, sir' and accused
him of thrusting himself on to the jury. All twelve were told,
'You shall be locked up without meat, drink, fire and tobacco
. . . You shall not think thus to abuse the court; we will have a
verdict by the help of God or you shall starve for it.' The jurors
were sent out to spend the night together and 'had not so much
as a chamber pot, though desired'. Next morning they returned
without the required verdict, at which the Lord Mayor
threatened to cut the throat of one juryman, then to slice his
nose; and, when Penn intervened, the Lord Mayor cried,
'Gaoler, bring fetters and stake him to the ground.' The Recorder observed that until now he had never understood why the
Spaniards operated an Inquisition, but if things went on like this
they would need one in England. Before sending the jury out
again he threatened to have them carted about the city 'as in
Edward III's time'. They returned on the following day, chilled,
dishevelled and uncommonly hungry, with the same verdict as
before. The Recorder, complaining 'you have followed your
judgments and opinions rather than the good and wholesome
advice which was given you', fined them forty marks each and
ordered them to be imprisoned until the money was paid. All
went to Newgate, including the two accused, for varying periods.
The sequel is told on the plaque at the Old Bailey: 'The case
of these jurymen was reviewed on a writ of Habeas Corpus and
Chief Justice Vaughan delivered the opinion of the Court which
established the Right of Juries to give their Verdict according to
their convictions.' The plaque does not say whether any official
displeasure was visited on the Recorder and London's First
Citizen.

George Fox, founder of the Society of Friends, had already
fallen foul of the courts. The Quakers, along with the innumerable other nonconformists, tended to be humourless, perfervid,
self-righteous, contemptuous of authority and incapable of
speaking save in terms of the Old Testament. Nor did some of
them endear themselves to the Bench by their habit of cohabiting

with women when 'moved of the Lord' to do so, without any
ceremony of marriage. This, said the judges, was mere adultery;
but the offenders retorted that of old the holy men of God took
unto themselves wives without being called upon to fee a minister.
The Quakers also objected strongly to the idea of feeing an
attorney in their defence. What was the judge for if not to
expound the law to the prisoner? A pamphlet signed 'G.F.'
entitled *An Instruction To Judges and Lawyers* (1657?) shows
the sort of thing judges had to contend with :

'And when the Judge is askt by the prisoner concerning the
hat, what Law and custom is for it and where he may read it?
Oh, cryes the Judge, and swells, and rages, and full of fury, I
do not carry my law books upon my back; but, saith the poor
prisoner, the Judges of old was legs to the lame, and eyes to
the blind, and a help to the helpless, and why wilt not thou . . .
inform me of the Law and custom that says, I must be fined a
hundred mark, and forty pounds, if I will not put off my hat to
you; why will you not instruct me in that law? . . . saies the
Judge, if you will put off your hat I will do you justice, if not
take him away Gaoler . . .'

The Judge, as Fox admits, showed displeasure if the gaoler
or the cryer knocked off a prisoner's hat and would order it to
be replaced, in order that it might be doffed by the wearer. A
similar pamphlet called *Truth Cleared From Reproaches And
Scandals Laid Upon It By Those Who Goes By The Name Of
Judges, And Who Went The Northern Circuit* (1654) describes
an episode at Appleby Assizes, where Quakers complained of
having been assaulted and robbed by the sheriff's trumpeters.
The judge is 'Judge Nudigate,' who is cautioned by the writer
not to lie, slander or blaspheme.

'Call Henry Howsman, saith the Clerk, Henry Housman of
Lupton come near, so I coming nearer, the Officers cryed, put
off thy hat, but I not regarding much, one took it off, and gave
it to me again; so going into the nearer room before the bench
I put it on again, which caused many to cry out, put it off, and
the Judge began to be angry with me, and some of them struck
it off; and the Judge said he would teach me what I did in that
place; I said, I was in the presence of God every day about my
labours as well as then, and my conscience told me that I did
work and had my hat on before the Lord; well, saith the Judge,
I know that, and that I am no better than thou, neither think

better of myself, but I must teach thee to give honour here, give
him the Book, said they, lay on your hand and be sworn, saith
the Judge, concerning these two men; I am sworn to speak the
truth always and now also, and that Book saith swear not all;
well, saith the Judge, that is in your Communications but when
you are before Authority you must swear the truth to end
controversie . . .'

For a judge to have his own hat knocked off was a rare
hazard, but this happened to Chief Justice Richardson at Salisbury in 1631. An offended labourer standing at the bar suddenly
hurled a brickbat at him (*jeta un Brickbat à le dit justice, que
narrowly missed,* as the court report has it), but as the Judge
was leaning on his elbow at the time the missile merely dislodged
his hat. This inspired him to say, 'If I had been an upright judge,
I had been slain.' Later the witty Judge was present when the
offender had his hand cut off before being hanged.

In Ireland, a circuit judge might wield military power. In
1691 Sir Richard Cox, of the Common Pleas in Dublin, rode
to Cork not only with Commissions of Oyer and Terminer and
Gaol Delivery but also with a commission to govern the county
and city of Cork. In his *Autobiography* he says: 'I soon raysed
and array'd eight regiments of Dragoons and three Foot, which
were under my command all that summer; they did great service
and did much execution upon the Irish and took from them so
much prey (to the value perhaps of £10,000) as set many of
them up after the war. I took no share of it myself though I
might have had the tenth, but in everything I acted the part of
a true Englishman . . .' With these forces Cox held an eighty-
mile frontier, losing fewer than ten men. He received a special
payment from the Government of £150 and the King gave him
an abatement of half his quit rent for ever. Earlier that year,
acting the part of a true Englishman, Cox and Lord Chief
Justice Reynell made £300 on their way to Cork by selling
'printed protections' to the Irish at sixpence each. It is a curious
picture of justice at work; but Ireland had its own rules, or lack
of them.

Even in less troubled times it was customary for the circuit
judges in Ireland to advance through the countryside at a
dragoon-like pace, with loaded pistols in front of the saddles. The
high sheriff led and a troop of horse brought up the rear. But
life was not too spartan; the saddle-bags held not only law books

and the circuit wardrobe but wine and delicacies.* The grada-
tions of rank were not too easy to observe at a judicial picnic,
but discipline seems not to have suffered.

The operation known as Gaol Delivery often brought sudden
death to those delivered, but periodically it also extinguished the
lives of the assize judges. In every court-room lurked the spectre
of gaol fever (typhus). One of the more awesome outbreaks had
occurred at Oxford in 1577, when the Chief Baron of the
Exchequer, Robert Bell, Mr Serjeant Barham, the high sheriff,
almost all the grand jury and numerous knights and gentlemen
all died within a period of forty days, more than three hundred
in all. At first they were supposed to have succumbed to 'a
poisonous steam that seemed to have broken forth from the
earth'. Then it was said that the cause of Oxford's Black Assize
was a 'saucy, foul-mouthed bookseller' and popish recusant called
Rowland Jenkes, who before his trial had called on an apothecary
and asked him to make up a 'strange and dangerous' substance
to burn with a wick.† Later Bacon expressed the view that the
pestilence had been brought by the prisoners from the gaol, 'it
being observed that they alone were not affected by it'.
Gradually and reluctantly, the authorities conceded that the
plague was a product of the noisome conditions in the gaols,
but it was a very long time before they did anything about it.
Some judges sought to parry the infection by sniffing at medica-
ments, as doctors did in poorhouses. Sir Edward Coke and Sir
Edward Montagu took to carrying long-handled fans. Many
diaries and obituaries contain references to gaol fever. In 1586
Mr Justice Flowerdew died from this cause at Exeter Assizes,
along with leading gentlemen of the county. In 1598 John
Chamberlain wrote, 'I hear that Justice Beaumont and Serjeant
Drew that rode the Northern Circuit are both dead, upon some
infection of the gaol as is most like.' Chief Justice Nicholas Hyde
was another victim. One judge who died of gaol fever was
unfortunate enough to contract it while lying in gaol. He was the
disreputable Sir Robert Wright, who fled on the fall of James II
and was locked up in Newgate to await impeachment. Lord
Campbell gloatingly tells how his body was thrown into a pit
with those of common miscreants.

Outbreaks came thick and fast in the eighteenth century. On

*O. J. Burke: *Anecdotes of the Connaught Circuit.*
†*Gentleman's Magazine,* 1750

the Western Circuit in 1730 the Lord Chief Baron, Thomas Pengelley, was one of 'some hundreds of persons' who died in the area of Taunton, thanks to the foul condition of some prisoners carted there from Ilchester. Twenty years later the Old Bailey underwent a Black Sessions. The court was crowded to hear the trial of a duellist accused of killing his adversary. Of the judges, two escaped; but Sir Thomas Abney and Baron Clarke died, along with the Lord Mayor and other dignitaries, the total death-roll being about fifty. This led to the custom of strewing dried herbs in each court and the issue of nosegays for the judges. As an extra safeguard, vinegar fumes were pumped into court. The incidence of gaol fever did not decrease until a generation later, when resolute efforts were made to clean up and ventilate the gaols. The moving spirits were John Howard and John Topham, MP for Taunton.

10

CASTING OUT DEVILS

Happy was the judge who rode the circuits without ever being called upon to sentence witches. It is easy to say that judges, by virtue of their training, should have been more sceptical than other men; that they of all people should have been able to recognise hysteria, self-delusion and juvenile perjury when they saw it. But when the Church said that to deny the existence of witchcraft was to deny the revealed word of God, in both Testaments; when the Wisest Fool himself openly protested about the 'fearful abounding' of 'these detestable slaves of the Devil'; when Parliament had passed a law to stop people feeding, rewarding or giving suck to demons; when doctors and surgeons saw nothing unreasonable in exploring the bodies of old women for unnatural teats; when 'witch-finder' was an accepted if not admired occupation, who was the assize judge to form a minority of disbelief? Even the subtle minds of the great jurists, like Bacon and Coke, were ranged against him, though occasionally the subtlety seemed a shade over-refined, as in this passage from John Selden's *Table Talk*:

'The law against witches does not prove that there be any, but it punishes the malice of those people that use such means to take away men's lives. If one should profess that by turning his hat thrice and crying *buz* he could take away a man's life (though in truth he could do no such thing) yet this were a just law made by the State that whomsoever should turn his hat thrice and say *buz* with an intention to take away a man's life shall be punished with death.'

Originally witchcraft was left to the Church to extirpate. There must have been judges who wished that the onus of dealing with it still lay on the Church courts. If a judge was anxious to secure the acquittal of a suspect it was useless to proclaim a disbelief in witchcraft, since that would only brand him as irreligious and the jury would be at pains to teach him a lesson. All he could do was try to discredit the evidence, to reveal perjury and conspiracy in their true colours. The community in which he found himself was usually in a state of intense animosity towards its victims, who in all probability had been maltreated or 'floated' in ponds. In the courtroom the judge would sense the hatred in the air. 'The justices, to their eternal discredit, often gave way to the mob when forced to choose between the legal murder of an old woman whom they knew to be innocent and a riot in which property might be damaged,' writes a student of witchcraft.* Others, to their eternal credit, risked a riot and saved a life.

Witch-hunting had quickened under Elizabeth but became a national obsession under the early Stuarts and the Commonwealth. For reasons insufficiently analysed, the nation plunged back into the manias and superstitions of the middle ages. If pigs or geese behaved oddly, the Devil was assumed to be at large in the farmyard. In 1629 Mr Justice Hyde in the King's Bench admitted evidence by two old clergymen about a murdered woman whose body, when touched, was said to change colour, sweat, open and shut its eyes three times and extend its marriage finger three times; and on the strength of this three persons were convicted and two of them executed.† James I must take his share of the blame for the hallucinations of his subjects, but though he firmly believed in the existence of demons he was not totally credulous. In 1616 he called at Leicester where two of his judges, Mr Justice Winch and Serjeant Crewe, had left nine witches for execution. There he interviewed the boy who had given evidence against them and pronounced him an impostor. By then it was too late to save the women. This caused some embarrassment to the two judges, though it does not appear to have set back their careers. Charles I personally intervened in another witch trial, ordering three Lancashire witches to be brought to London for his inspection. He told them that their lives were no longer at risk but had no freedom to offer them. The egregious Matthew Hopkins, Witch-Finder General, who

*Eric Maple: *The Dark World of Witches.*
†*Gentleman's Magazine*, 1851.

took as his text 'Thou shalt not suffer a witch to live' (Exodus 22, xviii), was responsible for the deaths of scores of women in East Anglia. Bury St Edmunds seemed to excel at offering up its crones for sacrifice. In 1645, when nearly two hundred persons were locked up there on charges of trafficking with the Devil, a special Commission of Oyer and Terminer was set up under Serjeant John Godbolt, with various justices of the peace and clergymen. Two sermons were preached before the Commissioners got down to work. Of the first batch the judges hanged eighteen, who 'dyed very desperately'. The approach of royalist troops disturbed the administration of justice, but a second batch of women were apparently tried and condemned.*

The post-Restoration judges were a shade less credulous. On the Western Circuit Chief Justice North showed how a jury could be persuaded into freeing a supposed trafficker with the Devil. Before him at Taunton was an old man charged with bewitching a girl of thirteen into spitting pins. The Judge, according to his brother's account, wondered why the pins were always straight, never crooked. He examined witnesses 'very tenderly and carefully', so that the jury should not guess how his mind was working. The aged 'wizzard' defended himself with great conviction, but the Judge still played for time, uncertain whether he could safely instruct the jury to throw out the evidence. On an impulse he asked for the opinion of a justice of the peace who had first interviewed the accused man. This gentleman, who said he had not realised he was allowed to speak, offered the theory that the girl put her head down close to her stomacher, took up pins from its folds with her mouth and then, righting herself, spat them out into the hands of bystanders. 'This,' says Roger North, 'cast an universal satisfaction upon the minds of the whole audience and the man was acquitted.' As the Judge left the court a hideous old woman approached him and said, 'God bless your worship! Forty years ago they would have hanged me for a witch and they could not, and now they would have hanged my poor son.'

The account has a naive, almost fairy-tale quality characteristic of all such reports. Awkward questions bristle. Did the girl teach herself the pin trick? Were her family and friends so stupid as not to be able to detect it, or so evil as not to wish to do so? Would the justice of the peace have let the man die

*Montague Summers (ed.): *The Discovery of Witches.*

if he had not been invited to speak? If the girl had spat crooked pins, would the Judge have been unsceptical? As a court report, Roger North's account is highly unsatisfactory, but so are most accounts of witch trials.

Exeter was the Bury St Edmunds of the West. At one assize, as Chief Justice North rode into the city with Mr Justice Raymond, their horses had some trouble in hauling the carriage up the ascent to the Castle. This, they learned, was because two particularly malevolent witches in custody in the town had cast a spell on the animals. North was afraid that, in view of the popular excitement, his colleague, whose duty it was to hear the criminal trials, would take the passive line and allow the women to die; and his fears proved justified. In 1682 North himself was unable to save the lives of three more women – Temperance Lloyd, Susanna Edwards and Mary Trembles – who were convicted of witchcraft at Exeter. One of them admitted having given suck to the Devil, another had sold her soul to a dark stranger, the third had allowed the Devil in the guise of a lion to seduce her. If women openly admitted such acts, how were they to be saved? The Chief Justice explained his difficulties in a dispatch to Secretary Jenkins. His fellow judge Raymond, who tried the women, had assured him that they were 'the most old, decrepit, despicable, miserable creatures he had ever seen', fit subjects for an artist who wished to depict such figures. 'They appear not only weary of their lives but to have a great deal of skill in convicting themselves,' wrote North. 'Their descriptions of the sucking devils with saucer eyes were so natural that the jury could not choose but believe them.' The Chief Justice conceded that some might think the evidence the result of confederacy, melancholy or delusion. 'We cannot reprieve them,' he said, 'without appearing to deny the very being of witches, which, as it is contrary to the law, so I think it would be ill for His Majesty's service, for it may give the faction occasion to set afoot the old trade of witch-finding, which may cost many innocent people their lives, which this justice will prevent.' It was a remarkable argument that the State should murder a few to prevent the mob from murdering more, but it seems to have been accepted. The three women were hanged amid popular rejoicing, with a clergyman in attendance trying to wring further confessions from them. When she had only a few moments to live, Temperance Lloyd denied that she had ever passed herself through a keyhole or ridden over the sea on a cow, though she said the latter feat had been performed by Susanna Edwards.

Yet even an Exeter jury could acquit. In 1685, in the midst of the Bloody Assizes, a woman charged before Jeffreys, who disbelieved in witchcraft, went free. That same year, however, Sir Matthew Hale, Lord Chief Baron, blotted a good judicial record when he allowed two women to be hanged at Bury St Edmunds. They were accused of bewitching children, who claimed that the presence of the women caused them to lose their hearing, become rigid and vomit pins. Serjeant Kelynge (later Lord Chief Justice) was dissatisfied with the evidence. As an experiment one of the child accusers was blindfolded and touched by a woman who was in no way under suspicion; the fact that the child still screamed seemed to give point to the Serjeant's objections, but the Lord Chief Baron was unimpressed by the experiment. In court was 'a person of great knowledge, Dr Brown of Norwich', none other than Sir Thomas Browne, the physician-philosopher who wrote *Religio Medici*. Asked for his opinion, he said he thought the fits might be natural, but that they were aggravated by the Devil in collusion with the witches; and, from his great knowledge, he added that there was much vomiting of pins in Denmark. Instead of summing up, the Lord Chief Baron said to the jury: 'That there were such creatures as witches he made no doubt at all. For, first, the Scriptures had affirmed so much. Secondly, the wisdom of all nations had provided laws against such persons, which is an argument of their confidence in such a crime. And such hath been the judgment of this kingdom, as appears by that Act of Parliament which hath provided punishments proportionable to the quality of the offence.' The Judge then invoked the help of God in directing the jurors' hearts, observing that 'to condemn the innocent and to let the guilty go free were both an abomination to the Lord'. With or without divine guidance, the jury returned a verdict of guilty. The women were 'much urged to confess but would not'. After the verdict the three child witnesses, with their parents, called at the Lord Chief Baron's lodging. They were composed and in good health, only one of them complaining of a slight pricking of pins in the stomach. The Judge was told that their recovery had begun within half an hour of the verdict being announced.*

State Trials.

Those who have tried to explain away Sir Matthew Hale's lapse at Bury St Edmunds have suggested that his piety and theological readings seemed only to have had the effect of making him the more credulous and unrelenting; or that 'the rectitude of his intentions while under the bias of strong prejudices might sometimes betray him into great mistakes'. The Earl of Nottingham had only praise for 'a Chief Justice of so indefatigable an industry, so invincible a patience, so exemplary an industry and as magnanimous a contempt of worldly things'. All he lacked was a contempt of unworldly things.

It was not only the mob who wanted to see witches destroyed. Judges came under pressure from gentry and landowners, since an unconvicted witch could constitute a threat to prosperity. During a trial at Salisbury, before Mr Justice Rainsford, Sir James Long called at the Judge's lodgings and said that, if the witch escaped, his property would be worth nothing, since all his people would leave. The woman was acquitted, but to save the estate and presumably to protect the woman, the Judge ordered that she should be kept in the city gaol at 2s 6d a week, at public expense, for which Sir James Long was suitably grateful. By the next assize he was asking the Judge to allow her to return to a room in the city at a saving of 1s a week.*

Lord Chief Justice Holt is usually credited with having done more than most to discourage witchcraft trials, though one may wonder what success he would have had in the days of Witch-Finder Hopkins. One after the other, persons tried before him were acquitted, notwithstanding all the inventions of their accusers. It seems inconceivable that the trick of vomiting pins still required to be discredited. In 1701 a London labourer called Richard Hathaway, who complained that a witch's presence caused him to perform this feat, was searched and his pockets were found full of pins. It had been noticed that these flew from his mouth only when his hands were free. He had also complained of having been bewitched into fasting for long periods. To the jury at Guildford Lord Chief Justice Holt said : 'I must leave you to consider with yourselves whether you have any evidence to induce you to believe that it would be in the power of all the witches in the world, or all the devils in Hell, to enable a man to fast beyond the time that Nature will allow. They cannot invent the laws of Nature . . . Tricks the Devil may play

Life of Francis North.

but not work a miracle; it is not to be thought that God should let him loose so far.'* This theological lesson convinced the jury, who acquitted without retiring. At the Judge's insistence Hathaway was prosecuted as a cheat, jailed and pilloried. Bury St Edmunds, that metropolis of evil, was still finding women who suckled polecats and children who could be bewitched into walking up walls, but even at Bury Lord Chief Justice Holt was able to set suspects at liberty.

One of his acquittals was obtained by making use of personal knowledge, which normally a judge should never do. The accused woman was said to have cast a spell, written on a scrap of paper. 'Let me see it,' ordered the Judge. She explained that 'a young gentleman' had once given it to her, to cure her daughter's ague. 'And did it?' asked the Judge. He was assured that it had cured her and many others. He then turned to the jury and said : 'Gentlemen, when I was young and thoughtless, and out of money, I and some companions as unthinking as myself went to this woman's house, then a public one, and having no money to pay my reckoning I hit upon a stratagem to get off scot-free. Seeing her daughter ill of ague I pretended I had a spell to cure her. I wrote the classic line you see and gave it to her so that if any is punishable it is I and not the poor woman.' After her acquittal the Judge settled his old reckoning with interest.

The knowledge that accusers were liable to end up in the pillory did something to abate the persecutions. So did an announcement, in 1712, at Essex Assizes by Lord Chief Justice Parker, who said that if a witch drowned while being floated all those concerned would qualify for a halter, no matter what King James' book said. The last woman sentenced to death for witchcraft may have been Jane Wenham, of Walkerne, Hertfordshire, in 1712. Mr Justice Powell, described by Swift as the merriest old gentleman he ever saw, poured scorn on the evidence. Informed that Jane was able to fly, he said, 'You may – there is no law against flying.' The jury did not care to see their beliefs ridiculed, and they knew that the local clergy were convinced of Jane's guilt; so, when invited to acquit, they did the opposite. In the face of popular anger against him the Judge delayed the date of execution and tried to secure a reprieve. The mob would have put the woman to death had not a 'sensible gentleman',

*F. C. Moncreiffe : *Wit and Wisdom of Bench and Bar.*

Colonel Plummer, of Gilston, taken her under his protection and installed her in a cottage, where she lived inoffensively and piously. Her accuser, a pregnant hussy, also lived inoffensively after her sweetheart took the trouble to marry her.*

In the work of enlightenment the clergy were of little help. At Devonshire Assizes in 1716 Baron Price would have discharged two accused but for the fact that the local parsons 'made a body and got in a quantity of affidavits [so] that he was forced to satisfy the Church by continuing them in prison and one of them died in prison'.† Rural mobs continued to harry and float the enemies of God until well into the nineteenth century. Few now believe in sucking imps with saucer eyes, but a great many believe in flying saucers.

*Francis Hutchinson: *An Historical Essay Concerning Witchcraft.*
†William Matthews (ed.): *The Diary of Dudley Ryder,* 1715–76.

11

GLORIOUS MILESTONE

The rays of the Glorious Revolution did little to cheer the lives of those judges who lay in the Tower or in Newgate, awaiting the displeasure of their enemies. However, the immediate recriminations are of little importance. For the judiciary, history had now reached a turning point.

The Act of Settlement of 1701 set out the new freedoms. Generations of subservience to the Crown were over. There was no longer any need to worship the rising sun. Judges ceased to be the cronies of the King's Closet, the bullies of the administration, the apologists of arbitrary taxes, the confederates of the bishops. Their function was to administer the rule of law, holding the balance between Crown and subject, and between man and man. They were answerable to no political party, though in practice their selection and advancement would still depend very largely on their political views. Henceforth they held their office *quamdiu se bene gesserint*, for as long as they were of good behaviour, and not for as long as they pleased the Sovereign. They were to be irremovable except by death or for misconduct of a kind to warrant an address presented in both Commons and Lords. Parliament alone had ultimate authority over them; and it was Parliament which would now assume responsibility for safeguarding the nation's liberties.

These ameliorations, it should be stressed, were not at once apparent to those who lived through the post-Revolutionary upheaval. All wrongs and corruptions and suspicions did not vanish overnight. In the year before the Act of Settlement was passed, Lord Chancellor Somers asked to be dismissed after a near-successful attempt in Parliament to saddle him with complicity in the piracies of Captain Kidd, whose freebooting voyage he had helped to underwrite. For a Lord Chancellor, it was a curious form of investment. Pope's vision of an English eventide in *The Rape of the Lock* (1711) suggests that the assize courts are not yet purged of human fallibility :

> Meanwhile, declining from the noon of day,
> The sun obliquely shoots his burning ray;
> The hungry judges soon the sentence sign,
> And wretches hang that jurymen may dine.

In *Gulliver's Travels* (1726) the legal system has not yet been reformed. 'In the trial of persons accused of crimes against the State,' writes Swift, 'the judge first sends to sound the disposition of those in power; after which he can easily hang or save the criminal, strictly preserving all the forms of law.' It is not unknown for satirists to attack abuses which have ceased to exist. However, Swift's gibes against Chancery – Gulliver had been ruined by winning a suit with costs – continued to be valid. Nor was he wholly without justification when he described how judges used precedents 'as authorities to justify the most iniquitous opinions', for by the end of the eighteenth century Bentham and others would be complaining loudly about the injustices of judge-made law, a complaint which is still voiced periodically today. The judges would be accused of living cut off from liberal society, in a world of their own laws devised for an earlier, harsher day.

Nevertheless, the result of the Act of Settlement was that, as the judges' independence was seen to be assured and their political aspirations were curbed, so their public reputation rose. Much less was now heard about corruption. As we shall see, a Master of the Rolls and a Lord Chancellor were still to disgrace their offices, but the notion that judicial favours could be bought and sold – except among the petty chisellers in Chancery – was not seriously entertained in the eighteenth century. Not even the execrated Stuart judges had been venal; they abandoned impartiality only under royal pressure. Henceforth judges might be abused for being high Tories, or for leaning to populist ideas, or for ignorance of the law, or for bad manners, or for ferocity, or for unseemly ambition, or for social pretensions, but their bitterest enemies did not cast doubts on their financial honesty.

The assize trumpets sent out a terrible sound, but the notes were unflawed.

The Master of the Rolls who fell short of the new standards was Sir John Trevor, a cousin of Jeffreys and a considerable gamester. His error, committed in his capacity of Speaker of the House of Commons, consisted of accepting £1,100 from the Common Council of London to bring forward a Bill. In 1695 as Speaker he was privileged to preside over a debate on his own conduct and when the motion was put, accusing him of a high crime and misdemeanour, he declared with suitable gravity, 'The ayes have it.' Next day he had an attack of colic and did not take the chair, but sent the Mace with an explanatory letter. The colic continuing, he was dismissed from the Speakership but allowed to remain Master of the Rolls, 'to the great encouragement of prudent bribery for ever after', as Professor Holdsworth remarks.* Had he committed a comparable offence as Master of the Rolls, presumably Parliament would have retained him as Speaker.

A touch of black farce also distinguished the case of Thomas Parker, Earl of Macclesfield, the avaricious Lord Chancellor who fell a victim, in 1725, to the speculations of his underlings in the South Sea Bubble. He was not the most popular of figures, being both ambitious and overweening; qualities to be expected, in the view of some, in the son of an obscure country attorney educated at a free grammar school. If he had not crashed in ruin he might have been remembered chiefly for his ruling that whereas a man who pulls down a brothel as a public nuisance may be guilty of a riot, a man who presumes to pull down all brothels usurps the Sovereign's right and commits high treason. At the time of the Bubble the Masters of Chancery were under no obligation to keep suitors' money in a separate account. It was their custom to invest it in whatever enterprises or funds they fancied and to pocket the interest. Obviously the prospect of earning several hundred per cent on the estates of orphans and lunatics was too much to resist. When the Bubble burst it was found that Master Fleetwood Dormer had left on a holiday trip to the Continent, his funds being £25,000 short, and that Master John Borret had died, leaving his accounts in a state which horrified even his dishonest colleagues. For a while Lord

*Sir W. S. Holdsworth: *A History of English Law.*

Macclesfield had hopes of hushing up the scandal. He sought by gentle blackmail to persuade the Masters to make up the deficiencies, but they blackmailed back by pointing out that he had already charged them extortionate sums for their offices. Some £10,800 of the missing money the Earl reluctantly made up himself. The cries of the cheated suitors were too loud to stifle and the Lord Chancellor was indicted before the House of Lords on twenty-one charges, which could be said to compare favourably with Bacon's twenty-eight. Most of the 'wicked and corrupt bargains' of which he was accused involved 'illegally, corruptly and extorsively' demanding sums in the region of £5,000 from candidates for masterships, which were not among the offices he was entitled to sell. He was also charged with inciting the Masters to make false statements to the inquiry set up by 'his most sacred Majesty out of his fatherly goodness to his people'. It was surprising, said the prosecution, that men of such small substance could produce such large sums to buy masterships, but not so surprising when it was realised that these sums were repaid out of public money. The prosecution did not spare the rhetoric. The guardian of orphans had proved their oppressor. The custodian of the widow's mite had added it to his own heap. The keeper of the King's conscience had prostituted his own. The man charged with reforming abuses had spent his days and nights in an ignominious traffic with the highest bidders. The scales of justice had been used to carry out the business of a usurer. Contrary to the Law of Nature, a suitor had been made the instrument of his own destruction. Such an example could not fail to be 'a warning and a terror to times to come'. To which the Earl replied that the practices of which he was accused were 'never before looked upon to be criminal or complained of as such'. In fact, the sale of offices had been banned in Plantagenet days but generations of Lord Chancellors had ignored the prohibition.

Master Francis Elde explained how some of his friends had 'put it into his head' that a vacant mastership might be an appropriate office for him. When he approached the Lord Chancellor he was told, 'Thee and I must not make bargains.' A secretary called Cottingham then acted as intermediary and when Elde suggested a sum of £5,000 Cottingham replied, 'Guineas are handsomer.' Elde got together the money, which was 'a great burthen and weight', so he put it in a basket and gave it to the secretary, who took it to the Lord Chancellor. Almost immediately afterwards Lord Macclesfield invited him to dinner and the appointment was confirmed. Some months later he asked for the basket back and it was returned to him empty. Another witness, Master Thomas Bennet, agreed that Cottingham was a great stickler for guineas.

The evidence of Master Mark Thurston shed interesting light on the functions of a Lord Chancellor's lady. Her role invites comparison with that of Mrs Clarke, the Duke of York's ex-mistress, in the Army commissions scandal of a later date. Thurston told the tribunal that he had paid 5,000 guineas for his mastership, though in view of what had happened, he would have given 5,000 guineas not to have it. When he first began angling for the post he was promised an interview with the Lord Chancellor who, he understood, would make inquiries into his character. As nothing appeared to be happening and he had heard a rumour that another candidate was being considered, and more particularly because the press had already announced his own appointment, he went to Kensington to call on the Lord Chancellor. He was seen by Lady Macclesfield, who said she left public affairs to her husband, but seemed sympathetic to him. 'Before I went away from the room where I did have the honour to be with the lady,' he said, 'I did leave upon the table bank notes to the value of £5,250.' These were in a package directed to the Countess. After two or three days he was sworn into his post. Some months later, shortly before the scandal became public, Lady Macclesfield sent for him and returned £3,250, saying she did not know why he had left such a large present. 'The other part,' said Thurston, 'she would appropriate to her own use.'

Moving one of the articles of impeachment, Lord Morpeth hinted at some dark secrets in the nation's annals. First he compared the Lord Chancellor's activities to 'a continued piratical trade' and suggested that robbing Chancery suitors was like stealing from the shipwrecked. What punishment could there be for such wickedness? 'My Lords, there have been crimes so unexampled and of so horrid a nature that the malefactors have been tried at midnight and immediately drowned, and the journal books burnt, in compassion to mankind, that the memory of the proceedings being destroyed the crime itself might not be propagated.'

The Lord Chancellor, who throughout the trial 'desired' a great many questions to be asked, sometimes to the annoyance of the prosecuting serjeants, unfortunately did not desire to be told more about these sinister midnight inquisitions; so we can only speculate.

For the defence it was argued that to convict the Lord Chancellor would spread 'a universal cloud of reproach and infamy' over those 'venerable sages of the law' who had done as Lord Macclesfield had done in earlier generations. 'Many most pure and upright men have sat in the marble chair . . . and all of them without any public censure and without any self-reproach have received gratuities on disposing of their offices.' There had always been a well-understood distinction between the sale of offices and the sale of justice.

Their lordships, at the risk of impugning the immaculate dead, found the Lord Chancellor guilty and ordered him to pay a fine of £10,000. Until it was paid he was to stay in the Tower, which was always ready to receive Lord Chancellors. The Earl never considered himself to have been guilty of more than a 'want of discretion', but he did not resume his seat in Parliament. A harsher view was taken by the populace who, according to Lord Campbell, proclaimed that Staffordshire had produced the three greatest rogues of the day: Jack Sheppard, Jonathan Wild and Tom Parker. The King, out of his fatherly goodness to his people, and perhaps out of shame at the way the keeper of his conscience had behaved, made contributions from the privy purse towards the cheated suitors. It is not known whether Lady Macclesfield was able to spare some of her £2,000 gratuity towards the cause. Dormer's creditors seem to have received about 5s. in the pound, which would teach them to stay out of Chancery in future.

In the Commons the Speaker, Sir Spencer Compton, expressed thanks to those who had managed the trial, saying, 'You have stopped the cries of orphans and dried up the tears of the widow; even those who must ever be insensible of the benefits they receive, idiots and lunatics . . . will be partakers of the fruits of your labours.'* Certainly the trial proved a warning and a terror to future Lord Chancellors, though yet another was to be tumbled from office for want of discretion. One temptation at least had been removed before the Earl of Macclesfield was

*The Macclesfield case is reported in great detail in the *State Trials*.

appointed, for Lord Chancellor Cowper had abolished the custom whereby expensive New Year gifts were made to the sage in the marble chair.

The trial of the Earl of Macclesfield shows the sort of cesspool Chancery had become. Its waters could not grow much muddier, but henceforth they were to grow slowly clearer. No doubt the Earl's defenders were correct in saying that, while offices had been sold, justice had not. Justice, however, was unpredictable enough to inspire John Selden's saying, 'Equity is a roguish thing, as variable as the Lord Chancellor's foot.' It was not necessarily the rogue Chancellors who gave the roguish decisions. Of the treacherous Shaftesbury in his judicial role (before the days of the Popish Plot) Dryden says:

> Yet fame deserved no enemy can grudge;
> The statesman we abhor, but praise the judge.
> In Israel's courts ne'er sat an Abbethdin
> With more discerning eyes or hands more clean,
> Unbribed, unsought, the wretched to redress,
> Swift of despatch and easy of access.
> Oh! had he been content to serve the Crown
> With virtues only proper to the gown . . .

The Earl of Nottingham, who thought the Great Fire had been brought about by papists, is credited with many sound equity rulings. It should not be forgotten how tremendous were the day-to-day pressures on any Lord Chancellor. He was left with all too little time in which to weigh the principles of pure justice and to temper the laws for a better age.

A judge whose career forms a strong and admirable bridge between the old era and the new is Lord Chief Justice Holt, whose scepticism in the matter of witchcraft has already been remarked. Like all too many of his brethren, he grew up in dissipation. In later years he tried one of his Oxford friends for a felony and called on him in gaol to talk of old acquaintances. 'Ah, my Lord,' said the prisoner, 'they are all hanged except myself and your Lordship.' Many of Holt's ideas were too liberal for his day. During an action before him in which a man sued for possession of various items of property, including a Negro, counsel argued that Negroes were items of merchandise, like monkeys; opposing counsel contended that an owner had no absolute right in them, since he could not kill them like oxen. Holt ruled that in common law Negroes were no different from other men and that there were no slaves in England. Lord Mansfield's famous ruling in 1772, in the case of the Negro Somerset, was little more than an echo of this.

Holt had his foibles. He insisted that prisoners should not be brought before him in irons, though manacled prisoners were still to be seen in the dock in the nineteenth century. He was strongly against the use of the military in quelling riots and would enter on the scene of the fray with tipstaffs in an effort to cool tempers (it was part of the Lord Chief Justice's duty to help put down disorders). He is said to have asked a soldier what he would do if the mob did not disperse and received the reply, 'Fire on them, as we have orders.' The Judge said, 'Have you so? Then take notice that if one man is killed and you are tried before me, I will take care that every soldier in your party is hanged.' This, if true, was neither judicial nor sensible, but the story may have been a concoction designed to show the Judge's humanity – to civilians, if not to the military.

In *The Tatler* Holt, as 'Verus', was praised by Sir Richard Steele as one who 'considered justice as a cardinal virtue, not as a trade for maintenance'. He showed unusual punctiliousness in acting as the prisoner's counsel. 'The prisoner knew that, though his spirit was broken with guilt and incapable of language to defend itself, all would be gathered from him that could conduce to his safety; and that the Judge would wrest no law to destroy him nor conceal any that would save him.'* Evidently there were judges from whom such elementary courtesies were not to be expected. A century later the Rev. Sydney Smith was to say some scathing words on the notion that a judge could be prisoner's counsel, but Holt tried to show concern for the undefended in a callous age.

Professor Holdsworth, an admirer of Holt, also praises him for trying to bring an element of rationality into commercial law, a subject scorned by other judges, whose concern in the civil courts was with wranglings over land, as it had been since the Conquest. But a new mercantile Britain was emerging and commerce needed judges who understood its problems, though it had to wait a very long time for them. Here again Holt was ploughing a furrow which Lord Mansfield would continue.

*No. 14, 1709.

Because, for the judges, the greater part of the eighteenth century was a period of quiet consolidation and strengthening of esteem – even though the laws they administered became steadily more brutal – the period does not loom large in these pages. An age which began in fear of Jacobites ended in dread of Jacobins; and the judges once more found themselves figures of controversy.

12

FIGHTING THE 'PHRENZY'

When the Gallic 'phrenzy' began to infect the minds of
Englishmen, the judges had no doubt where their allegiance lay.
In lauding the virtues of the finest constitution in the world, in
decrying the infamy that would seek, by violence of speech or
action, to undermine it, they did so in almost the same words as
their forebears had used when defending the same constitution
against the spies and plotters of Spain. Although no longer the
creatures of the Throne, they praised its occupant in fulsome
terms, sometimes discerning in him virtues which others had
failed to notice. All this the judges did of their own passion
and conviction, with some occasional guidance from the Lord
Chancellor. It may not have been their duty to hold the sky
suspended, but it was a function that they loyally and willingly
undertook. Mr Justice Ashhurst's rousing address to the Middlesex grand jury, in 1792, was printed as a penny broadsheet and
distributed by the Society for Preserving Liberty and Property
Against Republicans and Levellers. At the head of this document
was an assurance that it breathed so much the true spirit of the
English law and was 'so well suited to curb the Licentious Spirit
of the Times that it must be read with heartfelt satisfaction by
all true Englishmen'. Here was a nation, said the Judge, in
which no man was so high as to be above the reach of the law
and no man so low as not to be within its protection; but such
a happy state could not survive without subordination and a
Coercive Power to punish those who would live by rapine and
spoil. It was necessary to deter all men of 'dark and gloomy
hearts' who wanted Britain to follow France into an abyss of

misery, and who were organising societies to further that purpose.

Those who remained unsickened by the carnage across the Channel, who felt that it was still a hopeful, if no longer a blissful, dawn in which to be alive, found the sentiments of Mr Justice Ashhurst intolerable. Jeremy Bentham composed an angry, carping pamphlet, *Truth v. Ashhurst,* but did not allow it to be printed until 1823. It is decidedly not in his best vein. What mainly incensed him was the Judge's uncritical praise of English laws, which Bentham had been so long assailing. These laws, he said, were made by judges as a man makes rules for his dog; that is, by waiting for the dog to do something wrong and then beating him for it. The French, despite the abominable things they had done, were moving over to statute law.

Writing well after the event, the Whiggish Scots judge, Lord Cockburn, said: 'Firm but mild and judicious treatment and a little reliance on the tendency of time to abate epidemic follies would have made the British Constitution popular and the proceedings in France odious everywhere.'* Perhaps so; but the Government of the day was taking no chances. Between them Pitt, the Lord Chancellor (Lord Loughborough) and the Attorney-General (Sir John Scott, later Lord Eldon) favoured a policy of stamping out ideas and preserving minds from contamination. It is easy to mock their hopes and their zeal; but men of dangerous eloquence and vast assurance were going about the kingdom describing themselves as 'Friends of the People', addressing each other as 'Citizen', using phrases like *ça ira* and *vive la Convention,* threatening to sound the 'tocsin of revolt', scoffing at kings and denying the existence of God. Some of them aped the unbuttoned dress of Frenchmen and wore their hair unpowdered. Agitators like these were deemed more dangerous than pamphleteers and quickly became marked men; but that did not mean that pamphleteers and printers were to escape. Wild language could lead to wilder behaviour. So men were prosecuted for likening the wise King of England to Nebuchadnezzar or describing their rulers as a base oligarchy feeding their filthy vermin on the nation's vitals. Such expressions, in the view of the Crown, were 'calculated to degrade and bring into contempt the Sovereign, the Government and the Legislature, and to withdraw therefrom the confidence and

*Henry Cockburn: *Memorials of His Time.*

affections of the people and to fill the realm with trouble and dissension'.

It was not to be expected that Ireland, with all its ancient grievances, would escape the contagion. During the 1790s, plots and insurrections, fanned by the French, were put down with sword, fire and noose. Wolfe Tone's United Irishmen, founded in 1791, grew more and more radical. But there were United Scotsmen and United Englishmen too. As it turned out, the first major trials arising out of the Revolutionary fervour took place in Edinburgh, where meetings of a British Convention had been dispersed in 1793. It has been suggested that the reason for this venue was that the Scots courts had unrestricted power to punish sedition by transportation. The trials in question are those commemorated on the Martyrs' Memorial on Calton Hill, Edinburgh, which very nearly bore an inscription saying that the men were 'victims of judicial iniquity'.

The presiding judge was Lord Braxfield, variously described as the Jeffreys and the Ellenborough of Scotland, and the unchallenged original of Robert Louis Stevenson's Weir of Hermiston. He was Scotland's Lord Justice Clerk, the equivalent of England's Lord Chief Justice. Lord Cockburn has left an acrid, Whig's-eye-view of this formidable character, who gloried in his use of the vernacular: 'Unscrupulous, tyrannical, coarse, dissipated, illiterate, he was morally almost featureless. He had a hard heart, a tainted mind, a cross-grained, domineering nature and an uncouth exterior. A noble aspiration or a lofty motive he was incapable of experiencing. Without faith, without hope and without charity, he moved continually in a world of sordid interests and ignoble purposes.'* According to Cockburn, Braxfield scorned all natures less coarse than his own and forced people to enjoy, or endure, his indecencies 'by hearty laughter, energy of manner and rough humour'. In appearance he was 'strong-built and dark, with rough eyebrows, powerful eyes, threatening lips and a low, growling voice . . . like a formidable blacksmith'. His diversions were 'claret, whist and less pure enjoyment'.† Less trenchant critics make allowances for his humble origins. 'It was mortifying,' says Ramsay of Ochtertyre, 'to hear an aged judge revered for talents and usefulness swearing without provocation like an ensign of the last age in his

Memorials of His Time.
†Henry Cockburn: *Circuit Journeys.*

teens.'* Brougham spoke civil words about Lord Braxfield, emphasising his old-school politeness in female society. Sir Walter Scott dedicated a thesis to him. Nobody denied that Lord Braxfield had a great capacity for work. Though Cockburn calls him dissipated, there were harder drinkers on the Scots Bench, and drink did not impair his judgment. 'Illiterate' possibly means only that he lacked an interest in art and literature and scorned rhetoric.

James Boswell, who addressed a solemn, indeed over-solemn, letter to Lord Braxfield on his appointment in 1780 to the Scottish High Court, stressing the need for judicial decorum, made a point which was not without relevance to the trials of 1793–94: 'My Lord, have you never observed that a criminal trial in Scotland appeared on the part of the judges not so much an inquisition whether the prisoner was guilty as an anxious study that one already known to be guilty should not escape? Has your Lordship never remarked, in the Judiciary Court, that when witnesses were swearing *against* the prisoner, their testimony was received by the Bench with full credibility; but that when swearing *for* him distrust and suspicion were evidently expressed?' Possibly this was caused, Boswell thought, by the fact that a prisoner in Scotland had the benefit throughout the trial of counsel who could protect him from injustice, whereas in England the judge was traditionally the man who watched over the prisoner's interest. The fact remained that 'a better *spirit of office,* more propriety of behaviour and a more civilised mildness of manners' were to be found in the south. That this letter had any effect on Lord Braxfield's behaviour is wildly unlikely. His tendency to assume guilt was summed up in his saying, 'Bring me prisoners and I'll find you law.'

If Lord Braxfield used the Bench as a political pulpit during the sedition trials, it is clear that the prisoners used the bar for the same purpose. The initial impression afforded by the *State Trials,* which mercifully do not attempt to reproduce the vernacular, is of the Lord Justice Clerk's forbearance, even fortitude, when faced by arrogant harangues. However, in the trial of the advocate Thomas Muir, who had been disseminating the works of Thomas Paine, the Judge was able to summarise uninterruptedly for posterity the views of a Scots Tory of the day. Praising the 'happiest, the best and the most noble con-

Scotland and Scotsmen in the Eighteenth Century.

stitution in the world', he said : 'Is not every man secure in his
life, liberty and prosperity? Is not happiness in the power of
every man, except those perhaps who, from disappointment in
their claims of advancement, are discontented? And does not
every man sit safely under his own vine and his own fig tree and
none shall make him afraid?' This was not the most accurate
picture of the depopulated Highlands at the time, but Lord
Braxfield was speaking generally. He pointed out that the
accused man had sought to undermine this happy system and
had enjoyed contacts with Paris. 'I never was an admirer of the
French,' said the Judge, 'but I can now only consider them as
monsters of human nature'. On Parliamentary reform, which
was widely thought to be a cover for revolution, Lord Braxfield
held unequivocal views : 'A government in every country should
be just like a corporation; as for the rabble who have nothing
but personal property, what hold has the nation of them? What
security for the payment of taxes? They may pack up all their
property on their backs and leave the country in the twinkling
of an eye, but landed property cannot be removed.'

When the judges came to consider sentence, Lord Henderland said they had the choice of banishment, fine, whipping,
imprisonment and transportation. Whipping was too severe and
too disgraceful for a man of Muir's character and rank; and
banishment would be improper because 'it would only be sending
to another country a man dangerous to any, where he might
have the opportunity of exciting the same spirit of discontent'.
Eventually the judges decided to send this dangerous man to the
other side of the world for fourteen years, which did not count
as banishment; though fourteen years would seem a period in
which a man could work up a fair amount of discontent. Lord
Braxfield commented that the 'indecent applause' for Muir by
certain persons in court showed that the spirit of dissatisfaction
was still abroad. Muir said, 'Were I to be led this moment from
the bar to the scaffold I should feel the same calmness and
serenity which I do now.' There is a story to the effect that just
before Muir's trial began the Judge whispered to a juror whom
he knew, 'Come awa', Maister Horner, come awa', and help us
to hang ane o thae daamned scoondrels.'*

To Maurice Margarot, a delegate of the London Corresponding Society, which was campaigning for universal suffrage, the

*Henry Cockburn: *Memorials of His Time.*

court extended an astonishing degree of indulgence. Margarot was, as they must have known, a man with a ready and fearless tongue and many an ace up his sleeve. He began by demanding to know why the Lord Justice General of Scotland was not present. He protested because the doorkeepers were charging the public for admission and was told to mind his own business. The following dialogue is supposed to have occurred, though it does not appear in the *State Trials*: Lord Justice Clerk: Hae ye ony coonsel, man? Margarot: No. LJC: Dae ye want to hae ony appointit? Margarot: No. I only want an interpreter to make me understand what your Lordship says.* The prisoner went on to challenge not only the authority of the court but its integrity:

'A judge ought to be like Caesar's wife, not only spotless but even unsuspected; that is not the case with you, my Lords . . . You may, though you are now sitting upon that Bench, be brought to atone on your knees, perhaps with your lives, for any infraction of the laws you may be guilty of. My Lords, we well know that Cambyses ordered an unjust judge to be flayed and the skin of that judge covered the seat of his successor. We also know that in the reign of Alfred in one year forty-four judges were hanged; and you will know the fate of Jeffreys who, though the slow hand of the law could not overtake him, was torn to pieces by the people . . .'

It is unlikely that Jeffreys (who was not torn to pieces by the people) would have allowed a prisoner to get so far; but the Scottish Jeffreys gave the prisoner rein on the grounds that he was not a native of Scotland. Later in the trial Margarot sprang as nasty a trap for a judge as is imaginable:

Margarot: Now, my Lord, comes a very delicate matter indeed. I mean to call upon my Lord Justice Clerk and I hope that the question and the answers will be given in the most solemn manner. I have received a piece of information which I shall lay before the court . . . First, my Lord, are you on oath?

LJC: State your questions and I will tell you whether I will answer them or not. If they are proper questions, I will answer them.

M: Did you dine at Mr Rochead's at Inverleith in the course of last week?

LJC: And what have you to do with that, sir?

*Kay's *Edinburgh Portraits.*

Lord Braxfield:
'Bring me prisoners and I'll find you law'

Lord Ellenborough:
the foe of 'speculative humanity'

'An Interesting Trial for Murder,' as seen by Doyle, 1849

A new term opens in Westminster Hall, by Doyle

M: Did any conversation take place with regard to my trial?

LJC: Go on, sir.

M: Did you use these words: 'What should you think of giving him a hundred lashes, together with Botany Bay?' or words to that purpose?

LJC: Go on, put your questions if you have any more.

M: Did any person, did any lady say to you that the mob would not allow you to whip him? And, my Lord, did you not say that the mob would be the better for losing a little blood? These are the questions, my Lord, that I wish to put to you, at present, in the presence of the court. Deny them or acknowledge them.

The Lord Justice Clerk could have blustered or stormed, but there was a better way out.

LJC: Do you think I should answer questions of that sort, Lord Henderland?

Lord H: No, my Lord, they do not relate to this trial. Questions as to the facts which are at all material to the charges contained in this indictment my Lord Justice Clerk is obliged to answer, but not otherwise.

Lord Eskgrove: What may have been said in a private company cannot in any way affect this case . . .

Lord Swinton: Were he not a stranger here I should look upon it as an insult offered to the court.

The objection was repelled. It was an impressive show of judicial solidarity; but the trick was virtually won by Margarot.

Perhaps because of this challenge and the fear of worse to come, Margarot was allowed to make a very long speech in his defence, but his eloquence was of no avail. The sentence was one of fourteen years transportation, with the threat of 'death without benefit of clergy' if he returned prematurely to Britain. Margarot said, 'My Lords, I thank you.'

Lord Braxfield had not heard the last of that conversation at Inverleith. Joseph Gerrald reminded him of it when his turn came for trial; his case, he said, was already prejudged. This time Braxfield left the Bench, while Lord Henderland asked his brothers to consider the predicament of 'that respectable judge who has the honour to preside'. Lord Eskgrove thought Gerrald's statement showed the malevolence of desperation; Lord Swinton's view was that 'the insolence of his objection is swallowed up in the atrocity of his crime'. Lord Henderland said the conversation about which complaint was made appeared to have been a transient one about sedition and the punishment due to it, but was that any ground for declining a judge? The answer was, of course, no.

When Gerrald, who deliberately dressed in the French style, was found guilty, his counsel sought clemency on the grounds of his bad health. 'A man of high talents, of a cultivated understanding, is to be condemned to the communion of thieves and villains, the refuse and dregs of the human race . . . He is to be sent to the desolate shores of the remote southern ocean. From these hapless regions it may perhaps be impossible to return; but from his state of health it is highly probable that this gentleman will never even arrive at his miserable destination. His sentence of exile will have been to that "undiscovered country from whose bourne no traveller returns".'

Gerrald then spoke for himself, citing Hampden, Locke, Camden, Montesquieu, Blackstone, Cardinal Bellarmine, Burke, Hume and others who may or may not have been known to the 'illiterate' Lord Justice Clerk. He quoted Latin and Greek. He declaimed phrases like 'Oh! preposterous insult to the dignity of the human race' and 'Oh! blasphemy against the Author of all Goodness!' Lord Braxfield broke in to say, 'You would have been stopped before this if you had not been a stranger. All that you have been saying is sedition; and now, my Lords, he is attacking Christianity.' When Gerrald resumed he quoted St Augustine, Tully, Sir William Temple, Grotius, Hooker and Coke. It is said, though not in the *State Trials,* that he cited Christ as a reformer, which drew a comment from Lord Braxfield, 'Muckle He made o' t; He was hangit.'* Having overtaxed his strength, Gerrald was allowed to sit for a while, then he was up again quoting more poets and philosophers. Lord Braxfield was sufficiently impressed to say, 'I dare say he has eloquence enough to persuade the people to rise in arms.'

Gerrald: Oh, my Lord! My Lord! This is a very improper way of addressing a jury; it is descending to personal abuse. God forbid that my eloquence should ever be made use of for such a purpose.

LJC: Mr Gerrald, I did not say that you did so, but that you had abilities to do it.

Gerrald also was sentenced to fourteen years transportation.

*W. Forbes Gray: Some Old Scots Judges.

Had he protested that he would not live long enough to serve it, no doubt he would have been urged to serve as much as he could. He died of consumption five months after being shipped to Botany Bay, aged thirty-three.

The conduct of the trials and the severity of the sentences led to Whig protests in Parliament, which meant that the Government for party reasons was obliged to defend what happened. Charles James Fox began a tirade by picking on the 'strange assertion' by Lord Braxfield that no man had a right in the constitution unless he possessed landed property. 'Men of personal property, though they have immense sums in the funds, have no lot or part in the matter! How absurd, how nonsensical, how ridiculous!' Even under the Stuarts, protested Fox, the Bench had not behaved like this. Another of the judges had said that 'as he saw no punishment for sedition in our law he must go to Roman law . . . the Roman law left it to the learned Lord's discretion to give Mr Muir either to the gallows, or to the wild beasts or to Botany Bay!' Fox's last words were, 'God help the people who have such judges!' However, in the view of Pitt the judges would have been highly culpable if they had not used their discretionary powers to punish such 'daring delinquents'.* From high legal quarters Lord Braxfield received strong praise. The second Lord Mansfield said he knew of Braxfield only as 'a man of pure and spotless integrity, of great talents and with a transcendent knowledge of the laws of his country'. Lord Chancellor Loughborough said that 'if ever their Lordships should think proper to entertain an inquiry into the case he would pledge himself that they should find the conduct of the judges of Scotland had been such as their Lordships desired to find in men entrusted with functions so important'. Lord Thurlow also defended the proceedings, to the distress of Lord Campbell, who says the reports of the trials 'cannot now be read without amazement and horror mixed with praises to Heaven that we live in better times.'

Lord Cockburn, who published two volumes on the trials, says that at the time Scotland under the Tory grip was at the lowest point of political degradation, with no constitutional checks to private liberty, its only safeguard being the small Whig party. Lord Braxfield's culpability, he thinks, far exceeds that of his brethren. 'They were weak; he was strong. They

*Henry Cockburn: *An Examination of the Trials for Sedition.*

were frightened; he was not . . . Political reasoning and confident assumption of the truth of the charge were always conspicuous.' Lord Cockburn seems a little disappointed that the original inflammatory inscription proposed for the Martyrs' Memorial was watered down. 'How the judges' names are omitted I cannot understand. For it is in truth *their* monument.'*

What Scotland could do, England conspicuously failed to do. The year 1794 saw a bold attempt by the law officers at Westminster to convict a dozen agitators of high treason. The first was Thomas Hardy, founder of the London Corresponding Society, which advocated parliamentary reform. That it also advocated other things is evident from the resolution it passed that year at Chalk Farm condemning the 'arbitrary power' as exercised by the Court of Justiciary in Edinburgh, which 'ought to be considered as dissolving entirely the social compact between the English nation and their governors, and driving them to an immediate appeal to that incontrovertible maxim of eternal justice, that the safety of the people is the supreme and, in case of necessity, the only law'.† The evidence against Hardy, who was accused of conspiring to summon a convention, collapsed and he was drawn in triumph through London. John Horne Tooke was next up for trial, with ten others. This exhibitionist clerk in Holy Orders, who had supported Wilkes and quarrelled with him, who had been involved in much litigation and had cured himself of gaol fever in the King's Bench Prison by drinking claret (which gave him gout), had only himself to blame for the suspicion he had aroused; but he was plainly no potential regicide. Once again the jury acquitted. The trials caused tremendous public excitement and the Attorney-General, Sir John Scott, was hissed and booed in the streets. He has been blamed for trying to obtain a conviction for treason when the offences merely constituted seditious misdemeanour, but he was no more than a willing instrument of Pitt and Loughborough. When the prisoners were arrested they were examined by the Privy Council and judges were present at their questioning; the consensus seems to have been that they were guilty of high treason. Lord Campbell comments that such judicial procedure would have been regarded as intolerable in his day. No stigma

An Examination of the Trials for Sedition.
†Horace Twiss: *Life of Lord Eldon.*

is attached to Chief Justice Eyre, who presided at the trials of Hardy, Tooke and the others. He displayed 'some of the highest judicial qualities, patience, impartiality, and the power of sifting relevant from irrelevant matter and presenting the former to the jury in a luminous manner'.* Whether Pitt and Loughborough were grateful for such impartiality may be doubted.

In Ireland the 'phrenzy' culminated in the 1798 insurrection, a bloody miscalculation which was finally suppressed at Vinegar Hill. A small French force which landed in Ireland to help topple the Government was quickly mopped up (two years previously Wolfe Tone had sailed with a similar French expedition, but it had been scattered by storm). It happened that Chief Baron Yelverton was riding on circuit in County Mayo a month after the Vinegar Hill battle. Hanging in some profusion from the trees overhead were the fruits of the drum-head courts-martial. One lieutenant, tall and heavily built, had earned fame of a sort as a 'walking gallows', strangling rebels on his own back with the aid of his scarf.† The judicial party itself resembled a military force, with its advance escort of blunderbusses and two-edged swords, its troop of heavy dragoons in the rear. Moreover the Irish Bar were in uniform of scarlet with blue facings and yellow waistcoats; all, it was said, had faced death, if not in the line, then in the duelling field.‡ Oddly, there was little work for the circuit judges, but in Dublin the ringleaders of the rebellion faced an empty future. They did not expect expressions of sympathy for their nationalist aspirations. The Earl of Clonmel, Lord Chief Justice of the King's Bench in Dublin, had already laid down that 'God and Nature have joined England and Ireland together'. He said this in 1796 during the trials of the self-styled Defenders, after first expressing thanks to God that he was in a position which put him above politics. It was impossible, he stressed, for the two countries to be separated, 'and if bands of ruffians started up in every part they could not hold their dominion of murder for a month'. Dublin he described as 'the mint for coining treason and circulating it in small parts and making it current'. Equally baffled by the popular turbulence

*D.N.B.
†Jonah Barrington: *Personal Sketches.*
‡O. J. Burke: *Anecdotes of the Connaught Circuit.*

was Baron George. 'An amiable and virtuous Viceroy, the faithful representative of his Sovereign's goodness, is open to access and visible to those he governs. Every member of the administration is the same. None are afraid or ashamed to show their honest fronts to the mid-day sun.' Mr Justice Finucane said: 'The people of this country, before the introduction of French principles, were reckoned a shrewd and sensible people; but these phantoms raised in their minds have totally turned the heads of the unfortunate people . . . How much easier is it, if riches were their object, to grow rich by honest industry and the fair means which are in their power!' He added that sobriety and frugality were essential to this end.

The objects of these homilies died for the most part unrepentant. Among them was the Rev. James Coigly whose crime, said Mr Justice Buller, was 'directed against a prince whose virtues and whose mildness have excited applause and approbation from all mankind and against whom detraction itself cannot hint a fault.' The sentence on the clergyman was that he be hanged, drawn and quartered, the quarters to be placed at the disposal of the said mild and virtuous prince. In the event Coigly died on Pennington Heath without being mangled.

The disaffection towards the Government in Ireland was shared in unexpected quarters. In 1805 no less a person than a judge of the Common Pleas in Ireland, Mr Justice Johnson, was brought to trial at Westminster accused of publishing an anonymous libel against the King. It was, said the Attorney-General, a mischievous, scurrilous, unfounded and malicious attack, an 'offence the most alien from every sentiment of a liberal and ingenuous mind'. The libel had been supplied to William Cobbett, who had already been found guilty of publishing it. Cobbett did not shield his contributor, but said he had been ill used by him and had delivered up the manuscript to assist in tracing the writer. As a result Cobbett escaped punishment. Mr Justice Johnson was found guilty. Later a *nolle prosequi* was entered and he was retired with the usual pension for wrongdoers.

When the French menace was transformed into a direct threat of invasion by Napoleon, the judges were moved to new extravagances of denunciation. The monsters of iniquity who had dishonoured their God and murdered their king were mocked for being Catholics, Deists, Atheists, Mussulmen and anything that seemed expedient. In the assize towns of Wales Mr Justice Hardinge, warning the grand juries that the French would seize their crops and rape their women, described Napoleon as 'an Atheist at Paris, at Rome a Papist, in Egypt a Mussulman, a Military Pope at Paris again and a Jew in a Parisian synagogue'. He told the grand jury at Cardiff, in 1804, 'Let the Pope, that solemn prostitute of servility and of cowardice, transfer his diadem to the Idol of Paris.' In 1808 he declaimed to the Brecon grand jury, 'The times call upon me with an imperious voice to animate the high spirit of the day under your wing, if it should be the last breath of my life.'* Possibly this is what the grand juries wanted to hear; or they may have resented the notion that they needed an imperious voice to rally them.

Comically, in the occasional spells of peace with France, the judges were called upon to try pamphleteers and poets for stirring up bad blood with that nation. In 1787 Lord George Gordon had been rebuked by Mr Justice Ashhurst (who sounded the clarion against France in 1792) for making unkind references to the French Queen. Other nations, he said, were prone to think that the views of our press represented those of the State. 'It is beyond the power of the law,' he said, 'to rectify men's minds and to infuse into them that noble fire which burns in the breasts of good men and prompts them to the doing of praiseworthy actions and promoting the happiness of the country and the good of their fellow creatures.' But at least he could stop people from disturbing that tranquillity and he sentenced Lord George Gordon to three years in Newgate.

In 1803 a Frenchman living in England, Jean Peltier, was tried before Lord Ellenborough for vilifying Napoleon and seeking to bring him into hatred and contempt both with the British and the French. He had committed this offence in a poem. The Attorney-General pointed out that Napoleon was *de facto* the Chief Magistrate of France. 'He has been recognised by us in that character and in that character we made peace with him. Is it possible, then, that such a publication can be innocent or inoffensive?' Summing up, Lord Ellenborough told the jury, 'Gentlemen, I trust your judgment will strengthen the relations by which the interests of this country are connected

*J. Nichols (ed.): *Miscellaneous Works of George Hardinge*.

with those of France.' The jury obligingly found Peltier guilty. The editor of the *State Trials* adds, 'War between Great Britain and France being renewed soon after this trial, the defendant was never called upon to receive judgment.'

Not the least wickedness of the French was that they had taught Englishmen the habit of blasphemy. The judges had no doubt that it was their duty to save the Christian God from his detractors. In 1797 Mr Justice Ashhurst said blasphemy was an offence not only against the Almighty but against all law and government, 'from its tendency to dissolve all the bonds and obligations of civil society'. None believed this more strongly than Lord Ellenborough, the fierce, uncompromising Lord Chief Justice of those years of peril. The extract below is from the report of the trial, in 1812, of Daniel Isaac Eaton, a bookseller, charged with publishing a blasphemous libel :

Eaton: Let us examine and if possible discern the God who is supposed to have made this promise—

Lord Ellenborough: You are evidently coming to something reprehensible and it is necessary you should be checked.

E: My Lord, I have only two or three sheets more to read.

Lord E: It is not the length of the address which constitutes the offence but the matter of which it is composed. It is shocking to me and to every Christian present.

E: When the address is heard out it will be found to be relevant to my defence.

Lord E: You must omit those passages which cast any reflection on the Scriptures.

E: 'For I cannot nor ever could perceive any, the smallest, similarity betwen the God of the Jews and the God of the Christians, as supposed to be worshipped in the present day—'

Lord E: You must see that this is unfit for yourself to read and for us to hear. If you go on in this manner I must order your address to be handed to the officer and he, when reading it, must pause and omit every offensive sentence. I tell you once more that I will not permit the Christian religion to be reviled. Loiter a little at each passage before you read it and do not insult the court with offensive matter.

Eaton continued, but soon gave up and sat down. Then, surprisingly, Lord Ellenborough relented and allowed him to read his statement in full. After a hostile summing up the jury returned a verdict of guilty. Eaton was sentenced to eighteen months in Newgate and was ordered to stand in the pillory once a month.

The case aroused intense indignation in the breast of the poet Shelley, not yet twenty years old but already a master of polemics. His *Letter to Lord Ellenborough* was printed in Barnstaple but hurriedly withdrawn after copies had been circulated. Had it received wide public notice the poet would have been in deep trouble. The *Letter* referred to 'the unmerited sentence which you have passed on Mr Eaton' and went on, 'There are no laws which screen you from the reproof of a nation's disgust, none which ward off the just judgment of posterity if that posterity will deign to recollect you.' By what right, Shelley demanded, had Lord Ellenborough punished the bookseller? What 'antiquated precedents, gathered from times of priestly and tyrannical domination', could he adduce for such an insult to humanity and justice? 'Wherefore, I repeat, is Mr Eaton punished? Because he is a Deist. And what are you, my Lord? A Christian. Ha, then! The mask has fallen off; you persecute him because his faith differs from yours. You copy the persecutors of Christianity in your actions and are an additional proof that your religion is as bloody, barbarous and intolerant as theirs . . . From the promise held by your Lordship's zeal we need not despair of beholding the flames of persecution rekindled in Smithfield . . .'

In 1818 came a powerful shock for Lord Ellenborough, a shock which some say hastened his end. In that year William Hone was put up for trial three times in quick succession on charges of publishing sundry blasphemies, which included parodies of the Creed. At the first hearing, under Mr Justice Abbot (Lord Tenterden), the jury returned a verdict of not guilty. Lord Ellenborough chose to take the second trial and rapidly became incensed with the behaviour of the spectators, who were plainly on Hone's side. Calling for the sheriff and his assistant, he said, 'I have sent for you and your colleague, sir, as there is an absolute necessity for your presence. There have been most unseemly disurbances in court; you are the persons who are responsible and you *shall* be responsible, and therefore you will use your utmost activity in apprehending any persons who dare to interrupt the course of justice.' When Hone made a sharp retort to a judicial ruling, there was loud and unanimous

applause. Outraged, the Judge demanded to know of the sheriff why he was taking no steps to arrest anybody; and when he replied that everyone was at fault, the Judge ordered, 'Open your eyes and see. Stretch out your hand and seize the offender.' This jury again acquitted and the applause was deafening.*
Summing up in the third trial, the Lord Chief Justice said that in obedience to the Laws, to his conscience and to his God he had no hesitation in pronouncing Hone's works to be a most impious and profane libel. Believing and hoping that the jury were Christians, he had no doubt that they would be of the same opinion. The jury were not of the same opinion and Lord Ellenborough 'never held up his head again'. Blaming bad health, he resigned and died some months afterwards.

He will reappear in the next chapter.

---

* James Grant : *The Bench and the Bar.*

13

'UNHAPPY MAN ...'

It was a Victorian judge, Mr Justice Stephen, who described the penal laws of the early nineteenth century as 'some of the clumsiest, most reckless and most cruel legislation that ever disgraced a civilised country.' He added: 'If this bloodthirsty and irrational code had been consistently carried out, it would have produced a reign of terror quite as cruel as that of the French Revolution and not half so excusable.'*

This bloodthirsty code was directed in the main to the preservation of property, which now merited a capital P in the works of the poets:

> A wheaten garland does her head adorn.
> O Property! O goddess, English-born!†

The impious, light-fingered masses, corrupted by envy, seemed deaf to all exhortations to praise God and leave other men's candlesticks alone. Savage punishments seemed to be the only way to fight what Lord Chancellor Hardwicke called 'the degeneracy of the times, fruitful in the invention of wickedness'. Gradually, piecemeal, was built up that monstrous agglomeration of two hundred felonies punishable by death: picking pockets, shoplifting, stealing from bleaching greens, being found with a blackened face, consorting with gypsies and so on. The code had no more powerful defender than the harsh, irascible Lord Ellenborough, who became Lord Chief Justice in 1802; a man who believed that it was impossible for the law to be too severe, that terror alone could keep wrongdoers at bay.

*Cornhill Magazine, February, 1863.
†Ambrose Philips, quoted by D. B. Wyndham-Lewis in The Stuffed Owl.

Transportation he regarded as 'a summer airing by an easy migration to a milder climate'. Lord Ellenborough was the principal opponent of Sir Samuel Romilly when that tireless reformer began his campaign to whittle down the list of capital crimes. In 1808 Romilly, surprisingly, persuaded Parliament to abolish the death penalty for pocket-picking. Two years later, when he sought to remove the same penalty for stealing goods worth £2 or more from shops, Lord Ellenborough was ready to point the perils of 'speculative humanity'. Already, he said, they were seeing the effects of lifting the penalty from pickpockets, whose trade had increased enormously. If shopkeepers were not to have the protection of the gallows, losses would be such that 'in many instances bankruptcy must be the lot of honest, laborious tradesmen'. It was true that the full rigour of the law was seldom applied. 'Yet the terror was precisely the same; and such were the minds of those upon whom it operated that he believed the apprehension of no milder punishment would produce anything like safety to the public interest. Besides, it afforded an opportunity sometimes of bringing criminals to a sober consideration of their wickedness.' Lord Ellenborough said that he had consulted the other judges and they were all of his opinion; though two of them are believed to have dissented. He did not want to be thought inhumane :

'The duty of judges was very great, painful and arduous; and none could say but they were extremely anxious to extend mercy to every deserving case; and indeed they were entitled in this respect to more credit than was generally allowed to them. Few of their Lordships could estimate their feelings, or conceive adequately what they suffered when they laid their heads upon their pillows, at an assize town, and had to reflect that the next day would impose upon them the painful duty of pronouncing upon several of their fellow creatures their awful doom.'*

In the same debate Lord Eldon, the Lord Chancellor, also opposed Romilly's proposal. He said it would be manifestly wrong to execute a starving family for stealing a sheep, but what about those who made a trade of stealing sheep? He remembered trying a man for stealing a horse and finding that he had stolen eleven; moreover, he possessed fifteen turnpike gate keys to facilitate his plunder. Among those who voted in the Lords for retention of the death penalty on this issue were the Arch-

*Hansard, May 30, 1810.

bishop of Canterbury and six bishops. The Commons in the main were on Romilly's side.

It is familiar knowledge that in trials for theft juries brought in perverse verdicts of not guilty, or flagrantly valued the goods stolen at less than the amount which warranted death. Judges often connived with them. In Lord Mansfield's court, after the jury had undervalued some stolen clothes, the prosecutor exclaimed, 'Under forty shillings, my Lord! Why, the fashion alone cost more than double that sum!' To this Lord Mansfield replied, 'God forbid, gentlemen, we should hang a man for fashion's sake!' Even when convicted and sentenced to death, the prisoner often had a good idea whether the sentence was being imposed in earnest or as a formality, with the near-certainty of a reprieve. Lord Kenyon was much upset when a woman he was condemning for stealing goods worth more than £2 collapsed as if already dead. 'I don't mean to hang her,' he protested. 'Will nobody interfere and tell her I don't mean to hang her?' In the years 1801–09, according to Romilly's figures, only one-eighth of those capitally convicted in London went to the gallows, whereas fifty years earlier about three in four had died. In 1811 he showed that in the five preceding years 598 persons had been committed for stealing from shops, of whom 120 had been tried, and of these only twenty had been convicted and one executed.* The simple fact was that if a judge wanted to save a man's life he could do so, either by his conduct of the trial or by a recommendation to mercy afterwards. Those who sparingly exercised this privilege were known as 'hanging judges'. In Romilly's view it was wrong to leave so much discretion to the Bench; it was a power 'such as no man would desire to be vested with'. Judges were influenced, he said, by a variety of factors; one would be prejudiced by bad alibis, another would wish to make an example because the offence had occurred in a place where such deeds were rare, another because such deeds were common and ought to be checked, another because a prisoner had a bad record as a poacher.† According to Romilly a judge left three men to be hanged at Maidstone Assizes because none could produce a character witness.

Sometimes the Sovereign's own whim decided whether a man

*Hansard, February 9, 1810.
†Patrick Medd: Romilly.

should live or die. Lord Eldon has told how George III's ministers in council advised against a reprieve for a man guilty of robbery in Bedford Square, London, where Eldon and other judges had their homes. The Lord Chancellor advised that the man be spared on the ground that he had not used violence. 'Well, well,' said the King, 'since the learned Judge who lives in Bedford Square does not think there is any great harm in robberies there the poor fellow shall not be hanged.'* The Lord Chancellor's advice clearly carried weight, since it was his duty to review the evidence in capital cases. On taking the Great Seal, Eldon had been shocked at the careless way in which Old Bailey reports were reviewed, often by reference only to the Recorder's comments, not by re-examination of the evidence.

Until the year 1836 the law laid down that those charged with felony had no right to be represented by counsel; and without the services of counsel their chances of a successful defence were slim. On the judge fell the onus of seeing fair play for every prisoner, even when the accused crowded into the dock in triple or quadruple ranks. As the Rev. Sydney Smith pointed out, the judges who were supposed to be prisoners' counsel were of limited ability : 'Some have been selected for flexible politics – some are passionate – some are in a hurry – some are violent churchmen – some resemble ancient females – some have the gout – some are eighty years old – some are blind, deaf and have lost their power of smelling.' They could accept no previous instructions from their 'clients', nor could they receive any whispered communication during the trial. Attempts to change this law had been met with the remarkable objections that to employ counsel would be a serious expense for a poor prisoner and that it would produce an unseemly element of bickering between prosecution and defence at a time when a man's life was in the balance. Sydney Smith was inspired to high derision. A suitable speech from the court chaplain, he thought, would run as follows :

'You are going to be hanged tomorrow, it is true, but consider what a sum you have saved! Mr Scarlett or Mr Brougham might certainly have presented arguments to the jury, which would have ensured your acquittal; but do you forget that gentlemen of their eminence must be recompensed by large fees, and that if your life had been saved you would actually

*Horace Twiss : *Life of Lord Eldon.*

have been out of pocket above £20? You will now die with the consciousness of having obeyed the dictates of a wise economy; and with a grateful reverence for the laws of your country, which prevent you from running into such unbounded expense – so let us now go to prayers.'*

While Sir Samuel Romilly's attempts at reform were being thrown out by the Lords, criminals made the most of the ever-lengthening odds in their favour. Louder each year grew the cries of bankers, traders and others who saw depredators going totally unpunished. Bankers did not want to see forgers hanged; shopkeepers did not want to see shoplifters hanged; masters did not want to see dishonest footmen hanged; not even squires wanted to see poachers hanged; but all of them were anxious to see such offenders thwarted. Surely, they argued, lesser punishments, firmly enforced, were more likely to curb crime than ferocious punishments rarely inflicted? In 1819 this argument was advanced by numerous witnesses, including bankers, to a Select Committee on the Criminal Laws. By then Romilly was dead, by his own hand; the Committee was set up largely at the instance of Sir James Mackintosh, who had been a judge in India and was proud of the fact that crime in his district had been kept down with minimal assistance from the rope.

The Committee observed that the judges, though meriting all respect, were not the best witnesses on the effects of the penal laws. 'They only see the exterior of criminal proceedings after they are brought into a court of justice,' said the Report. 'Of the cases which never appear there and of the causes which prevent their appearance they can know nothing. Of the motives which influence the testimony of witness they can form but a hasty and inadequate estimate. Even in the grounds of verdicts they may often be deceived. From any opportunity of observing the influence of punishment upon those classes of men among whom malefactors are most commonly found, the judges are, by their stations and duties, placed at a great distance.'

At the Old Bailey, the Committee were informed, it was the custom to reserve sentence of death on offenders until the end of the session; only murderers were sentenced immediately after conviction, as the law required. Sir Archibald Macdonald, a

*_Edinburgh Review_, 1821–26 (four articles).

former Lord Chief Baron, said : 'I have thought for many years there was a great impropriety in passing the solemn sentence of death upon eighteen or twenty people, not one of whom could with any sort of propriety be left for execution; and most of whom, especially in London and other populous places, were very confident in their own minds that they would not be left for execution; my own idea being that the criminal law should be ingenuous and that it should speak distinctly what a criminal is to expect; and that the execution of that sentence should be as nearly infallible as possible; which, if moderate, could well be afforded, subject always to the interposition of the Crown.' The witness added that he knew of no instances in which the Crown had turned down a judicial recommendation of a reprieve.

The Rev. Horace Cotton, Ordinary of Newgate Gaol, told the Committee that terror of the death sentence was greatly weakened by the knowledge that it was unlikely to be carried out. 'I have seen [the prisoners] behaving in a most indecent manner while sentence of death is passed, so much so as to call for my reprehension afterwards. I have gone into their yard or cells and reproved them. I have seen them cracking nuts and looking up at the galleries and nodding to their friends and acquaintances . . .'

The Old Bailey catered for hardened offenders and no doubt it was easier to show fortitude as a member of a group. Yet from time to time, as the newspaper reports show, there were scenes of hysterical dread in the Old Bailey courtroom as the death sentence was passed and even the judges were 'visibly affected'.

Sentencing an offender, or a drove of offenders, to death was not just a matter of reciting a brutal formula laid down by statute. Most judges first called on the prisoner, whom they addressed as 'Unhappy man', to make his peace with God, or, as He was variously called, the Supreme Being, the Supreme Judge of Us All, the Searcher of All Hearts, the Fountain of Mercy, the Father of All Mercies and the Disposer of All Affairs. To this end, the condemned man would be urged to give himself up to 'the pious admonitions of the reverend clergyman whose office it will be to prepare you for your Awful Change'. Lord Eskgrove, a Scots judge whose eccentricity verged on imbecility, used to say, 'Whatever your religious persuasion may be, or even if, as I suppose, you are of no persuasion at all, there are plenty of reverend gentlemen who will be most happy to show the way to Eternal Life.'* These reverend gentlemen were eager to do what they could, but the prisoner was expected to co-operate. 'Knock with earnestness for your Redeemer at the Gate of Heaven and I trust the Gate may be opened to you,' said Mr Justice Park to two machinery-wreckers.† Admonishing a woman forger, Mr Justice Hardinge said, 'Never despair to meet those Angels in Heaven who have more joy over a penitent sinner than over that virtue and purity that want no repentance . . . Poor creature, kneel to me no more.'

The phrase 'Awful Change' was a much-used judicial euphemism, but it might be varied to 'the bitter draught you are about to take', or the prisoner would be reminded that he was 'trembling on the verge of eternity'. There were frequent references to 'this world of sin and sorrow' and 'this vale of tears'. Most of the grim judicio-clerical clichés are to be found in an address by Baron Vaughan to three prisoners at Winchester in 1831 :

'Unhappy men, you stand in the presence of God and in the face of your country convicted by the unanimous verdict of a most dispassionate and discriminating jury of the offence of demolishing, pulling down and destroying machinery employed in certain manufactories in different parts of the county . . . All that I can do (and it is the most friendly advice that I can now give you) is to implore you as you value your immortal souls to prepare for the Awful Change which you must speedily undergo. Your days are numbered. The gates of mercy on this side of the grave are closed against you for ever, and I therefore hope that without one moment's loss of time you will on leaving this place, prepare yourselves for your fate, that you will avail yourselves of the excellent spiritual assistance that is within your call, that on bended knee and with penitent and contrite hearts you will earnestly, fervently and immediately supplicate the Throne of Grace for pardon, remission and forgiveness of your sins.'‡

The more high-sounding the exhortation to penitence, the more brutal seemed the formal words of the death sentence at the close; and even more brutal was the death sentence when the

*Henry Cockburn: *Memorials of His Time.*
†*The Times,* January 17, 1831.
‡*Morning Post,* December 31, 1830.

judge, instead of saying '. . . hanged by the neck until you are dead, and may the Lord have mercy on your soul' substituted 'hanged by the neck till you are dead and your body to be handed to the surgeons, to be dissected and anatomised, according to the directions of the Act of Parliament, and may the Lord have mercy on your soul'. Not all judges appear to have found it necessary to include this statutory intimation; but prisoners well knew that the anatomy schools were avid for their remains.

There is a story, possibly apocryphal, about a judge who told the prisoner he could expect mercy neither on earth nor at the bar of Heaven. What is astonishing is to find how often judges assured the prisoner that there was absolutely no prospect of earthly pardon, when so often they were wrong. The knowledge that the judge had no ultimate control over the gates of mercy clearly sustained many a prisoner as he sat in what looked like stoical apathy, or cracked nuts.

In times of rebellion the condemned man often had little enough time to avail himself of the excellent spiritual assistance within call. For many of the Irish traitors death came next morning. Even when more time was available, some prisoners failed to use it in the prescribed manner. To Dennis Redmond, convicted at Dublin, Baron George said: 'Not satisfied with having brought yourself under the avenging hand of the law, you dedicate that time which should have been devoted to God, and during which you should have worn with your knees the very flags of your cell, to composing and endeavouring to get published one of the most wicked, remorseless, mischievous and ill-intended pamphlets that could possibly have been conceived.' Shortly afterwards he was executed 'upon the Coalquay'.*

Lord Ellenborough, who complained that it was difficult for an assize judge to sleep the night before a sentencing session, felt that undue emotion ought not to be engendered on the subject of severe punishments. When John and Leigh Hunt were in trouble, in 1811, for publishing a sensational article on flogging in the Army, the Lord Chief Justice said:

'There are punishments the nature of which cannot properly be discussed. Supposing a punishment to be a capital punishment, it is a grievous thing to consider – it is most mischievous

State Trials.

and painful to the feelings of the relatives and family of the individual. If such a topic was to be discussed in an inflammatory way you might be electrified – no man can say to what extent he might be disabled from discharge of his duty, where the question was life or death, if his feelings and sensibility were to be so strongly worked upon. It would disable those whose duty it is to pronounce the law and to draw the attention of juries to issues of that description. Therefore it is not cutting down the liberty of discussion to require that such subjects should be discussed moderately and that a person in the exercise of an allowed right should not create more mischief than he attempts to remedy.'*

Happily Lord Ellenborough kept a firm rein on his imagination until the end.

One judge who made a dubious parade of his emotions was Mr Justice Hardinge, senior justice of Brecon, Glamorgan and Radnor, who has already figured in these pages. His most notorious speech was to Mary Morgan, a servant girl aged seventeen, whom he sentenced to death at Presteigne in 1805 for premeditated murder of her bastard infant. He reminded her that she had selected a knife in advance to slay 'the new-born infant of your own sex, the off-spring of your secret and vicious love'. Then, dilating on the indulgence of 'criminal passions' and 'criminal pleasures', the Judge said, 'Thus it is that one guilt produces another; especially in your sex when seduced into its criminal intercourse with ours.' But Mary was not to despair. 'Look up to me, I can give you comfort,' said the Judge. 'To cut off a young creature like you in the morning of life's day (for it is little more than a day to the oldest of us all) is an infliction thrown upon me, which I have no power to describe, or to bear so well as perhaps I should. You must not think we are cruel; it is to save other infants like yours and many other girls like you from the pit into which you are fallen; your sentence and your death is mercy to them.' Later the Judge went on, 'You have heard the sentence and the imperious will of the law. It affects your body alone, your soul it cannot reach – it is in the hands of God . . .' Mary Morgan was hanged two days later. There is a story to the effect that a junior on the circuit rode to London to get a reprieve and arrived back an hour too late.

*States Trials.

Mr Justice Hardinge could have recommended Mary Morgan to mercy, but he held severe views on infanticide. Some weeks afterwards he 'blushed' to inform the court that another girl convicted of Mary's offence had had her sentence commuted to two years' imprisonment. 'This crime never occurs in the higher classes of life,' said the Judge. 'It is the guilt of the poor alone, almost universally in the pale of domestic servitude. It springs from a distempered conscience; a desperate and frantic remorse; a fear of poverty or of shame.' A religious upbringing might have saved 'the poor creature who perished at Presteigne', but she had 'scarcely even heard of the Saviour's name'. She had even prepared 'gay apparel' for her acquittal. 'Masters will do well to reflect upon the mischief done by them to their servants and through them to the community at large, if they are themselves men of dissolute habits or of low pursuits,' warned the Judge. They should not keep incontinent female servants in their households, for fear of corrupting others. As for the 'medical tribe', they would do well to be upon their guard against the sale of abortifacients.

Was Mr Justice Hardinge's own conscience 'distempered' by the thought of Mary Morgan's death? He was a prolific poet of sorts and occasionally his judicial labours gave him inspiration. Here are his lines entitled *On Seeing The Tomb Of Mary Morgan* :

> Flow the tear that Pity loves,
>   Upon Mary's hapless fate;
> It's a tear that God approves;
>   He can strike; but cannot hate.
> Read in time, oh beauteous Maid!
>   Shun the Lover's poisoning art!
> Mary was by love betray'd,
>   And a viper stung the heart.
> Love the constant and the good,
>   Wed the husband of your choice,
> Blest is then your children's food,
>   Sweet the little cherub's voice.
> Had Religion glanced its beam
>   On the Mourner's frantic bed,
> Mute had been the Tablet's theme,
>   Nor would Mary's child have bled.
> She for an example fell,

But is Man from censure free?
Thine, Seducer, is the knell,
It's a Messenger to thee!

But this poem is not more egregious than the epitaph composed by the Earl of Ailesbury on Mary's tomb. This says that
the 'victim of sin and shame', who was 'unenlightened by the
sacred truths of Christianity', was 'roused to a late sense of guilt
and remorse by the eloquent and humane exertion of her benevolent Judge, Mr Justice Hardinge', and that she 'underwent
the sentence of the Law with unfeigned repentance and a fervent
hope of forgiveness through the merits of a redeeming Inter-
cessor'.

Happily, it was unusual for a judge to be praised for benevolence on the tombstone of his victim.

Mr Justice Hardinge's biographer* has preserved his address
to another wayward Mary, whom he sentenced to death for
stealing goods worth more than five shillings from a house in
daytime. The Judge seemed especially indignant that among the
articles stolen by Mary Robert, a prostitute, was 'an old and
faithful servant of the poor creature whom you rifled', namely
a watch. After saying 'I disarm you of all hope to live,' he told
her that her vicious habits with men made her look ten years
older than she was. Truth, the Judge may have thought, was
beautiful at all times.

It remains to add that Mr Justice Hardinge's 'life's day' was
more than four times as long as that of Mary Morgan. In the
Dictionary of National Biography he is described as 'a pain-
staking judge', 'an honourable and benevolent man, witty and
sprightly in manner'. On the strength of his reputation as a
humorist, Byron includes him in *Don Juan,* and says that the
culprit up for condemnation always 'had his judge's joke for
consolation'.

Lord Cockburn, that sharp-tongued Scots judge of a later
generation, had heavy contempt for the religiose homiletics
of judges like Mr Justice Hardinge. 'There is a great art in
pronouncing sentence,' he wrote. 'The old judges used generally
to abuse the process. The feelings of a later age would not
tolerate this. But they have introduced a sermonising system
which it requires some courage in a judge to avoid. Even in the

*J. Nichols (ed.): *Miscellaneous Works of George Hardinge.*

slightest case – not extending beyond imprisonment – the prisoner must always be reminded of his latter end and of his immortal soul.' Lord Cockburn thought that strictly practical warnings as to the consequence of crime would be more likely to have an effect on worldly audiences and worldly villains. 'The misfortune of the religious plan is that as adherence to it is thought a duty, it is apt to lose its effect by being applied indiscriminately in every case. A proper mixture of the two would be the best thing.'*

Criminals in peril of the noose were said to prefer being tried by a 'real judge' in red robes, but they did not always qualify for the full pomp of an assize. Sir John Taylor Coleridge, a friend of Wordsworth, says in his *Diary* for 1827: 'Today I have been prosecuting an Exeter man for a capital forgery; he has been found guilty and sentenced to death by the Recorder . . . It is almost a more striking scene when such a circumstance occurs in this unusual way before a comparatively young man in an inferior court than when it happens before a judge in all the pomp and dignity of a court of assize. It was very aweful and affecting . . .' The scene was no less awful and affecting when the death sentence was passed, as it sometimes was, in the small hours, when the rest of the world slept. At Salisbury, in 1830, Coleridge defended in a trial which did not end until half-past two in the morning. 'Even then the court was crowded and I do not remember to have seen a more distressing sight than was presented by a father and two fine lads at the bar for their lives, and the mother, daughter and two other children in the witness box, the court dimly lighted, much of it lost in gloom, a furious judge summing up might and main against them.'†
As it happened, these accused escaped death; but many a man was notified of the Awful Change at an hour when vitality had sunk low, the air was vitiated and the candles were guttering to extinction.

That a judge should sentence someone to death just to give him a fright seems unlikely. Lord Chancellor Eldon is the authority for saying that Mr Justice Willes, son of a lord chief justice, sentenced a boy at Lancaster to die next morning without in the least intending it to happen. 'The judge awoke in the middle of the night and was so affected by the notion that he

*Circuit Journeys.
†Lord Coleridge: *This for Remembrance.*

himself might die in the course of the night and the boy be hanged that he got out of his bed and went to the Lodge of the High Sheriff and left a reprieve for the boy and then returned to his bed and spent the rest of the night comfortably.'*

Occasionally a judge managed to squeeze a jest out of the subject of hanging. Baron Heath, who believed that it was impossible to regenerate felons, heard at Gloucester Assizes that a witness came from Bitton. He commented, 'You do seem to be of the Bitton breed but I thought I had hanged the whole of that parish long ago.'† Two Scots judges are under suspicion of having joked with the men they sentenced. Lord Braxfield is supposed to have told an offender, 'Ye're a vera clever chiel, but ye'd be naun the waur o' a hanging;' and Lord Kames allegedly said to an old chess-playing crony, Matthew Hay, convicted of murder before him at Ayr in 1780, 'That's checkmate to you, Matthew.' Lord Cockburn said he got the story from Lord Hermand, then a counsel in the case, who was outraged by 'a piece of judicial cruelty which excited his horror and anger'.

There is no lack of judges to tell such tales about their brethren. Lord Campbell mentions a judge who, after sentencing a forger at Stafford Assizes for uttering a false £1 note, said, 'And I trust that through the merits and mediation of our Blessed Redeemer you may experience that mercy which a due regard to the credit of the paper currency of the country forbids you to hope for here.' This presumably was an attempt to ridicule a law which demanded a life for a £1 note. But what is one to make of Lord Eskgrove's celebrated rebuke to the tailor who stabbed a soldier to death: 'Not only did you murder him, whereby he was bereaved of his life, but you did thrust, or push, or pierce, or propel the lethal weapon through the belly-band of his regimental breeches, which were His Majesty's'? Lord Cockburn says he heard Eskgrove say it; he has written several pages in derision of this judicial scarecrow, who was more talked about in Edinburgh than even Napoleon. Whenever a group of lawyers suddenly fell apart in helpless laughter, it was a fair assumption that one of them had been mimicking the delivery of Lord Eskgrove.‡

In a category all his own comes Mr Justice Graham,

*Horace Twiss: *Life of Lord Chancellor Eldon.*
†F. C. Moncreiffe: *Wit and Wisdom of Bench and Bar.*
‡*Memorials of His Time.*

notorious for his extreme civility to all in court, including the
prisoners. It was said that 'people went away with a sense of
gratitude for his kindness, and when he sentenced a batch of
prisoners to death he did it in a manner that might make anyone suppose, if he did not know the facts, that they had been
awarded prizes for good conduct'. Mr Justice Graham was once
required to read out the names of a number of prisoners at the
Old Bailey before sentencing them to death. Afterwards he was
informed that he had omitted the name of John Robins. 'Oh,
bring back John Robins,' he said. 'By all means let John Robins
step forward. I am obliged to you.' Then apologetically,
addressing the prisoner, he said, 'John Robins, I find I have
accidentally omitted your name in my list of prisoners doomed
to execution. It was quite accidental, I assure you, and I ask
your pardon for my mistake. I am very sorry and can only add
that you will be hanged with the rest.'*

In 1820 three Bills abolishing capital punishment for various
forms of theft successfully passed through Parliament. Other
barbarous forms of retribution were also under attack; among
them the penalty of hanging, drawing and quartering for treason, and also the gibbet and the pillory. Lord Ellenborough is
credited with insisting that a traitor's body should still be
quartered after death, though he did not hold out for disem-
bowelling. As a result John Francis, the young man charged
with shooting at Queen Victoria in 1842, was ordered by Lord
Chief Justice Tindal to be hanged until dead and then divided
into four pieces, these 'to be disposed of in such manner as Her
Majesty shall see fit'. In the end he was transported for life.

Old-fashioned judges still ordered felons to be hung in chains
near the scenes of their crimes, but villagers had begun to
petition against this obscenity. According to a Bow Street
officer who gave evidence before a Parliamentary Committee in
1816, two men who had murdered revenue officers were gibbeted
in such a position that all sailors passing up the Thames could
see the carcases; the sheriff's only qualm was that the display
was 'so near Lord Spencer's place'.† Officially the gibbet ceased
to exist in 1827. The pillory had been under criticism on the
grounds that the mob either exalted the criminal or made out-

*Richard Harris (ed.): *Reminiscences of Sir Henry Hawkins*.
†Hone's: *The Table Book*.

rageous attacks on him. In 1780 a man pilloried for unnatural offences at Southwark was so maltreated by the mob that he was dead on removal. However, Lord Ellenborough thought the pillory was a useful punishment, 'as old as 1269', combining the elements of disgrace and exposure. There were 'several offences to which it was more applicable than any other that could be found,' notably perjury and fraud. In 1814 he caused a furore by sentencing Lord Cochrane to stand in the pillory opposite the Royal Exchange at midday for an hour, as part of his punishment for conspiring to defraud the Stock Exchange. Nothing was more calculated to rouse public and Parliamentary sympathy in favour of the cantankerous sailor-Member of Parliament than a sentence of this kind. Lord Ellenborough was virtually pilloried himself; he was insulted in the street and his house was attacked. Sir Francis Burdett said that if the sentence was enforced he, too, would stand in the same pillory; but the Government speedily saw to it that this part of the sentence was remitted. In the following year Michael Angelo Taylor sought leave of the Commons to introduce a Pillory Abolition Bill. 'The punishment was unequal,' he argued; 'to a man in the higher walks of life it was worse than death; it drove him from society and would not suffer him to return to respectability.'* In the Upper Chamber Lord Ellenborough opposed the Bill on the grounds already stated; but in 1816 the pillory was abolished except for perjury and subornation. By this time Lord Cochrane was mounting a thirteen-gun broadside in Parliament against the Lord Chief Justice, accusing him of 'partiality, injustice and oppression,' but the attack failed.

In 1832 Lord Eldon spoke against a Bill designed to abolish the death penalty for horse stealing and taking goods worth £5 or more from a dwelling-house. To steal £5 might seem a trivial sum to warrant death, said Lord Eldon, but to a poor man it might represent the fruit of five or ten years' labour. He himself would as soon hang himself as hang a man for forging a £10 note, but what was to be done with an attorney who forged documents and cheated beneficiaries out of £250,000? 'To say that such a man was not to be punished by death, out of respect for human life, was carrying the doctrine too far.'† Privately, Lord Eldon expressed pleasure that in his time on the Bench he

*Hansard, April 6, 1815.
†Ibid, June 25, 1832.

rarely had to leave persons for execution. Once he rejoiced because a woman he was due to sentence to death escaped from gaol – 'she was remarkably kind to me'.*

A taste for old-fashioned punishment survived among certain of Queen Victoria's judges. Shortly after John Francis had been sentenced to hanging and quartering in 1842, a deformed wretch, John Bean, presented a pistol at the Queen as she was driving to the Chapel Royal. Lord Abinger, having condemned the sort of person who strove for 'a kind of ignominious notoriety or an asylum for the rest of his days', warned that if anyone else imitated Bean's example, and was lucky enough not to be convicted of high treason, he would 'gain another species of notoriety by being publicly whipped at a cart's tail through any street in the Metropolis'. As it was, Bean escaped with a sentence of eighteen months in Millbank Penitentiary.

*Horace Twiss: *Life of Lord Chancellor Eldon.*

14

MACHINES ARE GOOD FOR YOU

In the late Hanoverian years, with the country torn by agricultural unrest, the judges emerged as bold defenders of the rights of capital, as apologists for mechanisation and as advocates of *laisser-faire*. It was not a role which became the judicial office; and the spectacle of a judge reading a lesson in economics to a batch of sullen labourers and then shipping his class to Botany Bay is scarcely the happiest.

Deepening distress was making the farm labourers desperate. Their future, like that of the factory workers, was linked with the new world of machinery, but the agricultural machines seemed designed to create further unemployment. George Crabbe in *The Village* had pointed to the inequalities suffered by the labourers :

> But yet in other scenes more fair in view,
> Where Plenty smiles – alas! she smiles for few –
> And those who taste not, yet behold her store,
> Are as the slaves that dig the golden ore –
> The wealth around them makes them doubly poor.

Certainly the temper of these hard-pressed illiterates was changing. They were less disposed than formerly to rely on the random benevolence of their superiors, less ready to accept the station into which it had pleased God to call them. They were even prepared to riot in markets if prices were too high. When labourers did this in Merthyr in 1801 Mr Justice Hardinge scolded them, saying, 'Nothing is more unjust than to be inflamed against a *market* because the general price of it is dear . . . You have a right, as you tell us, to be fed. But has not the owner of goods in a waggon or in a shop the right of selling his goods at the market price of the day, be it ever so high?' Death sentences followed.*

In earlier times the peasants had revolted *en masse* and had been suppressed, bloodily. Now the followers of King Lud and Captain Swing were waging another kind of warfare; not only were they burning ricks and smashing machines, but they were trooping round in gangs demanding money with menaces from parson and squire. The year 1830 was a particularly alarming one for the country gentry. Dukes put their personal cannon into working order and trained their footmen as artillerists. At Encombe, in Devon, Lord Chancellor Eldon's rural seat was in danger of being sacked, but the mob were cheated by a stratagem. Late that year Special Commissions were set up in several counties to exact retribution. The West Country, where the panic had been greatest, prepared for another Bloody Assize. In the gaols of Hampshire and Wiltshire lay nearly a thousand labourers whose excesses, whether against men or machines, had rendered them punishable by death. In many of the disturbances there is little doubt that the labourers were hoodwinked and manipulated. Sometimes the farmers for whom they worked assured them that their wages could not be raised unless the parson reduced his tithe demands; the farmers then stood cynically by while the mob coerced the parson into signing a promise to waive his due. However, it was the labourers, and only rarely a farmer, whom the grand juries delivered up for punishment.

On the eve of the Special Commissions *The Times* printed some cautionary words by Edmund Burke, inspired by the executions which followed the Gordon Riots in 1780 :

'It has frequently happened in occasions of this nature that the fate of the convicts has depended more upon the exceptional circumstances of their being brought earlier or later to trial than to any steady principle of equity applied to their several cases. Without great care and sobriety criminal justice generally begins in anger and ends in negligence. The first that are brought forward suffer the extremity of the law, without circumstances of mitigation in their case; and after a time the most atrocious delinquents escape merely by the satiety of punishment. A small number of executions is seriously recommended because it is

*J. Nichols (ed.): *Miscellaneous Works of George Hardinge.*

certain that a great havoc among criminals hardens rather than subdues the minds of people inclined to the same crime . . . Men who see their lives respected and thought of value to others come to respect that gift of God themselves. I have ever observed that the execution of one man fixes the attention and excites awe; the execution of multitudes dissipates and weakens the effect.'*

At Winchester a hundred capital convictions were recorded over the Christmas period. The Special Commissioners were Baron Vaughan, Mr Justice Parke and Mr Justice Alderson, the last of whom had only just been appointed to the Bench and who was to confer death on his fellow beings almost before he had adjusted his wig. The gentry turned out in strength to welcome, and show solidarity with, the judges; they included three hundred yeomen on horseback and the leading families in their carriages, headed by Lord Shaftesbury. Throughout the Commission the judges were escorted by that distinguished soldier, Sir Colin Campbell; and the most distinguished soldier of all, the Duke of Wellington, until recently Prime Minister, was there to sit with them on the Bench, as Lord Lieutenant. On the grand jury were nine baronets, four knights and ten esquires, of whom six were Members of Parliament. There were three hundred prisoners.

After the Assize sermon Baron Vaughan read the economic lesson. He pointed out that whoever condemned the use of threshing machines must also banish the use of spade, hoe and axe. 'If this right were conceded to the agricultural labourer what reason can be assigned for denying the exercise of a similar right to those who are employed in the fabrication of cloth, linen, cotton . . . ?' The result would be general economic collapse. How could employment be secured by the ruin of the farmer, by destruction of property? At this stage Baron Vaughan expressed the fear that he might be trespassing on 'a question which it is not within our province as ministers of the law to discuss'. The function of the judge was merely to declare, expound and execute the law. His self-rebuke had little effect, for he went on : 'It may be sufficient to observe that it is the undoubted right of every subject . . . to employ his capital and conduct his business, whether engaged in agriculture, commerce or manufacture, in such manner as he may think most conducive

*The Times, December 22, 1830.

to his own interest, unless where the wisdom of Parliament has controlled him by legislative restriction.' The Judge found it difficult to distinguish the difference in moral turpitude between destroying a machine to advance an individual's private interests and felonious appropriation of property for that person's own use. However, he would now dismiss all questions of political economy. The fact was that machines were protected by law. Those who were dissatisfied with the law should 'appeal to the ordinary tribunals of the country for redress', and not attempt to sit in judgment on their own wrongs, which was the way of barbarism. Parliament had a 'sacred and paramount' duty of framing and, if expedient, of reforming the laws; but it had not reformed the laws which forbade the smashing of machines. The Judge ended his hour-long speech by urging the grand jury, on their return home, to exert themselves to restore peace and stop the innocent from being seduced by the delusions of the wicked.*

Mr Justice Taunton, at Lewes, was bitterly critical of those who represented the rich as oppressors of the poor. 'It would be impertinent of me to say anything to you as to your treatment of labourers and servants. That man must know little of the gentry of England, whether connected with the town or the country, who represents them as tyrants to the poor, as not sympathising in their distress and as not anxious to relieve their burdens and to promote their welfare and happiness.'† These remarks offended *The Times,* which thought Mr Justice Taunton should have 'dealt more in warnings to the rich and less in vapid and unmeaning eulogies'.

At Reading Mr Justice Park addressed the grand jury in the same strain. Never was there a country which showed such concern for the young, old, deaf, blind, widowed, orphaned and 'every child of wretchedness and woe'. He said: 'There is not a calamity or distress incident to humanity, either of body or mind, that is not humbly endeavoured to be mitigated or relieved by the powerful and the affluent, either of high or middling rank, in this our happy land, which for its benevolence, charity and boundless humanity has been the admiration of the world.' The grand jury's task was to 'inculcate a firm, earnest and zealous allegiance to His Majesty's throne, a strict submission to the law and a profound attachment to religion'. At the same

*The Times, December 21, 1830.
†*Ibid.,* December 22, 1830.

time there must be no weakening in the high or middling ranks. 'Probably something of blame must attach to persons who too tamely submitted to the threats and intimidation held out by these lawless and wicked men . . . it is alleged that in some places magistrates have encouraged persons to lay aside their thrashing machines and to comply with the demands of the rioters. Such conduct is most impolitic wherever it has taken place.' A magistrate needed firmness, resolution and decision, not 'luke-warmness, negotiation, compromise or cowardice'.* At Aylesbury the same judge sternly condemned those who had sought to force a reduction in tithe payments. 'It was highly insolent,' he said, 'to require of gentlemen, who had by an expensive education qualified themselves to discharge the sacred duties of a minister of the Gospel, to descend from the station and reduce themselves to the station of common labourers.'† This was what many a rector would have liked to say, but dared not.

Mr Justice Alderson made his first address to a grand jury at Dorchester. Over-population, he explained, was contributing to the disorders. Men had been encouraged to contract early and improvident marriages, making them partly dependent on the poor rate; and at the same time growing literacy had sharpened their sense of inferiority without enabling them to understand the reason for their plight. The magistrates, said the Judge, should try to keep these new literates free from the contagion of dangerous publications, while not restraining discussion of all subjects within the limits of decency and good order.‡

Some of those who appeared before the Commissions were legally represented, others not. If the crime was a capital one, a man had no right to counsel. The Rev. Sydney Smith would have exploded at the scene. At Winchester, Baron Vaughan asked a Mr Bosanquet, who happened to be there, to watch the evidence on behalf of the undefended prisoners. He added that he and his fellow judges would also perform that function, but 'he was sure he should not appeal in vain to charitable feelings in any of the gentlemen whom he saw before him'.† It was a strangely casual way of ensuring justice for simple men in smocks who faced the noose; but greater men than these had

*Ibid, December 28, 1830.
†Ibid, January 15, 1831.
‡Charles Alderson: *Selections from the Charges of Baron Alderson.*
§*The Times,* December 2, 1830.

gone to their deaths without benefit of counsel. At Reading Mr Justice Park rebuked a defender who asked a question intended to screen his client at the expense of another. 'I beg you to understand, sir,' said the Judge, 'that every person who cannot afford to employ counsel is *my* client; and be assured that I shall not be so negligent of their interests as to allow you or anyone else to hang one of my clients in order to save your own.'* These were splendid words, and doubtless sincerely meant. But it is impossible to doubt that many a simple man found guilty might have got off if he had had a skilled lawyer to defend him. No prisoner was allowed to plead that his actions had been brought about by distress or to argue economic theory; such matters were fit only to be mentioned, and then discarded, by judges.

It would not have surprised Burke to learn that the first men to be sentenced were treated severely and that later leniency set in. The Winchester judges went into recess early one day to discuss which men should die and which should live, and in this they appear to have received the assistance of the Duke of Wellington. In a private letter Mr Justice Alderson wrote: 'I am thoroughly sick of this business and hate it. We have such a terrible responsibility and I feel to be ashamed and angry with myself for suggesting, as I must do, that the life of this or that man should be sacrificed. As to some there is no doubt; but then as to others there is the necessity of example on the one hand and the real ignorance and unconsciousness of the people that they were doing what was likely to sacrifice their lives on the other. I have convicted dozens of robbery whom I feel sure I might have safely left in the room with my purse without their stealing it.'†

Out of one hundred men capitally convicted, the Winchester Special Commission left six for execution. After the death sen-sentences 'Mr Justice Alderson put down his face upon his hands, deeply affected.' The six men refused to be unduly downcast, despite the assurance that 'all hope of mercy is excluded for you'. In the end the lives of two men were exacted. All the prisoners were turned out to watch the execution. One of the men, dressed in rags, had lost all fortitude; the other was composed and firm of step and, though pinioned, held 'a pamphlet of a religious

*Ibid, December 30, 1830.
†Charles Alderson: *Selections from the Charges of Baron Alderson.*

Opening the Assize at Stirling, 1873: the judges' procession

'Justice After Dinner': a *Punch* view of
judicial indulgence at the Old Bailey

Lord Chancellor Brougham: 'he shivered to atoms
the House of Fraud and Decay'

Lord Chancellor Eldon:
'he was addicted to over-doubting'

nature' which he read intently, until the moment of the Awful Change*; a credit to the Chaplain and the Judge.

Many were transported. For all his sensibility Mr Justice Alderson was unable to send men to this fate without rubbing salt into their wounds. The sentence, he assured them, was one of permanent banishment from the land of their birth; they would never see their relatives or friends again; they were going to a land where they would be akin to slaves and where the profits of their industry would go to others; and this punishment was lighter than their crimes merited. Baron Vaughan said almost the same words; it was part of the judicial patter. The thought of being akin to slaves was perhaps the least oppressive aspect of the prisoners' fate. In Crabbe's *The Village* the labourer says :

> These fruitful fields, these numerous flocks I see,
> Are others' gain, but killing cares to me.

Among the labourers transported were two or three 'whose names we did not catch', as the reporters apologetically put it. The names they did catch included those of the dignitaries who took their seats on the Bench with the judges. At Salisbury the Marquess of Lansdowne and the Earl of Radnor claimed this privilege; the Act of Richard II forbidding strangers on the Bench was ignored or forgotten. Despite this show of strength, threatening letters were left for the judges in the Salisbury court-room and also delivered at their lodgings.†

The Special Commissions stifled for a time the active insubordination of the farm labourers, but did not prevent them banding together to force up wages. In 1825 an Act of Parliament allowed workers the right of combination, but limited it to those who attended meetings; there was to be no persuading of others. This law was widely disregarded. In 1834 another newly appointed judge sat at Dorchester to hear charges against the six men of Tolpuddle, who had been concerned in administering illegal oaths. This they had done at a secret meeting, which was dominated by a large figure of Death and a sign which said 'Remember Thy End'. The law under which they were prosecuted had been aimed at sedition but was used against 'confederacies' of all kinds; any organisation which administered

*Hampshire Advertiser, January 15, 1831.
†*Ibid,* January 15, 1831.

F

unlawful oaths was automatically illegal. Baron Williams held that the gravity of the affair lay in the attempt to withdraw from the authority of the law and perform acts unobserved by the world; the behaviour of men who operated by stealth could not fail to grow worse. His sentence of seven years' transportation was regarded as unduly severe on men who were victims of superstitious folly. In 1836 the six 'martyrs' were pardoned.

Agricultural mobs . . . Reform mobs . . . Chartist mobs . . . all were straining the forces of law and order to the limit. In 1842 Special Commissions were dispatched to the North of England, where Chartist armies had been intimidating workers into leaving their jobs. The attendant excesses had included machinery-wrecking, arson, extinguishing of boiler fires and 'plug drawing'. The *Morning Post* thought it possible that the workers of Britain might be brought some way to their senses if the Government were to circulate, as a broadsheet, extracts from an address to the grand jury at the Staffordshire Special Commission by Lord Chief Justice Tindal. 'The great difficulty with the English common people,' said the *Morning Post,* 'is to make them receive any advice with reverence.' They paid no attention to admonitions from the Church, but 'the power and authority of a great criminal judge is a palpable thing, of which they are all conscious.' The judicial views which the newspaper wished to see disseminated included a condemnation of the 'despotic tyranny' of calling men from their work. 'If there is one right to which a man is entitled,' said the Lord Chief Justice, 'it is the right of exercising his own skill, knowledge and labour with a will free and unshackled by any control or dictation; yet, strange to say, this right which the discontented claim for themselves to the fullest extent, they, by a stranger perversity and selfishness, refuse to others.'*

Baron Alderson (as he now was) voiced similar views at one Special Commission or another. If the Grand Turk were to order men to stop working, he said, the world would cry, 'What tyranny!' At Chester he found an opportunity to defend the wealthy classes. 'Some people appear to think that the rich are idle,' he said. 'This is not the case. They work, though their labour is of a different description from that of the prisoners. The judges who now sit in these courts have a great deal of labour to perform and they belong to the labouring classes . . .'

*Morning Post, October 11, 1842.

The greatest stir, as it turned out, was made by Lord Abinger, Lord Chief Baron. For some two or three years he had been inveighing against the mob law which would pull down the monarchy and aristocracy, the folly of a universal agrarian law with every man wielding his own spade, the absurdity of trying to replace power and property as the two great elements of the political edifice. In 1842, at the Cheshire Royal Commission, Lord Abinger resumed his theme, in words which would have commended themselves to Lord Braxfield: 'It must be known that the House of Commons as at present constituted would never allow every man in the kingdom, whether having property or not, to have a vote for our representatives or allow their Members to sit without a property qualification . . . But even if the Commons should consent the Lords would to the last resist the destruction of their privileges. Finally, was it to be expected that the Sovereign would, without force or violence, consent to the changes proposed by the Chartists?' Having taken it upon himself to interpret the views of both legislative chambers and the Sovereign, Lord Abinger next complained, at the Lancashire Special Commission, that the Government was pursuing a policy of mistaken lenity. Mob leaders had boasted that all Britain was girding for the fight, that Birmingham was fielding one hundred thousand men armed with steel. 'Gentlemen, I am at a loss to know what distinction there is between conspiracy to subvert the Government and impose force and restraint on all branches of the Legislature, in order to have a particular measure passed into law, and the crime of high treason.' The judges of England, he said, had always held that conspiracy to use force to restrain the will of the Sovereign was an overt act of high treason, for which the lives of the offenders were forfeit.*

Lord Abinger's use of the Bench as a political platform was heavily criticised in Parliament and in the newspapers. The *Morning Advertiser* condemned his 'liberticide harangues' and went on: 'By his Lordship's exposition the mere fact of seeking any change in the system of government, by means calculated to alarm the authorities, is equivalent to an overt act of treason; so that the people in such case have nothing to do but to hug their chains, lest their very rattles may disturb the repose of their taskmasters.' It often happens that the provincial newspapers use more excitable language than the national organs. The

*Morning Post, October 12, 1842.

Macclesfield Chronicle, after describing Lord Abinger as 'this renegade Whig,' said: 'There is scarcely a single man whose office leads him to animadvert on human wickedness in whose history may be found crowded a greater mass of political infamy.' A long selection of opinions like these was read to the House of Commons by Thomas Duncombe, the best-dressed firebrand of his day, who had presented to the House the Chartists' petition with 3,315,752 signatures. He described Lord Abinger as 'partial, unconstitutional and oppressive' and accused him of having spoken to the prisoners in a 'rancorous, malignant, political and party spirit'. No one would have gathered from such criticisms that the Chartists had, in fact, posed a very potent threat to lives and property; the mobs they fomented were far from passive. Duncombe made a useful debating point when he quoted the words of Sir James Scarlett a few years earlier: 'No man detests a political judge more than I do. No man in my opinion ought to be made a judge on account of his politics; at any rate he ought not to carry them with him on the Bench.' Sir James Scarlett became Lord Abinger in 1835.

When Duncombe had expended his indignation – some of it ill-supported by the facts – the Attorney-General told Members that in his view the Judge was right to point out how those who carried 'the terrors of something very closely resembling civil war' into every parish should be reminded how close they had come to committing high treason. By a vote of 228 to 73 the House endorsed this view.*

Baron Alderson was still on the Bench when the tumults of 1848 threatened the governments of Europe. On all sides, he told the grand jury at Chester, we heard of wars and rumours of wars. 'We have felt famine. We are dreading impending pestilence. Around us are the seas and waves of popular assemblies tumultuously roaring. The powers of the world seem shaken and falling. Europe in the last year has been convulsed to its very centre. Its ancient dynasties, where are they? Even the mighty fabric of ecclesiastical power seems crumbling to pieces at its seat in Rome; and he whose great predecessors claimed presumptuously to confer and take away kingdoms is now a fugitive, it seems, from his own people's infatuated violence.'†

Lord Chief Justice Crewe could have said it a little better.

*Hansard, February 21, 1843.
†Charles Alderson: *Selections from the Charges of Baron Alderson.*

But Baron Alderson did not base his case wholly on rhetoric. He had been conducting economic research and was anxious to share the fruits of it with the grand jury. The richest nations were those which ate the most meat. In Paris in 1789 the citizens devoured 147 pounds of meat per man. By 1817, when the Empire had crashed, consumption had been reduced to 110 lb 9 oz. After the 1830 revolution the figure had dropped to 98 lb 11 oz. 'God knows,' said the Judge, 'what it is now.' The grand jury were asked to observe 'how the period of the lowest political rights was the period of the highest physical comforts among the poor; it shows therefore, that the one is not necessarily connected with the other'. He did not mean, of course, that political rights were of no importance – 'no doubt it may sometimes be desirable to obtain freedom even at the hazard of suffering'. His point was that those who agitated for such things should first count the cost. There followed an appeal to show affection for the poor, to educate them, to explain that 'the accumulation of capital in manufacturing districts is really a blessing to the public', and that 'the large and expensive estates of our nobility and gentry are really a blessing by being kept together not for private luxury but as enabling their possessors the better to promote agriculture, the more easily to establish schools and build churches . . .' To end the sermon, the learned Baron read from a book upholding the law of primogeniture. In France, where this fine old law had been abandoned, resulting in 'universal and compulsory sub-division of land', there was ruin and decay; one quarter of the land had passed into the hands of strangers, to whom it yielded but two per cent while they paid eight per cent for borrowed money.*

For a quarter of a century Baron Alderson regaled grand juries with his orthodoxies and unorthodoxies, social, economic and political. Presumably Lord Chancellors could have asked him to desist, but there is no evidence that they did. In 1854, at Hereford, he was attacking the Government's proposals to alter the poor relief laws. In 1856 at Liverpool he was criticising 'our active but not very judicious philanthropists, who have been attempting to abolish the punishment of transportation alto-gether'. Transportation offered men redemption in a new world, whereas in our own gaols hardly any criminals were reformed and nobody wanted to employ them afterwards, even as cheap

Ibid.

labour. Ideally, men should be transported with their wives and families. The real incorrigibles would remain here; 'we have no right to inflict on the colonies people who are incapable of being reformed in any country at all.'

Back in 1830, when he sentenced droves of West Country labourers to transportation, the Judge had not stressed the redemptive aspects of their sentence; instead he had emphasised that they were being parted for ever from their friends and banished into slavery. But he had been a new judge then and anxious, possibly, not to give any initial impression of weakness. Perhaps it is unfair to have singled out the views of Baron Alderson for such close attention; but in the main they were representative enough of those of his brethren. In some respects he was in advance of them; for instance, in his desire to see an end of capital punishment and a relaxation of the game laws. In the *Dictionary of National Biography* Baron Alderson is described as 'a strong churchman of moderate tendencies' and 'a man of much religious feeling and a humane judge'.

Lord Cockburn, writing in 1888, indulged in many a snort about the way in which his predecessors converted the circuit seat into 'a platform from which Tory judges preached Toryism to the Tory authorities beneath them'. They 'exerted themselves powerfully as political trumpets and would harangue about innovation, Jacobinism and the peculiar excellence of every abuse'.* No judge of his own day, said Lord Cockburn, could last a month if he indulged in such excesses. But political judges who were a shade more cautious in their utterances survived into our own time.

*Circuit Journeys.

15

SOBERING UP

After the Regency manners underwent a gradual refinement. It is highly likely that Lord Eldon was the last Lord Chancellor to have been deposited in a whore-house by his royal master, by way of a practical joke. The royal master was the Prince Regent, who worked out the jape in conjunction with Sheridan. Beyond grumbling at having to pay for a room and a woman he did not use, and further grumbling at the indignity of having to hire a cab home from a house of ill fame, the Lord Chancellor seems to have taken no great umbrage.*

Nature did not always help to make a judge a figure of majesty. There were crooked, spindle-shanked judges straight out of Gillray or Rowlandson and judges with great swag-bellies coated with snuff. For every judge who strode there was another, like Lord Eskgrove, who 'hirpled'; for every judge with a deep organ voice there was one who sounded like a flawed flute. However ill-favoured, most judges had a suitable regard for their turnout. Wigs did not necessarily lend to dignity; it has been said that wigs make the wise look foolish and the foolish look wise. The least prepossessing English judge of his day was possibly Sir Charles Wetherell, Recorder of Bristol, described as 'one of the greatest slovens who ever walked'. He is said to have escaped mob fury in Bristol disguised in a clean shirt and a pair of braces.† One of his Parliamentary performances drew the comment that 'the only lucid interval was that between his waistcoat and his breeches'.‡

*James Grant: *The Bench and the Bar.*
†Serjeant Ballantine: *Some Reminiscences of a Barrister's Life.*
‡D.N.B.

Writing of the England of 1815, Halevy says: 'A judge might be a man of humble birth, hampered by an unsuitable wife, a former mistress or an uneducated and unpolished woman of the lower middle class. Nevertheless he was treated with respect by the noblest families in the land . . .'* Halevy no doubt had some particular judge, or judges, in mind. History is remarkably reticent about judges' wives. They are never mentioned in reports of assizes, of judicial banquets, or in books of legal anecdote. Yet even 'hanging judges' had wives, who presumably took a sympathetic interest in their husbands' work. Judges were not natural bachelors; indeed, a close study of Foss will show that a thrice-married judge was no rarity. One story of a judge's courtship has been preserved. Lord Braxfield, having found a likely candidate, said, 'Lizzy, I am looking out for a wife and I think you just the person that would suit me. Let me have your answer, off or on, the morn and nae mair aboot it.'† To this direct appeal the lady returned a direct answer; she accepted.

The tribute 'as sober as a judge' had yet to be earned. In some quarters the state of the judges on the Bench, notably at the Old Bailey, had been a source of comment. Too many observers have testified to the speeding up of justice after a good dinner for the charges to be dismissed out of hand. It was the custom for the City sheriffs to give two dinners each day – at three o'clock and five o'clock – for judges, aldermen, the Common Serjeant, the City pleaders and a few members of the Bar. Both dinners were identical, the first course being 'rather miscellaneous', though commonly featuring marrow pudding, and the second consisting always of beefsteak. Only one man dined at both. This was the ordinary, or chaplain, who said grace on each occasion and did not care to affront the company by failing to eat each meal.‡

Sergeant Ballantine remembered the Old Bailey dinners. The hospitality was genial enough, 'but one cannot but look back with a feeling of disgust to the mode in which eating and drinking, transporting and hanging were shuffled together. The City judges rushing from the table to take their seats on the Bench, the leading counsel scurrying after them, the jokes of the table scarcely out of their lips, and the amount of wine drunk not

*England in 1815.
†Kay's *Edinburgh Portraits*.
‡*Quarterly Review*, February 1836.

rendered less apparent from having been drunk quickly . . .'
One Recorder, the Hon. Charles Evan Law, used to take a
tray of coffee with him on the Bench. Once he spilled it, but
said not a word. Next morning he had more coffee brought in
and spilled it over the clerk of arraigns below him. This called
for an apology, not to the clerk but to the jury: 'Gentlemen, I
have constantly begged that the desk should be made broader.'
Ballantine mentions that on the last day of the Old Bailey
sessions 'a decently dressed, quiet-spoken man' would take a
glass of wine with the diners. 'This he drank to the health of
his patrons and expressed with becoming modesty his gratitude
for past favours and his hopes of favours to come.' He was
John Calcraft, the hangman.*

According to Mr Justice Hawkins, post-prandial trials at the
Old Bailey 'did not occupy on the average more than four
minutes each.' They went like this:

Prosecuting counsel, to first witness: 'I think you were walking
up Ludgate Hill on Thursday, 25th, about half-past two in the
afternoon and suddenly felt a tug at your pocket and missed
your handkerchief, which the constable now produces. Is that it?'

'Yes, sir.'

'I suppose you have nothing to ask him?' says the judge. 'Next
witness.'

Constable stands up.

'Were you following the prosecutor on the occasion when he
was robbed on Ludgate Hill? And did you see the prisoner put
his hand into the prosecutor's pocket and take his handkerchief
out of it?'

'Yes, sir.'

Judge to prisoner: 'Nothing to say, I suppose?' Then, to the
jury, 'Gentlemen, I suppose you have no doubt? I have none.'

Jury: 'Guilty, my Lord,' as though to oblige his Lordship.

Judge to prisoner: 'Jones, we have met before – we shall not
meet again for some time. Seven years transportation. Next case.'

Time: two minutes, fifty-three seconds.†

It reads like *Punch*; and as it happens *Punch* was hammering
away at this very subject. In 1844 it commented on the roseate
tinge, the look of fulness on Justice in the evening compared
with 'the pallid nun-like maid that summed up in the forenoon'.

*Serjeant Ballantine: *Some Reminiscences of a Barrister's Life.*
†Richard Harris: *Reminiscences of Sir Henry Hawkins.*

The Court of Aldermen, it seems, had been discussing whether the after-dinner sittings at the Old Bailey should cease. 'The proposition was, however, negatived; the majority of the Court doubtless feeling that justice never had so soft a heart as when her belly was full, and that though proverbially blind nothing so infallibly cleared her intellectual vision like sparkling Burgundy and fine full-bodied port.' *Punch* described the acceleration of justice that was to be observed after the dinner recess and added: 'How often, too, has a Recorder passed a tremendous sentence on an offender simply because he has seen his iniquity double.'

Not all that often, perhaps. On another occasion *Punch* asked: 'How many a convict owes an extra seven years of slavery to the indigestion of the learned baron who tries him! With only the difference of a few grains of calomel, how different had been his doom! Nevertheless, the offender is sentenced – he has no appeal from the hard bowels of the man who judged him – and away he goes.'

In Scotland, with its tradition of hard drinking, it was the practice of judges, before 1800, to send for wine and biscuits when the business seemed likely to be protracted. Black bottles of strong port were set down beside them, along with carafes of water. For decency's sake the judges pretended at first not to see this refreshment; then they poured out a little water, then put a little wine in it, and soon were pouring out bumpers to the envy of the gallery. Lord Cockburn says that even that tolerant age looked askance at the custom. The strong-headed judges like Lord Braxfield were unaffected, but the 'feeble or twaddling' ones like Lord Eskgrove showed signs of muzziness. However, all had cultivated the art of sitting and looking judicial even when the bottles were nearly drained.*

This custom was not observed on circuit, according to Lord Cockburn. At inns the judges went off to dinner, 'after which they returned again to the transportation and hangings'. It was said that in the evening processions the judicial step was less true to the music than in the mornings. One of the deepest drinkers on the Scots Bench was Lord Hermand, who regarded liquor as productive of virtuous actions. He addressed the court in a murder trial as follows: 'We are told that there was no malice and that the prisoner must have been in liquor. In liquor! Why, he was drunk! And yet he murdered the very man who

Circuit Journeys.

had been drinking with him! They had been carousing the whole night – and yet he stabbed him. Good God, if he will do this when he is drunk, what will he not do when he is sober?'* Another Scots judge, Lord Newton, is said to have emptied three large bottles of claret at a sitting and then dictated a sixty-page law paper. A French visitor who had made Lord Newton's acquaintance was greatly impressed when, entering Parliament House in Edinburgh one morning, he saw on the Bench, full of dignity, the man he had left in a state of intoxication an hour earlier, after an all-night session.† Lord Braxfield held his liquor well and could show lenity towards those whose capacity did not rival his. To two young advocates he said, 'Gentlemen, ye maun jist pack up yer papers and gang hame, for the ane o' ye's riftin' punch, and the other's belching claret, and there'll be nae gude got oot o' ye the day.'‡

When courts sat, as they did, long into the night, and even through until breakfast, no one should be surprised that judges resorted to stimulation. It is very hard to see why these long sessions were tolerated. Mr Justice Abbot began the experiment of sitting late out of shamefacedness when he found that Lord Ellenborough, though severely ailing, had tried seventeen defended cases in a day while he himself had got through only five. After four or five late nights he desisted, on representations from barristers who had no time to read briefs or make consultations. Some judges apparently took pride in their powers of endurance and even taunted counsel for wilting or asking for adjournments. In the trial of Lord George Gordon in 1781 Thomas Erskine (Lord Erskine) made a long, post-midnight speech and the verdict was given at 5.15 am, the court having sat since 8 am the day before. When the Irish barrister brothers Henry and John Sheares were on trial for their lives in Dublin in 1798 their counsel Curran rose to speak for them after a sixteen-hour session with only a twenty-minutes interval. He asked for a respite, but the Attorney-General said Curran could not be more tired than anybody else.§ The jury went out after seven o'clock in the morning and shortly afterwards brought in a verdict of guilty. Judgment was pronounced at three in the

*Ibid.
†Kay's *Edinburgh Portraits.*
‡*Ibid.*
§W. H. Curran: *Life of J. P. Curran.*

afternoon and the brothers were hanged next day. Sir John Taylor Coleridge says that he sat at Exeter for twelve hours on a Monday and for nineteen on the Tuesday; 'I went in at eight a.m. and sat until three a.m., summing up with as much freshness and perhaps more perspicuity than I had done in any other case at the assizes.'* It is hoped that the jurors' mental faculties were as fresh as those of the Judge, but it seems unlikely. From this distance it is scarcely credible that the practice of marathon sittings could have been thought compatible with the administration of justice. The custom still persisted under certain judges late in the Victorian years.

Although a judge could keep the court in session until all hours the jury were not encouraged to do so. When the quack St John Long was being tried in 1830 for his part in a woman patient's death the judges retired to dinner at five o'clock, first locking up the jury. It was a Saturday night in November. Dinner proceeded merrily, says one account, and the steaks were renewed again and again. The well-known counsel, Mr Adolphus, told all his best stories and the chaplain was about to be challenged for a song. Then the court keeper reported that the jury had sunk into a 'deep dead lull', which augured a long delay. Baron Garrow suggested waiting until midnight and then discharging the jury, but Mr Justice Park, 'a warm admirer of the times when refractory juries were carried round the country in a cart', said he would wait until ten o'clock and then tell the jury they must be locked up without food, fire or candle until a reasonable hour, say nine o'clock, on the Monday, by which time he trusted they would have reached a unanimous verdict. Very shortly after digesting this message the jury decided to convict.† At this time the law still allowed a jury to be kept 'without meat, drink, fire, candle or lodging', but by 1870 they were allowed to have fire and refreshment at their own expense.

The reader may wonder how the needs of nature were provided for during a long sitting. Lord Ellenborough, it appears, had a 'vase' beside him. 'I have myself often heard his large seals dangling from his watch chain rattle against the vase, as he took it in his hand *coram populo,* decorously turning his back,' says Lord Campbell. Lord Kenyon had 'a porcelain vase with a handle' placed at the extremity of the bench, near the

*Lord Coleridge: *This for Remembrance.*
†*Quarterly Review,* February 1836.

box where the students sat. A tale that seems too good to be true has it that one day a student, finding his ink too thick, discharged some of it into his Lordship's vase. The Judge soon afterwards visited his corner and almost immediately afterwards was seen to be in a state of distress, convinced that he had contracted a mortal disorder. His hand shook so much that he had to be led from court, but as he entered his carriage the student responsible for his anguish came up and apologised.* Instead of being committed for contempt he was invited to dine with the Judge. Only the judges were equipped with vases. They could always point out that the Speaker in the Commons had similar provision for his comfort. What the jurors did has escaped the record.

By modern standards, the degree of incivility offered by counsel to judges was often excessive, but so was the provocation given by judges. It was not unknown for the Bench to be provided with a selection of newspapers. Lord Mansfield would pick one up and begin to read it as a hint that counsel was becoming prolix. To Lord Campbell a brief glance at a newspaper was a permissible hint, but he thought the practice in his own day was being carried to 'an indecorous and offensive length'. He had seen a judge methodically turning the pages of *The Times* while counsel was opening a case.† Some judges, of whom Lord Eldon was one, wrote private letters on the bench. According to Lord Campbell, counsel would lay traps for the Lord Chancellor, saying they wished to invite his attention to a new argument, which had already been developed by six or seven previous speakers; and the Lord Chancellor would nod his head and agree that it was an interesting new point. Lord Brougham was not above catching up with his correspondence while he sat in Chancery. Sir Edward Sugden (a future Lord Chancellor) once paused in his argument until Brougham looked up and said, 'Go on, Sir Edward, I am listening to you.' Sugden's reply was, 'I observe that your Lordship is engaged in writing and not favouring me with your attention.' To this the Lord Chancellor retorted, 'I am signing papers of mere form. You might as well say that I am not to blow my nose or take snuff while you speak.' One version of the tiff says that Brougham offered to show Sugden what he was writing, possibly

*Lord Campbell: *Lives of the Lord Chief Justices.*
†*Ibid.*

to reassure him that he was not busy on an article for the *Edinburgh Review*. There was bad blood between the two at the time. Brougham may have been aware that Sugden was the author of the jest 'If the Lord Chancellor knew a little about law he would know a little of everything.' Lord Campbell held that, if the newspaper trick failed, it was legitimate for a judge to check absurdity 'by a rebuke or a sneer, a sarcasm or even a look of exhausted patience or of suppressed ridicule'. He himself, when severely taxed, would stride up and down the bench, pausing to strike attitudes of despairing boredom and sometimes 'presenting a not inconsiderable amount of back surface to the audience'.*

The dignity of the Bench was not heightened by those judges who took pet dogs into court with them, thus presenting counsel with another object on which to fawn. One of the many clashes between John Curran, the Irish counsel, and the Lord Chancellor of Ireland, Lord Clare, arose from the presence on the Chancery Bench of his Lordship's Newfoundland. Curran paused in mid-argument, as the Judge fondled his pet, and when invited to proceed, said, 'I beg pardon. I thought your Lordships were in consultation.'† Mr Justice Hawkins at a later day went every-where with his dog Jack, which not only sat beside him on the Bench and in his carriage but had to be given a privileged seat at other functions.

If the standard of behaviour in the English courts was not always what it might be, the Irish courts were often the scene of buffoonery. When Lord Norbury was sitting in Dublin a hubbub of merriment came from his court. This Chief Justice of the Common Pleas in Dublin is said to have boasted that he began life with £50 and a pair of hair-trigger pistols. Lord Chancellor Clare opposed his elevation to the chief justiceship – 'make him a bishop or an archbishop, anything else!' Nicknamed Puffendorf from his habit of blowing out his cheeks, Lord Norbury was noted for 'a broad humour and an absolute indifference to propriety'. Even attempts to restore order seemed destined to provoke mirth, as when Mr Justice Mayne, sitting beside Lord Norbury, rebuked a spectator with, 'I see you sitting there like a wild beast with your hat on.' The story that Lord Norbury once sat on the bench in a green masquerade costume has received

*Serjeant Ballantine: *Some Reminiscences of a Barrister's Life.*
†W. H. Curran: *Life of J. P. Curran.*

clarification; he wore the masquerade dress under his gown – but not altogether invisibly – because it was the lightest apparel he had and the weather was hot;* he is thus no more and no less culpable than a flying officer who puts on his uniform over his pyjamas to fly an air officer commanding to an inspection. Daniel O'Connell made one of several attempts to unseat the merry Chief Justice on the grounds that he had slept during a murder trial and was unable to furnish any notes. Not until two years later, at the age of eighty-two, was he bought off the Bench by being offered a peerage as Viscount Glandine and Earl of Norbury (he had been Baron Norbury), with a special remainder to his second son and a pension of over £3,000.

The Irish Bar seems to have been more amiably disposed towards Lord Norbury than it was towards the Earl of Clonmel, Chief Justice of the King's Bench in Dublin. So overbearing and quarrelsome was this Judge that, after he had shown exceptional incivility towards a barrister called Hackett, the Bar resolved that until he publicly apologised no barrister would hold a brief, appear in the King's Bench or sign any documents in court. The ultimatum was effective. The judges took their seats on the bench but no counsel were present and the attorneys had other engagements. On the following day an ample apology appeared in the newspapers, contrived to make it appear that it had been written of free will immediately after the original offence.† ('Mutinies' by the Bar were not always successful; serjeants who staged a 'dumb day' before Chief Justice North in the Common Pleas, on a matter of self-interest, climbed down rapidly when he announced that, on the following day, he would hear arguments from all comers.)

Curran's son and biographer maintains that the 'vivacity of eloquence' in the Irish courts did not affect the course of justice. No doubt it was shocking to hear counsel pathetically reminding the judge of the convivial meetings of their early days, but 'the judges who showed the utmost indulgence and sensibility to these episodes of fancy were ever the most conscientious in preserving the sacred stability of the law'. Certainly the Bench had much to contend with from counsel. One judge called on the sheriff to be ready to arrest anyone whose behaviour ruined the decorum of the court. Curran, who suspected he was

*Jonah Barrington: *Personal Sketches.*
†*Ibid.*

being got at, said, 'Do, Mr Sheriff, go and get ready my
dungeon; prepare a bed of straw for me; and upon that bed I
shall repose with more tranquillity than I should enjoy were I
sitting upon that Bench with a consciousness that I disgrace it.'
It was Curran who, when told by Mr Justice Robinson, 'If you
say another word, I shall commit you,' replied, 'Then, my
Lord, it will be the best thing you have committed this term.'

Curran's son argues that an impassioned style of oratory was
necessary since the jurors were men in whose minds political
prejudices were uppermost. It was necessary to play on these
passions, 'to prey on their eternal fears' and even teach religion
and morality.

Sir Jonah Barrington in his *Personal Sketches* says that the
judges of Ireland appeared to be sent there from England because
they were no use for anything else. Barrington, an Irishman,
was a judge in the Court of Admiralty in Dublin, in which
capacity, over a period of years, he appropriated some of the
moneys paid into his court. The offences were brought to light
by a commission of inquiry into the Irish courts in 1830. In that
year, as a result of addresses in both Houses of Parliament,
Barrington was removed from office, in the manner prescribed
by the Act of Settlement.

Scotland did not derive its judges from England. It grew and
nurtured its own, tolerating in them an alarming degree of
eccentricity. Some have already been mentioned. Lord Monboddo, who appears in Boswell's *Johnson,* resembled 'an old
stuffed monkey dressed in a judge's clothes.'* A lover of ancient
Greece, he held flower-strewn 'Attic banquets' at which he
ventilated unorthodox theories, including the then hilarious
notion that men and orang-outangs came from the same family.
It was his view that a carriage was 'an engine of effeminacy and
idleness', and since it was unknown to the Greeks he rode to
court on horseback. On judicial issues his views rarely coincided
with those of his brethren, with whom at various times he lost
all patience. To mark his disapproval he would refuse to sit on
the bench with them and give his judgments from the clerks'
table. His finest hour was when he visited the King's Bench in
Westminster Hall and sat tight when the court emptied on a
sudden rumour that the building was about to collapse. His
deafness made it difficult for him to realise what was going on.

*W. Forbes Gray: *Some Old Scots Judges.*

Afterwards he said he 'thought it was an annual ceremony with which, as an alien, he had nothing to do'.*

Lord Gardenstone, whose hobbies were philanthropy and town planning (notably at Laurencekirk), shared his bedroom with a favourite pig. To a guest who tripped over it in the dark, he said, 'It's just a bit sow, poor beast, and I laid my breeches on it to keep it warm all night.'† Lord Kames was noted for his addiction to the word 'bitch'; his brother judges were bitches and equity was his bitch goddess. His sense of propriety may be gauged from this dialogue with a witness in a murder trial:

Sir, I have one more question to ask you and remember you are on your oath. You say you are from Brechin?

Yes, my Lord.

When do you return thither?

Tomorrow, my Lord.

Do you know Colin Gillies?

Yes, my Lord, I know him well.

Then tell him I shall breakfast with him on Tuesday morning.

As the nineteenth century progressed the circuits became more and more anachronistic. The old assize towns were dwarfed by the new cities of the Industrial Revolution; yet Birmingham had to wait for an assize until 1859 and Sheffield, incredibly, until 1956. Even when railway travel left some of the old assize towns difficult of access, local pride and local interest, notably that of innkeepers, could be relied upon to fight any proposal to re-draw the circuits. Much time-wasting ceremony attended every judicial visit, even when the gaols had no prisoners to be delivered; but the parade of power and the display of solidarity between the judges and the town authorities was thought to serve a useful purpose in discouraging potential wrongdoers. When the peculiar Lord Eskgrove was told that a prisoner in Ayr gaol had cut his throat on hearing the assize trumpets, even though he was not on a capital charge, the Judge is said to have expressed delight that the assize still brought wholesome terrors with it.‡ Such an incident would not have surprised James Boswell. In his *Letter to Lord Braxfield* he had argued that the full apparatus of pomp could inspire more reverence, and prevent

*Ibid.
†Ibid.
‡Henry Cockburn: *Circuit Journeys.*

more crimes, than 'thousands of executions'; and for that reason
he had strongly opposed the tendency to pinch pennies on the
judicial equipage, as by abolishing the special baggage waggon
and storing legal papers in the boot of the carriage, along with
the boot brushes.

In the cities, where folk were less easily impressed by ceremony, the spectacle of scarecrow judges lifting their skirts as they
minced through puddles, with a pantomime escort of bored
javelin men all out of step, by no means drove offenders to
slash their throats in terror. It still depended very much on the
high sheriff whether the parade enhanced judicial dignity,
whether the judges came in with an escort of Lancers or a flock
of jeering urchins. In 1834 Baron Alderson noted with satisfaction at Lancaster (scene of Mr Justice Allybone's discomfiture) that the sheriff met him with eighty persons all on grey
horses, that the coach was drawn by six greys and had seven
outriders also riding greys, plus a second carriage behind. If a
sheriff provided a single coach, with four unmatched horses, no
outriders and the merest dribble of apathetic gentry, a judge
might ask himself whether the Sovereign's dignity was being
sufficiently respected. At Leicester a sheriff was once fined by
Mr Justice Best because the 'bad ways' of the town had caused
excessive bumping to the judicial carriage. Baron Platt at
Newcastle Assizes informed the grand jury that the high sheriff
had escorted the judges in a plain clarence carriage instead of
with the 'usual garniture' of javelin men, outriders and trumpeters. When the high sheriff protested that he was as loyal a
subject as any in the kingdom, the Judge retorted that, for a
gentleman of ample means, he had failed to evince a suitable
show of respect for the Queen's Commission.* At Aylesbury
Mr Justice Hawkins grumbled to the grand jury that his
lodgings would have been rejected out of hand by an Army
billeting officer. He could not find his bedroom because of the
smoke from a choked chimney. 'I congratulate you, gentlemen,'
he said, 'not only on there being very few prisoners, but also on
the fact that you are not holding an inquest on our bodies.'†
Since the Judge was notorious for sitting in an airless fug, with
the court-rooom window pasted over, the grand jury may have
wondered what he was grumbling about.

*A. H. Engelbach: *Anecdotes of Bench and Bar.*
†Richard Harris: *Reminiscences of Sir Henry Hawkins.*

Circuit judges had no option but to stay in their designated lodgings, where their marshal, butler and cook made them as comfortable as they could. The lodgings might be mansions kept specifically for the purpose, or villas vacated for a fee at assize time, or portions of official buildings; they might be full of flowers provided by the sheriff's wife or full of cockroaches. At Cambridge judges had the right to lodge with the Master of Trinity, an arguable privilege. Except in Scotland, judges and barristers were not allowed to stay at inns, where unprofessional familiarity might break out; the more impecunious juniors huddled together in one rented sitting-room and shared the cost of coals. Normally the judges entered the town ahead of the barristers, who were by no means avid to hear the sermon which followed the reading of the Commission. The Bar were not allowed to listen to the judge's charge to the grand jury, a prohibition for which there seems to have been no sensible reason; in any event, they could find out from the solicitors what the judge had said, or, if it was newsworthy, they could read it next day.

One of the least-loved features of the assize was undoubtedly the sermon. In Queen Anne's day an assize sermon preached at Derby by Dr Henry Sacheverell had set the whole country by the ears. It was an intemperate harangue on 'The Communication of Sin' and, in the view of Parliament, reflected gravely on the Sovereign, the Government and the Protestant succession. The preacher, as insolent as he was vain, was called to the bar of the Commons and suspended from preaching for three years, his writings being burned by the hangman. He vastly enjoyed his notoriety. Since then the assize sermon had tended to be non-controversial and soporific. There were Biblical passages which a tactful preacher refrained from choosing, like Luke xviii 2 ('There was in a city a judge which feared not God, neither regarded man'), but some preachers, from a sense of mischief or with misapplied wit, selected texts warranted to embarrass the judge. Lord Cockburn recalls a clergyman who chose as his text, 'And Samuel went from year to year in circuit to Bethel, and Gilgal, and Mizpeh,' when it was very obvious to the congregation that he was alluding to Jedburgh, Dumfries and Ayr, the more so since one of the judges listening was called Samuel. Cockburn considered that any minister who prostituted the pulpit by punning 'should be thrashed on the spot'. As for the content of assize sermons, he commented: 'There are few things more curious than the decorous appearance of patience with which sensible people can sit and hear a man with an unattractive manner roar out two-and-a-quarter hours of *sheer absolute nonsense*. Yet nothing so common.'*

Apart from preaching the sermon and intoning prayers, the assize chaplain had little to do publicly but say 'Amen' after the death sentence. In private he strove to prepare prisoners to meet their God and sometimes he laboured hard and long. When Mr Justice Hawkins sentenced a soldier to death at Winchester, the man retorted 'Curse you.' The chaplain worked on the offender for ten days to persuade him to withdraw this incivility to God's representative at Winchester and only narrowly succeeded. The Judge read the apology as the man was being executed.†

In some assize towns, as at Exeter, the links between the judges and the military were emphasised. In theory the judge commanded the garrison and an officer would call on him, salute and report the strength of the troops. The judge, who might not know one end of a rifle from the other, would nod gravely and give permission for the soldiers to be let out of barracks. It all helped to show miscreants what they were up against. There had been a time when judges were wary of a standing army, fearing that troops would set free the prisoners from the gaols.

Lord Brougham often criticised the circuit system in Wales, where the same judges followed the same itineraries, year in, year out. They kept meeting the same magistrates, the same gentry, 'almost the same tradesmen', the same witnesses and attorneys. In England judges changed their circuits, but as the years went by they, too, met the same magistrates, the same influential families; they kept on collecting the same souvenirs from the same lord mayors, the same requests for school holidays from Shrewsbury or Winchester. Not least, they kept consuming the same banquets and attending the same balls wherever they went. The extent to which judges feasted with squires and sheriffs, mayors and lord lieutenants, parsons and colonels was not the happiest feature of assize time, especially when the gallows stood awaiting its prey. Judges were perfectly capable

Circuit Journeys.
†Richard Harris: *Reminiscences of Sir Henry Hawkins.*

of preserving their integrity, if not their figures, amid the fleshpots, and retaining their modesty in face of fulsome toasts, but in the eyes of poachers, radicals and, increasingly, trade unionists it looked like an alliance between 'them' and 'us' – and 'them' constituted State, Bench, Army, Church, Town Hall and even Masters of Foxhounds all drinking to each other's health.

When there were no prisoners to be tried, the judge would receive his pair of white gloves, smilingly congratulate the grand jury and accept any suitable offer of hospitality in the neighbour-hood. The sheriff would disband his javelin men and back they would go to work on his estates. A conscientious judge had plenty of time on circuit to ask himself whether he was earning his salary. If he had no nobleman's seat to visit he might spend his time hobnobbing with bishops, or kissing the ring of the nearest cardinal, or indulging in general sightseeing, or sitting in his lodgings and writing verses, or preparing moral reflections or crochety complaints for the next grand jury. Some even made a point of seeing the insides of the gaols they helped to fill. It was an agreeable enough life, for a man unconsumed by ambition, with an interest in cathedrals and antiquities. Lord Lyndhurst enjoyed going on circuit, finding it 'pleasanter to try larcenies and highway robberies than to listen to seven Chancery lawyers on the same side upon exceptions to the Master's report.'* The circuit judge also enjoyed a solatium in the form of a tax-free allowance, in the spending of which the Bar were willing to give every assistance. But from the taxpayer's point of view the circuit system badly needed overhaul.

---

*F. C. Moncreiffe: *Wit and Wisdom of Bench and Bar.*

16

GOADED BY BROUGHAM

To rid the criminal law of its barbarities had been difficult enough, but it was a quick task compared with that of freeing the civil law of its delays and injustices. Nowhere were these more glaring, in the early part of the nineteenth century, than in the Lord Chancellor's own department, the Court of Chancery, which had been a source of dissatisfaction, and not infrequently of scandal, for centuries. It was the court which dealt with trusts, wills and settlements, along with the backwash of bankruptcy and lunacy.

The task of Lord Chancellor was far too great for one man. His duties as a member of the Cabinet were onerous enough, but he was required also to distribute his time between the Palace, the Privy Council, the House of Lords and the Court of Chancery. Lord Thurlow, when asked how a Lord Chancellor was able to get through the work, replied, 'Just as a pickpocket gets through a horsepond; he *must* get through.'* Until 1813 the only other judge on whom the Lord Chancellor could lean for help was the Master of the Rolls.

Common law judges were never too busy with their own jurisdictional squabbles to unite in resentment at the assumption of purer and nobler standards by the Chancery Bench. A cynical judge, asked to explain the difference between common law and equity, said, 'At common law you are done for at once, whereas at equity you are not so easily disposed of; one is prussic acid and the other laudanum.' The trouble with Chancery was that it denied justice by refusal, or inability, to decide. Jeremy Bentham complained of 'the business of hours spun out into

*Horace Twiss: *Life of Lord Eldon.*

years'. The spinning out was achieved by a proliferation of
costly paper, in the form of affidavits, declarations, pleas, injunc-
tions, rejoinders, surrejoinders, replications, traverses, rebutters,
surrebutters, references to masters, masters' reports and so on. No
juries had any say in these causes, which were settled over the
years, and sometimes over the generations, by the lawyers and
the Lord Chancellor, by which time most of the moneys at stake
had been engulfed in fees. It was said that when a case once
entered the Court of Chancery in Lord Eldon's day – and his
day lasted twenty-five years – 'it was quite uncertain whether it
would be decided in the lifetime of either of the parties, supposing they were to live for upwards of a quarter of a century'.*
Occasionally some slight acceleration might be achieved by the
payment into the Masters' department of Gratuity Money, in
other words a bribe.† Some of the delays were undoubtedly
caused by the tendency of testators to draw up complex and
obscure wills, tying up their estates in such a way as to afford
perennial legal employment; other delays were caused by the
obduracy of litigants or by their thoughtlessness in dying or
going mad. Notoriously, some Chancery litigants were unhinged
before they went to law; and some said that anyone who went
to law must be unhinged.

Parliamentary critics who hammered away at delays in
Chancery blamed shortage of judges, the ever-growing com-
plexity of the laws, the alarming rise in the number of bank-
ruptcies and the equally alarming increase in lunacy petitions.
All this detritus of human frailty and folly was tipped on the
table of the Lord Chancellor, to whom it brought not only
ennui but fat fees. In 1811, according to Michael Angelo Taylor
in Parliament, three hundred appeals were waiting to be heard
and at the rate they were called they would take twenty years to
finish. Two years later a Vice-Chancellor was appointed; his
court eventually inspired the jest that whereas the Lord
Chancellor believed in *oyer sans terminer* the Vice-Chancellor
observed the rule of *terminer sans oyer*. Another Parliamentary
critic, John Williams, cited the case of Ware v. Horwood, in
which an ingenious solicitor had rendered accounts to his clients
containing such items as:

'For writing a long letter to his Lordship [the Lord Chancellor]

*James Grant: *The Bench and the Bar.*
†Brougham: *Hansard,* February 22, 1831.

and importuning particular attention to it, 9s 6d; for attending the court to get the cause reinstated on the paper, 13s 4d.

'For attending the Lord Chancellor in his private room when his Lordship begged for further indulgence until tomorrow, 13s 4d.'

According to Williams (though not everybody believed him) charges of this kind had been repeated until the bill came to £1,030. But solicitors' charges were small compared with those of counsel. Every time a barrister stood up to 'move' in a case he charged the client a substantial sum of guineas for expressing the hope that the Lord Chancellor could see his way to do something at his convenience.

It must seem surprising that men of honour should have been content to spend a professional lifetime operating a system of licensed rapine in a court which was set up for the purpose of securing equity and justice. The caustic Henry Brougham, who described the Court as 'the greatest calamity to which the people of England was exposed,' said that some honest practitioners had withdrawn from it, 'notwithstanding the effects of early education, fixed habits and their rising glory.' All these considerations 'had been put to flight in their candid and ingenuous minds by having daily exhibited before them the wounded feelings of suitors whose hardship sprang from the same source whence they were drawing fame and fortune'.* One of those to whom he referred was Sir Samuel Romilly. The Lord Chancellor who bore the brunt of Brougham's attacks was Lord Eldon, whom he was destined to succeed on the Woolsack. In 1825 Brougham, in his most sarcastic vein, was pressing Eldon to resign, a course the overworked Chancellor regarded as unthinkable – 'a more chimerical apprehension never entered the brain of a distempered poet'. In 1826 Brougham complained that Eldon had done nothing in sixteen years of Parliamentary excoriation to ease the abuses of Chancery, though they were palpable and glaring as noon-day. 'The noble lord at its head had not made a single reform; had not made one improvement; had not advanced a single step; had not put himself in motion nor moved even the little finger of his left hand to procure the remedy of one evil.' The reason? According to Brougham : 'His doubting disposition amounted to a positive mental infirmity. He was addicted to

Hansard, June 5, 1823.

over-doubting – to too nice subtlety – which led him sometimes from an anxious observance of close and intricate points to lay a trap, as it were, for his sound and excellent judgment.' Brougham conceded that the Lord Chancellor had integrity and learning, 'a mind large and capacious filled with ample stores of learning' and 'an extraordinary subtle and nimble fancy'.*

Nothing sums up the state of Chancery under Lord Eldon more poignantly than his opening sentence in the judgment on Radnor v. Shafts: 'Having had doubts upon this will for twenty years there can be no use in taking more time to consider it.'† The papers in such causes did not lie reproachfully in front of him all that time, for his staff maintained a rotation of delays. A solicitor who wrote to Eldon complaining about a long silence received an unapologetic letter saying 'the papers were long ago taken from my table'; however, he would make an effort to find them again.

Defenders of Lord Eldon, while conceding a certain indolence, agree with Brougham that over-doubting was his trouble, which may or may not have been intensified by a 'prodigious capacity' for port wine. When he was Chief Justice of the Common Pleas his mania for exploring all hypotheses, and elaborating all points of distinction, had left many a jury fatally confused. Yet confusion was the one thing he was anxious to prevent; only lucid order would satisfy him. It was his wish that the doctrines of equity should be as settled and uniform as those of common law, while still capable of being tempered to special circumstances. He said he would be pained to think that rulings could change with each successive judge and that people would say that 'equity varies like the Chancellor's foot'.

The attacks by Brougham and others eventually resulted in the appointment of a commission to investigate the Court of Chancery, but this was stultified by Lord Eldon's insistence on being appointed as chairman. It was known that he was wholly against any reform of his beloved court, in which he had spent half a century as barrister or judge, just as he was against abolition of capital punishment, emancipation of Roman Catholics, Parliamentary reform and – in Bagehot's phrase – 'the danger of making anything more, the danger of making anything

Ibid., May 18, 1826.
†Lord Campbell: *Lives of the Lord Chancellors.*

less'. It must have been a wry moment for rooked suitors when
his estate was announced as £700,000. For an indolent man
it was no mean figure.

As a law reformer Brougham pledged himself to trim judicial
patronage, a system which was not greatly abused but gave
critics an endless opportunity to cry corruption and nepotism. It
was part of the system of the day, in which the Sovereign doled
out preposterous offices at Court, regiments in the Army were
bought and sold and optimists offered substantial sums in the
newspapers for official appointments. The Lord Chancellor had
the right to sell a variety of legal offices, said to be worth
£24,000, and to nominate persons to a great many other posts,
including some hundreds of Church livings. This meant that
he was under constant pressure, royal, political and social, to
reward other people's favourites. When the Rev. Sydney Smith
thanked Lord Chancellor Erskine for the gift of the living at
Foston-le-Clay, Erskine replied, 'Oh, don't thank me, Mr Smith.
I gave you the living because Lady Holland insisted on my
doing so; and if she had desired me to give it to the Devil, *he*
must have had it.'* There was no sensible reason why the
grant of livings at this date should have been vested in the
Lord Chancellor, but occasionally the facility proved useful.
Lord Loughborough, after delivering a judgment which reduced
an innocent clergyman to beggary, approached him immediately
afterwards and offered him 'a vacant living which I happen
fortunately to have at my disposal'.†

Of Lord Eldon it was said that 'his distribution of patronage
was on the whole injudicious, being chiefly determined by the
caprice of the Royal Family or any other influences which might
be powerful enough to overcome his habitual indolence.'‡
Requests from royalty, as Lord Eldon pointed out, were tantamount to commands and superseded promises given to others.
He complained that most applications for livings – he received
'I think I may almost say, thousands of applications' – were
impudently framed. He was capable of disobliging countesses,
believing it no part of his duty 'to make the Crown a trustee
of its advowsons for every considerable family in the kingdom.'§

*Hesketh Pearson: *The Smith of Smiths.*
†Foss: *A Biographical Dictionary of Judges.*
‡*D.N.B.*
§Horace Twiss: *Life of Lord Chancellor Eldon.*

Like most Chancellors he was not averse to keeping a few good things in the family.

Not only the Lord Chancellor but the Lord Chief Justice of England had patronage at his disposal; and this included appointments which he was entitled to sell. In defence of the system it was argued that judicial salaries were so low as to need augmentation if the right men were to be attracted. In practice the rewards fell haphazardly. A man who held office for only a short time might benefit from the falling in of numerous lucrative appointments, whereas no benefits whatever might accrue to a man who held the post for a far longer period. The three offices of most value which the Lord Chief Justice had in his gift were the chief clerkship of the King's Bench, the post of *custos brevium* and the clerkship of the outlawries (the chief clerk in turn had the gift of lesser offices). It is said that Lord Ellenborough was riding in Hyde Park when he heard of the death of his chief clerk. At once he dismounted and took steps to appoint himself to the clerkship, so that in due course he could pass it on to his son; meanwhile, it was worth an extra £7,000 a year to him.* In 1825 a major assault on judicial patronage was made in Parliament under cover of a proposal to pay judges a fixed salary. The Chancellor of the Exchequer, Frederick Robinson, drew cries of 'Hear, hear' when he said the sale of offices was inconsistent with judicial dignity and independence. Nor was the system of levying fees much happier. Judges had to swear an oath every quarter testifying to the amount they had received in fees, thus putting themselves into the role of 'public accomptants'. If suitors hesitated to pay the required fees to the judge, argued the Chancellor of the Exchequer, it must be extremely painful to the judges to enforce payment of them; and yet this was absolutely necessary so long as they constituted a part of the remuneration. Much argument revolved round what was a suitable salary for the King's judges. Thomas Denman (later Lord Denman) was taken aback by a proposal to pay ordinary judges £6,000 a year, a sum thought necessary by the Chancellor of the Exchequer 'to check too violent aspirations after preferment'. Such a rise, Denman argued, would be injurious to the judges' dignity. Showing a nice sense of class, he said, 'It was impossible by any increase in their salary that they could ever be raised to an equality with the great. At present

*Lord Campbell: *Lives of the Lord Chief Justices.*

they might be said to be at the head of people of middling fortune, which was better than being at the foot of the higher order.' In his view they should be content to live in Russell Square, where they enjoyed considerable respect, rather than to seek the rarer atmosphere of Grosvenor Square. John Cam Hobhouse advanced the curious proposition that 'it was characteristic of human nature that a man might be tempted from his honesty by £6,000 a year whose integrity would not be shaken by £4,000'. According to the Attorney-General, Sir John Copley, Lord Ellenborough's total income, thanks to the sale of offices, had been £16,000 a year and Lord Chief Justice Eyre had disposed of £30,000 worth of offices in his lifetime.* Members urged that salaries should be such as to attract men under sixty, with pensions high enough to induce a man to retire, thus sparing the nation such judges as the late Chief Baron Wood who had gone on circuit when he had 'lost one eye and both ears'. Brougham's contribution to the debate was to stress the dangers of judicial promotion. 'Independence of the Bench must always be equivocal, if not nugatory, as long as the Crown exercises the power to promote judges,' he said. 'This looking up for promotion on the Bench as in the Church naturally tended to make men look up to their maker rather than to the public good.'†

When the issue was debated in the Lords the new Lord Ellenborough insisted that the proposed salary of £10,000 a year for a Chief Justice of the King's Bench was unrealistic. 'No man could in prudence accept a peerage who had only a salary of £10,000 a year to depend on, independently of what he might have saved,' he assured the Lords. If they abolished remuneration from the sale of offices and from fees judges would have no inducement to exertion. He argued that since there was no objection to the sale of an advowson to a living, there should be no objection to the sale of a ministerial office.‡ The view of Parliament, however, was that chief justices ought not to be dependent on sales and fees. Under the Judges' Salaries Act of 1826 it was laid down that the Chief Justice of the King's Bench would receive £10,000, the Chief Justice of the Common Pleas £8,000, the Chief Baron of the Exchequer £7,000, the Master

*Hansard, May 16, 1825.
†Ibid., May 20, 1825.
‡Hansard, June 22, 1825.

of the Rolls £7,000, the Vice-Chancellor £6,000 and the ordinary judges £5,500 (soon afterwards cut to £5,000); all were to receive suitably graded pensions.

There were those who thought it high time the Lord Chancellor was put on a fixed salary, instead of trafficking in offices. Much Parliamentary time was wasted in attacking his supposed abuses of patronage. In 1831–32 critics spread their fire to include the Lord Chancellor of Ireland, Lord Plunkett, who was alleged in the press to have distributed £36,000 worth of appointments among his family, mostly in legal offices but also in church livings. In the House of Lords Lord Plunkett at first adopted an attitude of scorn. 'What! Are noble Lords to be called upon to defend themselves in Parliament against every stupid calumny which mortified but most impotent vanity or the virulence of faction may insert in a newspaper?' He had six sons and he had certainly done his best to provide for them, as was his duty. 'Two of my sons are in the Church and two at the Bar. I defy even calumny to impeach their conduct at either. My eldest son derives no emoluments from the public and all my family occupy but that station in society to which I am persuaded they are fully entitled.'* The Marquess of Londonderry thought that Lord Plunkett would do better to offer less disdain and more information, and quoted O'Connell to the effect that there was 'not a more pernicious legislator for Ireland or a more venal politician than Lord Plunkett'. The Lord Chancellor was strongly defended, however, by the Duke of Wellington, who said that it was a Chancellor's duty to look after his family and friends, as all previous incumbents had done. The post was ill-paid and no one would accept it unless he could avail himself of the traditional ways of looking after his dependents. Lord Plunkett had a large family and was 'perfectly right in placing them in those situations to which their abilities and pretensions were adequate'. Finally, the Duke condemned 'this senseless outcry against public men for not having overlooked the ties of blood and Nature in dispensing the patronage of office'. Lord Plunkett was grateful for this 'manly declaration' by the Duke and consented to give further details of the family appointments, which made it obvious that the charges against him were wide of the mark.†

*Hansard, March 2, 1832.
†Ibid., March 12, 1832.

To his distress Lord Eldon, who had vacated the Woolsack in 1830, was dragged into this controversy. In the Commons a Member called Spring Rice referred to a Committee report that Lord Eldon's son held six profitable legal offices. 'No doubt had there been six sons, thirty-six offices would have been distributed among them,' said this speaker, who demanded to know why so much virtuous indignation was being reserved for the Lord Chancellor of Ireland.* Apologetically, Lord Eldon rose in the Lords to make a personal explanation. When he first became Lord Chancellor in 1801, he said, the King had pressed him to accept patents of certain offices in the Court of Chancery. For a long time he refused, but the King importuned him and in the end he 'thought it a matter of duty no longer to resist the wishes of his Sovereign'. The press had said his son drew £12,000 from those patents, though nothing but the reversion of the offices had been secured to him, even after twenty-seven years. Lord Eldon contended that he was out of pocket in many directions and that the value of all his son's offices could not reimburse him for all his out-payments.† (To be importuned by his Sovereign was one of Lord Eldon's perennial misfortunes; he had wanted to remain Chief Justice of the Common Pleas but the King had pressed him to take the Woolsack.)

That same year the question of sinecures sparked off a Parliamentary brawl between the new Lord Chancellor, Lord Brougham, and Sir Edward Sugden. Nettled by a Parliamentary question from Sugden about two sinecures which he had pledged himself to abolish, but had meanwhile filled, Brougham likened his questioner to a reptile, a wasp, a spider and a bug (as a rhetorician he was singularly repetitive). Surely, argued the high-minded Brougham, he was entitled to the emoluments of these offices until the law deprived him of them? The House of Lords took no exception to the Lord Chancellor's language but the House of Commons did. 'How,' asked Sir Robert Peel, 'are we to perform our duties in this House if we are liable to be abused for so doing by the noble and learned peer who presides over the other branch of the Legislature?'‡

In 1833 the Lord Chancellor lost his power to sell offices and was put on the same salary as the Lord Chief Justice : £10,000.

Ibid., March 6, 1832.
†*Hansard*, March 12, 1832.
‡*Ibid.*, July 27, 1832.

He still retained wide patronage, but henceforth it would be exercised in a spirit of disinterested benevolence.

Brougham had found much to say about the judiciary in his famous six-hour speech in Parliament on law reform, in 1828. He repeated his earlier warning that judges should not look for promotion, but argued that they should have some sort of incentive on top of their salaries. 'So long as the door is thus closed to all ambition, so long must we find a tendency in them, as in all men arrived at their last resting-place, to become less strenuous in their exertions than they would be if some little stimulation were applied to them . . . I therefore would hold out an inducement to them to labour vigorously, by allowing them a certain moderate amount of fees . . . as an incentive.' He added that 'such fees should not be in proportion to the length of a suit or the number of its stages'. This proposal for a productivity agreement seems not to have been followed up.

Brougham went on to deplore a 'custom above the law' which laid down that party, as well as merit, must be studied in appointing judges. 'One half of the Bar is thus excluded from the competition; for no man can be a judge who is not of a particular party. Unless he be the known adherent of a certain system of government, unless he profess himself devoted to one scheme of policy, unless his party happen to be the party connected with the Crown or allied with the ministry of the day, there is no chance for him; that man is surely excluded. Men must be on one side of the great political question to become judges . . .' The Whigs in this respect were no better than the Tories. After citing instances of men who had changed their party in order to reach the heights of their profession, Brougham commended Scotland for its more liberal approach to the appointment of judges. Why could not England abandon 'this mischievous system by which the empire loses the services of some of the ablest, the most learned and most honest men within its bounds?' Hammering the point home, he went on : 'The judges have this leaning – they must have it – they cannot help having it – you compel them to have it – you choose them on account of their notoriously having it at the Bar; and you vainly hope that they will suddenly put it off when they rise by its means to the Bench. On the contrary they know they fill a certain situation and they cannot forget by whom they were placed there or for what reason.'

These were severe reflections on the impartiality of the judges. A century and a half earlier the complaint had been that the judges looked to the rising sun, which wore a royal crown; now, if Brougham was right, they looked to the party sun. But if the judges were invidiously chosen, what of those who heard legal appeals in the Privy Council? This was the court of ultimate appeal for the whole of the overseas empire, yet it had neither a regular Bench nor a regular Bar. Of the lawyers only the Master of the Rolls attended, assisted by an ex-ambassador or 'now and then a junior Lord of the Admiralty who has been neither ambassador nor lawyer, but would be exceedingly fit for both functions only that he happened to be educated for neither'. Such was the composition of 'that awful Privy Council' which sat at Westminster, allotted nine days a year to 'Plantation appeals', dispensed the law for eighty million people and disposed of all their property. Brougham said he once saw the fate of possessions worth £30,000 a year settled in a few minutes by the Privy Council, who reversed a decision reached by overseas judges after nineteen days of most earnest consultation.

The six-hour speech closed with a much-quoted passage:

'It was the boast of Augustus – it formed part of the lustre in which the perfidies of his early years were lost – that he found Rome of brick and left it of marble; a praise not unworthy of a great Prince, and to which the present reign also has its claims. But how much nobler will be the Sovereign's boast, when he shall have it to say, that he found law dear and left it cheap – found it a sealed book and left it a living letter – found it the patrimony of the rich and left it the inheritance of the poor – found it a two-edged sword of craft and oppression and left it the staff of honesty and the shield of innocence.'*

Most of the reforms urged by Brougham on this occasion were carried out in his lifetime, many of them by himself when, to the nation's surprise and his own, he became Lord Chancellor in 1830. The Court of Chancery was singled out for overhaul. 'In an instant,' said the Rev. Sydney Smith, exaggerating somewhat, 'the iron mace of Brougham shivered to atoms the House of Fraud and Decay.' Brougham sat long days in court and cleared the backlog of more than a hundred appeals, while the parasites of the Chancery Bar wrung their hands for their lost refreshers. A Vice-Chancellor had been asked by the Chancery

Hansard: February 7, 1828.

The Highest Court of Law in the Kingdom:
the Lords hearing appeals, by Doyle

The Court of Queen's Bench, 1880

An Old Bailey trial, 1881

The Lord Chancellor's Court at Lincoln's Inn Hall

Commissioners whether three judges could get through all the work of the court. 'No, nor three angels either,' he replied. Brougham did the work of three angels and his decisions aroused little or no dissent; but even he was forced within two or three years to apply for extra judges and by 1841 there were three Vice-Chancellors. By 1853, when Dickens' *Bleak House* appeared, Lord Denman complained that its picture of Chancery abuses was hopelessly out of date; the evils, he said, had been rectified without any help from the novelist. To this, Dickens replied that at the time of publication there was a suit before the Court of Chancery which had been begun twenty years before, in which from thirty to forty counsel had appeared at one time, and in which costs of £70,000 had been incurred. It was a friendly suit but it was no nearer its end than when it began. There was another well-known suit, still undecided, which had swallowed up twice that much money since it was launched in the previous century. Dickens said a Chancery judge had assured him that any imperfections in the system were due to public parsimony in not increasing the number of judges. Even if *Bleak House* exaggerated the evils, even if the Court of Chancery no longer had its decaying houses and its blighted lands in every shire, its worn-out lunatic in every mad-house, it continued to earn widespread public suspicion.

As well as breaking the great log-jam in Chancery, Brougham was responsible for setting up the Judiciary Committee of the Privy Council, introducing an independent Court of Bankruptcy and instituting the Central Criminal Court. He paved the way for the present system of county courts, a scheme which was bitterly blocked by vested interests at Westminster Hall. Lord Lyndhurst was their chief spokesman. Two-thirds of the legal business of Westminster, he complained, would be transferred to provincial tribunals. Barristers would 'convert themselves into provincial barristers . . . inferior in learning, inferior in talent, inferior in intelligence, inferior in all those great and glorious qualifications which had so long distinguished the Bar of England'. Under the existing system the judges at Westminster sat together, consulted each other daily and if need be hourly, were subject to each other's criticism and were answerable to an acute and vigilant Bar, all of which helped to ensure certainty, precision, freedom from corruption and freedom from pressures exerted by persons resident on the spot. The judge chosen from

G

the sad ranks of provincial barristers would be cut off from intellectual challenge and develop into a mere drone; 'he would ask their Lordships whether a man of such character, aye of such a class, was a fit person to be Lord Chancellor?' The whole idea would 'involve judges, barristers and attorneys in one common poverty and ruin'.* Brougham retorted by citing a case in which a firm claiming payment for a pound of butter had been saddled with £30 costs, thanks to the excellences of the courts at Westminster. Many merchants and shopkeepers had abandoned all efforts to claim payment of debts and the dishonest flourished exceedingly; but Lord Lyndhurst spoke for the lawyers, caring nothing, it seemed, for the aggrieved public. Not until 1846 was this reform driven through. As it turned out there was no difficulty in finding barristers willing to become judicial 'drones'. The county courts quickly proved to be of enormous benefit to the trading community.

Brougham might have wrought even greater reforms but for his intolerance, asperity and increasing lack of balance. Even though his conduct inflamed his enemies and distressed his friends, he remains the nineteenth century's law reformer *par excellence* and the liberating impetus he gave was slow to die away. In 1852 the Lord Chancellor, Lord Truro, fathered the Common Law Procedure Act which had as its object 'to make the progress of a suit as short, as economical and as simple as is compatible with the safe and satisfactory administration of justice'. According to its begetter, it was the biggest revision of procedure in common law since the days of Edward I. But Sir Alexander Cockburn (later Lord Chief Justice) wanted to see a more fundamental reform yet: the amalgamation of the systems of common law and equity, along with a codification of the laws, which as they stood were a disgrace to a civilised country. 'They were a sealed book to the subjects of the realm,' he said, 'and it would require a whole life of a man to make himself acquainted with them.'†

It was for Lord Chancellors to initiate reforms, but sometimes the ordinary judge could lend a useful hand. Mr Justice Maule is said to have done much to stimulate divorce reform by the ironical rebuke he gave to a bigamist at Warwick Assizes in 1845. The prisoner, who was penniless, had 'married' his second

Hansard: June 17, 1833.
†*Hansard*: June 3, 1852.

wife after his first had run off with a hawker. Before sentencing him to four months hard labour, for trifling with the laws of matrimony, the Judge said :

'I will tell you what you ought to have done; and if you say you did not know, I must tell you the law conclusively presumes that you *did*. You ought to have instructed your attorney to bring an action against the hawker for criminal conversation with your wife. That would have cost you about £100. When you had recovered substantial damages against the hawker you would have instructed your proctor to sue in the ecclesiastical courts for a divorce *a mensa atque thoro*.* That would have cost you £200 or £300 more. When you had obtained a divorce *a mensa atque thoro* you would have had to appear by counsel before the House of Lords for a divorce *a vinculo matrimonii*.† The Bill might have been opposed in all its stages in both Houses of Parliament. Altogether you would have had to spend about £1,100 or £1,200. You will probably tell me that you never had a thousand farthings of your own in the world; but that makes no difference. Sitting here as a British judge it is my duty to tell you that this is not a country in which there is one law for the rich and another for the poor.'‡

The ironies of Mr Justice Maule sometimes misled juries into bringing in a perverse verdict. In this instance they may well have been lost on the prisoner (who in some accounts is said to have been given only one day's imprisonment) but the speech seems to have had considerable impact on public opinion. In 1857, following a Royal Commission, a Court for Divorce and Matrimonial Causes was set up in London. The middle classes derived some limited benefit from it, the poor none at all. There was some pressure to allow the county courts to grant divorces, but the law officers felt that these were inappropriate tribunals for hearing evidence of sexual transgressions. The *mores* of the day can be judged from a statement by Lord Chancellor Cranworth : 'It was possible for a wife to pardon a husband who had admitted adultery; but it was hardly possible for a husband ever really to pardon the adultery of a wife'; and from a recommendation by the Bishop of Lincoln that adulterers should be

---

*From bed and board.

†From the bond of matrimony.

‡Jacob Larwood: *Forensic Anecdotes*. For another version, see report of Royal Commission on Divorce, 1912.

put in the criminal dock alongside forgers and burglars.* The press was grateful for a new source of news. In 1859 Queen Victoria wrote to the Lord Chancellor saying, 'The Queen wishes to ask the Lord Chancellor whether no steps can be taken to prevent publicity of the proceedings before the new Divorce Court.' Lord Campbell attempted a measure but failed.†

From mid-century onwards the Inns of Court were under pressure to shoulder once again those responsibilities for legal education which they had shed more than a century before. Almost everything a barrister knew was picked up in the courts, where by no means every judge was as assiduous in expounding the law to students as Lord Mansfield had been. The universities virtually ignored the practical side of the law. In 1852 a Council of Legal Education was set up, with the nominal co-operation of the Inns, but it was obvious that these otiose bodies were prepared to make minimal efforts. So long as would-be barristers ate the appropriate number of dinners, the Inns were content. Sir Richard Bethell bullied them in his capacity of Attorney-General and they at length conceded the necessity of examinations; but the examinations they set proved to be not worth the sitting. In this respect the lawyers lagged behind the doctors, who themselves were by no means distinguished for educational zeal.

Regrettably, Sir Richard Bethell, as Lord Westbury, is remembered, not for his efforts at reform, but as the last Lord Chancellor to bring disrepute on his office. His initial fault was to authorise some dubious traffic in bankruptcy registrarships, one of which went to his wastrel son, and to agree to paying pensions to officials who should have been prosecuted. By the time the scandal broke, in 1865, the Lord Chancellor was offering his son £1,000 a year to leave the country and live 'in Dresden or some other proper place'. Lord Westbury's worst sin, it may be thought, was to mislead Parliament in an effort to cover up. Nor was he alone in so doing. In the course of the affair a previous Lord Chancellor, Lord Chelmsford, made an elaborate avowal of innocence on a linked matter, only to hear Earl Granville read out a letter which gave the lie to what he had been saying. However, the House could not be bothered to chase two limping hares at once. The Member who led the attack on Lord Westbury in the Commons, G. W. Hunt, accused him of 'want of

*Hansard, May 19, 1857.
†Report of Royal Commission on Divorce, 1912.

vigilance, supineness and, I might almost say, fatuous simplicity'
– the same fatuous simplicity which brought down Bacon. In
mitigation the Attorney-General pointed out that Lord Westbury
had forsworn the gift of three hundred livings, 'many of them
of no inconsiderable value', and had appointed judges from the
opposing political party. The Commons acquitted Lord Westbury of corrupt motives but said that his 'laxity of practice and
want of caution' in granting the pensions were 'calculated to
discredit the administration of his great office.'* Announcing
his resignation to the Lords, the Lord Chancellor said the dictates
of conscience would have prompted him to step down many
months before, but he was not free to do so without permission
of the Government. 'The holder of the Great Seal,' he felt,
'ought never to be in the position of an accused person.'† But
being an accused person did not disqualify him from continuing
to hear appeals in the Lords. He once said, 'A Bench, no matter
what you may say, is a damned fine thing to sit on.'‡

In the years 1873–76 the system of courts was at last rationa-
lised and a truce called in the long war between common law
and equity. Lord Selborne, the Lord Chancellor who introduced the Supreme Court of Judicature Bill in 1873, pointed
out that the disctinctions between the two codes did not exist in
other nations, except those which had modelled their constitu-
tions on ours. The system was 'not only unsatisfactory in itself
but . . . productive of the greatest possible inconvenience and
obstruction to the administration of justice in its actual result'.
Now a single Supreme Court with undivided jurisdiction would
be formed of all the superior courts of common law and equity,
and under the same roof would come the Probate and Divorce
Court, the Admiralty Court and the Central Court of Bankruptcy. This Supreme Court would have two divisions: a High
Court of Justice to exercise original jurisdiction and hear appeals
from inferior courts; and a Court of Appeal. There were to be
twenty-one judges, the senior being styled Lord Chief Justice of
England.

Some opposition came from members of the Equity Bar who
did not relish the idea of depriving Chancery of the power to
teach other courts high principles and to exercise a 'beneficial

*Hansard, July 4, 1865.
†Hansard, July 5, 1865.
‡F. W. Ashley: *My Sixty Years in The Law.*

interference'. The barons of the Exchequer resented the loss of their ancient title. Of Chief Baron Kelly, last of the chief barons, it was said that he did not oppose the Judicature Acts, but simply ignored them, except in so far as they affected details of procedure. No one who valued the Judge's goodwill would refer to the Exchequer Division of the High Court of Justiciary. When he heard that one of his new judges was to be called Mr Justice Hawkins, he ruled that, if the ancient title of baron was to be denied, he must be called Sir Henry Hawkins.*

The constitution of the Court of Appeal was decided only after much wrangling. It replaced a variety of appellate bodies and finally emerged as a court in which the Master of the Rolls sat with lords justices of appeal, along with ordinary High Court judges as occasion demanded. A further appeal was still possible to the House of Lords, as it had been since baronial days. As a court, the House of Lords consisted only of the 'law lords' : the Lord Chancellor, the ex-Lord Chancellors, lords of appeal in ordinary and peers holding high judicial office. The Judicial Committee of the Privy Council, which heard overseas appeals, also had the services of the Lords of appeal in ordinary, sitting with the Lord Chancellor.

Not long after the Judicature Acts were passed the Judges ceased to sit in Westminster Hall, where they had heard cases for more than six centuries. In 1883 they moved to the 'monastic Gothic' of the present Law Courts in the Strand, the cost of the building being defrayed from the estates of those who had died intestate down the generations. The surroundings were imposing and the acoustics were terrible.

The great reorganisation of 1873–76 still did not provide for a Court of Criminal Appeal. On numberless occasions campaigns had been launched to stir the imagination of Parliament on this issue. One such attempt was made, in his more vigorous years as a barrister, by Chief Baron Kelly, in 1844. *Punch* had lent him support. In a civil action involving property, it pointed out, the losing party had a right of appeal; now 'Mr Kelly would make human characters and human freedom as valuable as chattels and money'. Kelly described to the House how he saved a man's life by incessantly importuning the judge who had doomed him to take the opinion of his brothers on the Bench. When the judge at last agreed to do so the sentence was modi-

*A Generation of Judges, by Their Reporter.

fied. Sir James Graham, the Home Secretary, was unimpressed.
It was of the utmost importance to the public, he contended,
that punishment should follow quickly upon crime; half its
deterrent value was lost by a delay. Such was the quality of
our judges that the innocent were very rarely punished. It now
seems scarcely believable that the country had to wait until 1907
for a Court of Criminal Appeal. Introducing a Bill for that
purpose, the Attorney-General, Sir John Walton, said that, at
long last, it would put liberty on an equality with property.
Our judges were unsurpassed, but even so justice had blun-
dered. 'Innocent men have been convicted and the numbers of
the victims during the last few years has not been inconsiderable
. . . An enterprising press has rushed in where jurists have feared
to tread and retrial by newspaper threatens to take the place
which ought to be occupied by the process of rehearing by a
judicial tribunal.'* This was a reference, no doubt, to the case
of Adolf Beck, twice wrongly convicted. One effect of setting
up the new court was to make judges think harder about the
lengths of the sentences they imposed. The Court's functions
were taken under the wing of the Court of Appeal in 1964.

Hansard, April 17, 1907.

17

'THE JUDGES ARE PREJUDICED'

Brougham, it will be recalled, inveighed against the appointment of political judges. It was a topic to which he often returned. Like Bacon, he believed there was nothing so much to be dreaded as a popular judge, but a party judge was always detestable; men honest enough not to be corrupted by money were not always proof against corruption by party. He had hardly ceased to issue warnings on this subject when, in 1868, Parliament decided to give judges the task of hearing election petitions, which was the least suitable role for a political judge. Hitherto the complaints of defeated Parliamentary candidates who alleged that they were the victims of corruption had been heard by committees of Parliament. Could the Bench lend an impartial ear in such disputes? The Judges did not welcome the task. The Lord Chief Justice, Sir Alexander Cockburn, wrote to the Lord Chancellor as follows :

'In conformity with your Lordship's wishes I have consulted the judges and I am charged by them, one and all, to convey to you their strong and unanimous feeling of insuperable repugnance to having these new and objectionable duties thrust upon them.

'We are unanimously of opinion that the inevitable consequences of putting judges to try election petitions will be to lower and degrade the judicial office, and to destroy or at all events materially impair the confidence of the public in the thoroughgoing impartiality and inflexible integrity of the judges, when in course of their ordinary duties, political matters come incidentally before them . . . We are at a loss to see how Parliament can, in justice or propriety, impose upon us labours wholly beyond the sphere of our constitutional duties and which no one ever contemplated the possibility of our being called upon to perform.'*

The letter had no effect. In another context Lord Chief Justice Cockburn demanded, 'Is Her Majesty's Commission to be neglected, are the gaols to remain undelivered and the assizes untried while Her Majesty's judges are encouraged to investigate all the unclean matters in a rotten borough?'† Unfrightened by this prospect, the Cabinet adhered to its decision. Her Majesty's judges would be given many more extra-judicial tasks warranted to fill them with insuperable repugnance (in 1854 they had resented being called upon to serve on a tribunal to adjudicate on railway fares).

Elections in those days, thanks to a long and vigorous tradition of malpractice at the hustings, used to be followed by a crop of disputes. Sir Henry Dickens says that as late as 1906 he had three retainers to act in such petitions, and in 1911 six.‡ Judges heard evidence about money paid to 'screaming women' (women hired to disorganise meetings), 'watchers' (who were supposed to see that voters were not kidnapped) and other recipients of illegal payments. It was necessary to distinguish between corrupt treating and reasonable hospitality. A bad judge could make a bad hash of such a hearing and that is what Mr Justice Grantham did. Known throughout the country as the most fervid of Tories, he should never have been allowed, or have allowed himself, to hear any issue with a political content. He had been an active Member of Parliament, a ruthless critic of Gladstone and a speaker who could be relied upon to give old-fashioned views with 'manly vigour'. At various times his forthright statements had delighted or offended most sections of the community. He was what the Scots call a kenspeckle figure. Like Lord Monboddo he despised carriages and rode to court on horseback – probably the last judge to do so. In 1906 Mr Justice Grantham's decisions in two election petitions upset a great many Members of Parliament and at one time his seat on the Bench appeared to be in danger. At Great Yarmouth the Judge had seen nothing wrong in the giving of an 'at home'

*E. B. Rowlands: *Seventy-Two Years at the Bar.*
†Quoted by S. O. Buckmaster, *Hansard* July 6, 1906.
‡Sir H. Dickens: *Recollections.*

by the Conservative candidate because, in the Judge's view, the election was not imminent; yet at Bodmin he held that a party given by the Liberal candidate, at a prior date to the Yarmouth 'at home', was highly improper because it was on the eve of the election. The nature of the treating was not quite the same in each case, but 347 Members of Parliament were sufficiently shocked by the apparent inconsistency to demand a debate. The Attorney-General (Sir John Walton) recalled the view of Sir Robert Peel that to remove a judge there must be 'corruption, partisanship, intentional moral delinquency', and said that such charges could not be applied to Mr Justice Grantham. There was much criticism of an after-dinner joke in which the Judge, expressing thanks for hospitality, said that his mayoral host ought to be proceeded against for corrupt treating. This was said at Great Yarmouth while the petition was being heard. However, A. J. Balfour argued that a corrupt judge would never have made such a jest; there was 'no more transparently natural, candid man' than Mr Justice Grantham. Less charitable was the Prime Minister, Sir Henry Campbell-Bannerman, who thought it had been a deplorable mistake on the Judge's part 'not to avoid, as he could have avoided, as others have avoided who were conscious of having partisan feeling, being selected from the rota for the trial of these petitions . . . No one more strongly condemns his conduct than I do.' The Prime Minister ended by saying, 'Have we not given him such a lesson that he is not likely to repeat these ill-considered actions?'*

For five years Mr Justice Grantham brooded over this rebuke, which threw the strongest possible doubt on his impartiality. Then, on the twenty-fifth anniversary of his first visit to Liverpool as a judge, he followed his address to the grand jury with a complete repudiation of his supposedly partisan behaviour in 1906, together with reflections on the integrity of Parliament. This brought him his second severe rebuke from a Prime Minister. Herbert Asquith said the House normally was scrupulous to avoid censuring judges, but there was a reciprocal obligation on their part not to reflect on the proceedings of Parliament. 'That obligation, usually so loyally recognised on the Bench, appears on this occasion to have been signally violated.'† The Prime Minister asked for time to consider what

Hansard, July 6, 1906.
†*Ibid,* February 8, 1911.

action was advisable. Some three weeks later he announced that no steps would be taken to dislodge Mr Justice Grantham; he had observed 'with satisfaction and without surprise that the speech . . . has been universally and emphatically condemned by professional and public opinion'.* Such unanimity, one might have thought, would have been a good reason for unseating the Judge. Mr Justice Grantham died later that year, having done his best in an appointment beyond his capacity. It was said in one of the debates in Parliament that no member of the Bench had had more experience of the painful results of judicial review. There is a story to the effect that Lord Justice Vaughan-Williams commented to Montague Lush, K.C., 'I see, Mr Lush, that in this notice of appeal there are no fewer than seventy-three grounds of appeal,' which drew the reply, 'Yes, my Lord, but this is an appeal from Mr Justice Grantham.'†

Mr Justice Grantham was one of the much-criticised political appointments of Lord Halsbury, who first became Lord Chancellor in 1885 and held the Great Seal, off and on, for seventeen years. He was also under fire for showing preference to family connections. When asked whether, *ceteris paribus,* he would appoint the best man to the job, he is said to have replied, '*Ceteris paribus* be damned, I'm going to appoint my nephew.'‡ The Duke of Wellington would have approved.

Lord Halsbury's judicial appointments were often subjected to withering comments by the legal journals and even by the national newspapers. It is possible to defend the elevation of Members of Parliament to the Bench on the grounds that their minds have been rendered more flexible and that they have acquired more knowledge of the world than if they had been reared wholly in the cloistered pieties of the law. But this was not the governing reason for political appointments to the Bench. A notorious letter by Disraeli, in 1868, shows how the system operated. It was addressed to the Lord Chancellor, Lord Chelmsford:

'Dear Lord Chancellor, After all, I regret to observe that Mr Justice Shee is no more. The claims of our legal friends in the House of Commons, supported as they are by much sympathy on

*Hansard, March 1, 1911.
†F. J. de Verteuil: *Fifty Wasted Years.*
‡R. F. V. Heuston: *Lives of the Lord Chancellors* 1885–1940.

our Benches, must not be treated with indifference, and therefore I venture to express a hope that you will not decide on the successor of Mr Justice Shee with any precipitation. Yours very faithfully, B. DISRAELI.'*

Lord Chelmsford took grave offence at this 'dictation'. Within a few days he was out of office and his successor agreed to Disraeli's nominee for the vacant judgeship. There was a whiff of James II about this transaction, but the system continued unaltered. Professor R. F. V. Heuston, who has analysed the controversial Halsbury selections at length, quotes telling passages from Halsbury's correspondence. In 1897 Lord Salisbury wrote to the Lord Chancellor saying that there was no clearer statute in the unwritten law of the party system than the rule that 'party claims should always weigh heavily in the disposal of the highest appointments'. Any alteration in this system would 'give our party arrangements a wrench'.†

Rather than give the party arrangements a wrench, Lord Halsbury saddled the country with some four or five judges whom lawyers now unite in denigrating. At the time they were named the Bar visibly trembled. For one of them an ancient joke was revived; he was nicknamed Necessity because he knew no law. It could have been applied just as well, some thought, to one of his stable mates, who was notorious for delaying judgment in difficult cases and then giving his decision without stating any reasons, not even echoing Lord Kenyon's 'I swear to God it is so'. Obviously, in creating thirty judges, Lord Halsbury could not create thirty paragons. The conclusion of Professor Heuston is that out of the total not more than seven appointments were dubious and that of these seven, four had been Tory Members of Parliament when elevated. In the distribution of blame Lord Salisbury must not be overlooked, though even he jibbed at one of the Lord Chancellor's appointments. It is perhaps superfluous to say that Lord Halsbury himself had fought several elections in his day and had been looked on as a strong party man.

Professor Harold Laski, who was fascinated by the links between law and politics, produced statistics to show that out of 139 judges appointed between 1832 and 1906 eighty were Members of Parliament at the time of nomination and eleven

*Lord Birkenhead: *Points of View.*
†R. F. V. Heuston: *Lives of the Lord Chancellors,* 1885–1940.

others had been candidates; and that out of eighty-three judges who left Parliament for the Bench sixty-three were appointed by their party while in office. All he inferred from these results was that membership of Parliament was of 'distinct assistance' to a lawyer who wanted to be a judge. What did impress him was that with one exception every Lord Chief Justice for sixty years had been an Attorney-General; and he asked whether a man who had fought to get a controversial measure through Parliament was the right person to preside over an action which involved its interpretation.

The 'right' of the law officers of the Crown to step into high judicial posts had not gone unchallenged. After the passing of the first Judicature Act in 1873 the Gladstone Cabinet pointed out that this succession had never been properly established. In future promotion would be governed by legal qualifications and service only. Tradition, as it turned out, was not effectively broken until after World War Two. Neither Lord Goddard nor the present Lord Chief Justice, Lord Parker, held political posts before their elevation.

From the earliest days of organised labour, it had been the complaint of working men that judges were politically prejudiced against them and could be relied upon to interpret the laws in their disfavour. The first attempts at industrial organisation had been regarded as criminal conspiracy in restraint of trade. Tolpuddle had become a legend. In troubled times the judges had to interpret the laws with little or no help from Parliament and it is not surprising if, as they surveyed the perennial threats to ordered society as they knew it, they took decisions in the light of their own deeply held convictions, which some would call prejudices. The contract between employer and employed, in their view, was a voluntary one, agreed by parties who met on equal terms; a man who thought his wage was inadequate was at liberty to work for somebody else. If he was injured in the course of that employment, that was his own misfortune; he recognised the risks and, by taking employment, accepted them. He had no claim against his employer and was lucky to have been given a chance to earn his bread. In 1837 Lord Abinger, in a judgment which was to doom thousands to misery, dismissed a claim by a butcher's boy against his employer for damages in respect of injuries received when an unstable cart collapsed. It was intolerable, Lord Abinger thought, that an employer should be liable in such an action; the possible repercussions were too painful to contemplate. From his judgment evolved the doctrine of 'common employment', which laid down that those who voluntarily worked for an employer had no claim against him for injuries caused by their fellow servants, though an outside party could claim damages in full. It was in modern eyes a monstrous concept; but it is all too easy to blame the judges for the injustices which flowed from it. Parliament could have changed the law if it had felt its conscience to be outraged, yet Parliament took sixty years to do so. During that interval employers honoured their obligations to total strangers but not to those who worked for them, save in so far as minor tinkerings with the law forced them to put their hands into their pockets. By 1897, when the Workmen's (Compensation for Accidents) Bill was before Parliament, only twelve men in a hundred injured in accidents received any form of compensation. Indignant Members chose to assail the judges rather than admit the guilt of the Legislature. Herbert Asquith was only one who lamented the 'fictitious – and I venture to say, fantastic' doctrine of common employment 'invented by the Bench'.* Augustine Birrell, Member for West Fife, said:

'Satan finds mischief still, not only for idle hands but for subtle and logical brains to do; and Her Majesty's judges had taken upon themselves not only to interpret contracts between employer and employed but to invent them and to introduce terms into the contracts which neither employer nor employed had ever heard of. The doctrine was only invented in 1837. Lord Abinger planted it; Baron Alderson watered it; and the Devil gave it increase.' (Laughter.)†

Birrell went on to complain about 'the most highly trained intellects of the country playing fast and loose with men's lives', a phrase which he could have applied with equal justice, along with some slight immodesty, to Members of Parliament. The great object of the Bill, as he saw it, was to put aside 'that discredited common law of England and adopt a law which knew nothing of common employment or contributory negligence or *volenti non fit injuria.*'‡

In the same debate Joseph Chamberlain urged that the House

Hansard, May 3, 1897.
†*Hansard*, May 3, 1897.
‡No wrong is done by one who consents.

should legislate in such a way as to avoid the use of the courts, thus foreshadowing the twentieth century policy of excluding the judges as far as possible from any say in social legislation. 'My experience,' he said, 'is that good employers do not grudge compensation to workmen injured in their service, but they do grudge compensation which goes into the pockets of the lawyers.'

Unfortunately, the 1897 Act was no masterpiece of drafting and the Bar continued to do well out of litigation arising from this Act and later ones. There were complaints that judges still interpreted the law harshly, as much from lack of sympathy with working men as from ignorance of labour conditions; a common allegation was that they missed no chance of discovering contributory negligence. The poor, according to Professor Harold Laski, 'could be pardoned if they had the impression that the law was an instrument rather for their control than for their service'.

By the turn of the century another explosion over 'judge-made law' was imminent. In 1859 the unions had won the right to exercise peaceful persuasion. By Acts of 1871 and 1875 they obtained a species of charter under which the stigma of illegality was removed and they were allowed to make rules to defend their funds from litigants and their own embezzlers. Nevertheless they found themselves increasingly under attack in civil law. What was 'combination' and when was it illegal? In 1900, by what the unions called a judicial *coup d'état*, the Taff Vale Railway Company obtained the right to sue the Amalgamated Society of Railway Servants, whose members had been 'besetting' its strike-breakers. Mr Justice Farwell in the Chancery Division threw out the argument that unions were not subject to the same laws as private individuals. 'It would require very clear and express words of enactment,' he said, 'to induce me to hold that the Legislature had in fact legalised the existence of such irresponsible bodies with such wide capacity for evil.' As a passing example of that evil he cited the rattening which had disfigured Sheffield some years previously. To strike was legal, said Mr Justice Farwell, but a society undertaking to manage and direct a strike was responsible for the way in which it was carried out. 'It is not a question of the rights of members of the society,' he ruled, 'but of wrong done to persons outside the society.' The Court of Appeal overturned Mr Justice Farwell's decision; then the House of Lords overturned the Court of

Appeal. The Lord Chancellor, Lord Halsbury, held that if the Legislature had created a 'thing' which could own property, which could employ servants, which could inflict injury, it must impliedly have given the power to make it answerable in court for injuries purposely done by its authority and procurement. *The Times* was not the only newspaper to express satisfaction that the unions, which had been using their 'vast pecuniary resources' to promote labour conflicts, had been shaken from their 'complacent irresponsibility'.* The cost to the union involved was in the region of £40,000. In the Commons Keir Hardie asked whether the Government would introduce legislation to restore the protection which the unions had enjoyed for thirty years and was told by A. J. Balfour, 'No, sir, it is not proposed to introduce legislation.'† At that year's Trade Union Congress the Taff Vale decision was condemned as an 'astounding' development in judge-made law. Many leading unionists, however, welcomed the judgment, holding that it would introduce some much-needed discipline into the movement; and Sidney Webb did not think the unions had been justified in claiming total immunity.‡ Yet, only five years later, when a Liberal Government was returned to power, the legislation that Keir Hardie had demanded was forthcoming. Two Trade Dispute Bills, one sponsored by a private Member, one by the new Government, were introduced into Parliament, with the object of restoring 'the original position that trade unions should be exempted from the law' (the phrase is that of the private Bill's sponsor). The discussion of the Government measure was marked by criticism of the judges from both the Attorney-General and the Solicitor-General, a rare spectacle. The Attorney-General, Sir John Walton, said recent judicial decisions had 'seriously disturbed preconceived notions' of what was permissible; the undoubted right of peaceful persuasion had been 'cut down to the point of extinction'; and funds contributed to provide against sickness or misfortune or unemployment had been held liable to claims arising out of repudiated acts of unauthorised persons. Thanks to a jungle of judge-made law there existed, said the Attorney-General, 'a feeling of insecurity and a sense of injustice'.

*The Times, August 2, 1901.
†*Hansard*, September 4, 1901.
‡Clegg, Fox and Thompson: *History of British Trade Unions Since* 1889.

What they proposed to enact was that if a deed was not criminal when performed by an individual, then it should not be criminal when performed by a union.* At the second reading the Solicitor-General took up the lament, saying that the courts had 'broken down the safeguards with which Parliament vainly thought it had protected trade unions'. He had an affectionate respect for the judges, who were only human and they 'naturally and properly gave effect to their own sincere convictions as to the character and purpose of organisations like trade unions'. Among these sincere convictions he cited the opinion voiced in Quinn v. Leathem by Lord Lindley, who said, 'A threat to call men out, given by a trade union officially to an employer of men belonging to the union and willing to work with him is a form of coercion, intimidation, molestation or annoyance to them and to him, very difficult to resist.' Sir Edward Carson (Lord Carson) could not see why unions should be in a privileged position. 'The decision in the Taff Vale case,' he said, 'was a decision absolutely in consonance with equity and with the general law of the land.' To Lord Robert Cecil it was very obvious that the reason for the measure was the increase in Labour votes. Rufus Isaacs (Lord Reading) declined to say that the judges had altered the law, but they had given voice to opinions 'contrary to the views of the vast majority of lawyers practising in the courts'. Of this 'vast' majority F. E. Smith (Lord Birkenhead) did not form part. In a withering speech on the private member's Bill he congratulated Keir Hardie on his Front Bench captures. The Government had voted against 'their deliberately formed and twice repeated convictions because they dared not face a mutiny which they could not quell'. He asked a question which nobody answered: Why, if peaceful persuasion was the real object, was it necessary to have a hundred men to persuade one?†

Trade unionists now enjoyed a twentieth-century equivalent of 'benefit of clergy', but the rulings of the courts were still not to their liking. In 1911 Parliament once more introduced a Bill to offset the effect of a judicial decision; it now became legal for unions to collect funds for political purposes. This time the debate was noteworthy for a sharp attack on the judges by Winston Churchill, as Home Secretary. He deplored the per-

Hansard, March 28, 1906.
†*Hansard,* March 30, 1906.

petual litigation to which, in the past decade, the unions had been subjected; he spoke of 'all kinds of legal decisions which came with the utmost surprise to the greatest lawyers in the country'; he thought it was not good for the unions to be brought into contact with the courts, nor was it good for the courts. Uproar came when he said that where class and party issues were involved it was impossible to pretend that the courts commanded general confidence. 'On the contrary they do not and a very large number of our population have been led to the opinion that they are, unconsciously no doubt, biased.' There were cries of 'No,' 'Withdraw' and 'We do not attack the judges', but Mr Churchill went on, 'I have not the slightest intention of withdrawing and I repeat what I said that it is unfortunate that these collisions occur between the courts and the great union bodies.' What the country needed was a bulwark between the unions and the courts.*

Mr Churchill's remarks were by no means unrehearsed. Two months earlier he had been questioned in the House about a statement he made to a deputation from the Parliamentary Committee of Trade Unions, in which he accused judges of 'using language reflecting on trade unions which was extremely ignorant and out of touch with the general development of modern thought, and which has greatly complicated the administration of justice and added bitterness to a sense of distrust of the administration of the law'. The Home Secretary was asked to say which judges used this language and when. Would he move an address to the King for the removal of these judges? Mr Churchill said he had nothing to add or subtract.†

These exchanges make piquant reading today, when trade unions are far from being the downtrodden and victimised bodies they were then represented to be. But it has always been a tenet of faith in the Labour movement that judges have been anti-Labour and anti-union. *Hansard* is strewn with the speeches of Labour MPs who say that on every social issue for a century and a half the judges have always been in the wrong. The literature of the movement, notably in the 1920s, is replete with statements of the kind. In the Poplar rumpus of 1924 the judges were accused of trying to thrust their own political doctrines down the throats of an elected majority. The Labour-controlled

*Hansard, May 30, 1911.
†Ibid., March 20, 1911.

Poplar Council had fixed a minimum wage of £4 for its adult workers, but the District Auditor, regarding the wage as excessive, had surcharged members of the Council. The divisional court supported the District Auditor, the Court of Appeal reversed the decision and the House of Lords reversed the Appeal Court's ruling. According to Lord Atkinson, the proposal to pay £4 a week was unreasonable, motivated by 'eccentric principles of socialistic philanthropy'. The left-wing outcry was loud; this was only what was to be expected from the prejudiced old men on the Bench. However, it would be wrong to suppose that the elected majority in that decade was necessarily in favour of such 'philanthropy', though it may well have been in Poplar.

In 1927, when the Government forced through a Trades Dispute Bill to outlaw general strikes, the judges attracted a great volume of Labour fury; so, for that matter, did juries. Philip Snowden was one of those who dared the judges to send five million workers to prison. From such outbursts the visitor from Mars might have supposed that judges dictated the affairs of the country. At the third reading of the Bill Sir John Simon attempted a defence of the Bench. If, he said, critics meant that judges were fallible creatures, with limitations to their experience, it was perfectly true; it was true of us all. He then made the observation quoted on page ten of this book, but was interrupted by a cry that judges were free to gratify their prejudices. Some of the stronger attacks were made outside the House, notably by the general secretary to the Trade Union Congress, Walter Citrine (Lord Citrine). He told his delegates: 'Did anyone believe that a judge could escape from his environment and be uninfluenced by his surroundings? They could have little confidence in the impartiality of the judges where trade union matters were concerned. The head of every Division in the High Court had formerly been a party politician and the majority of the highest court of appeal, the House of Lords, were or had been party politicians.'* In a speech under the auspices of Ruskin College, Citrine said: 'We have nothing, generally speaking, to thank the judges of this country for. Our whole experience has been that the judges have regarded the working class movement as a sort of excrescence on the body politic, something which legitimately had no right to exist at all in our

*The Times, April 30, 1927.

industrial life.' These remarks were described as 'outrageous' by Professor J. H. Morgan, writing to *The Times*.* Amplifying what he had said, Citrine asked : 'How can we respect the impartiality of a House of Lords appeal which might, quite likely, on a trade union case, come before men of the type of Lord Birkenhead and Lord Carson, whose venom against trade unionism has displayed itself repeatedly? . . . Professor Morgan may rest assured that the trade union movement has not the slightest confidence either in the impartiality or the competence of judges to deal equitably with trade union affairs.' He ended with a quotation from Professor A. V. Dicey, the jurist : 'If a statute . . . is apt to reproduce the public opinion not so much of today as of yesterday, judge-made law occasionally represents the opinion of the day before yesterday.'†

Which may well be true. It is an open question whether the sum of human felicity would have been increased if judges had taken to voicing the opinion of tomorrow or the day after tomorrow. The good judge tries not to elevate his own instincts and convictions into principles of law, but if the Legislature leaves wide areas to his discretion, can his decision be other than subjective? Camden said, 'The discretion of a judge is the law of tyrants.' It may be that critics of judge-made law would be better to attack Parliamentary draftsmanship.

Ibid., May 5, 1927.
†*Ibid.*, May 7, 1927.

18

PRESTIGE AT STAKE

In the years between the world wars the judges saw, or thought they saw, their function and prestige being undermined on many fronts. The 1914–18 war had turned many of them into tools of the Executive; one after another they had left the Bench, uncomplainingly, to sit on commissions, tribunals and committees. The Lord Chief Justice, Lord Reading, went on overseas missions, returning at intervals to his court, a bizarre division of duties. By the war's end the cry went up that the judges should cease to be linked with departments of State and return to their Benches. Not the least reason for restoring them to their traditional duties was unusually heavy congestion in the King's Bench Division and the Divorce Court.

The dissatisfactions felt by the judges were to find expression in the following ways:

Attacks from the Bench on the 'new despotism' of rule by the Executive;

Distaste, verging on 'insuperable repugnance', of the Bench at being involved in divorce litigation;

Protests by the judges at an economy cut in their salaries, with a threatened Petition of Right.

Winston Churchill had argued that industrial disputes should be settled without the aid of the judges and he was not alone in his belief. As the twentieth century progressed new measures of social welfare were designed so as to involve only the minimum of reference to the courts. Judges, the argument went, had been given their chance and had abused it; now decisions on social matters – pensions, health, bus services and much else – were to be taken by tribunals staffed with experts in their field. The judges did not fail to notice that they were being legislated out of a new society which had no wish, apparently, to hear their political or social views.

It may or may not have been a feeling of rejection which made the judges increasingly captious at what they saw as encroachments by the Executive, an attempt to assert a *droit administratif.* In 1909 Mr Justice Darling complained that an order issued by a public department was being accorded the absolute finality and effect of an Act of Parliament; and Mr Justice Jelf deplored that Government departments were putting themselves beyond reach of the courts. In 1911 the Master of the Rolls, Sir Herbert Cozens-Hardy, said that 'administrative action generally means something done by a man whose name they did not know sitting at a desk in a Government office, very apt to be a despot if free from the interference of the courts of justice'. Through the 1920s the judicial grumbling went on. In 1928 the Government, under heavy fire from lawyers, abandoned a proposal in a rating Bill which would have entitled the Minister of Health to submit doubtful points of law to the High Court for an opinion. The idea, warmly defended by Neville Chamberlain, was to save the money of those who could not afford to test an action in the courts, but legal opinion saw the procedure as a revival of the Stuart practice of holding a one-sided consultation with the judges on an issue which, at a later date, they might have to decide on the Bench. The law courts, said Sir Henry Cautley, were for litigants only and the new procedure would be 'a very vicious one'. Dennis Herbert said the Executive proposed 'to go privately to court and ask the court to give an opinion such as they wish to have, without any person who is affected by it being necessarily before the court, putting the case in their own words and by that means forging what I should describe as a most dishonourable weapon in order to bully a subject of this country and deprive him of his ordinary right of access to the courts'. It was the ship money controversy over again. Eventually Sir Kingsley Wood, Private Secretary to the Minister of Health, said the Government would scrap the proposal rather than let it appear that the judges were subject to, or advisers to, the Exchequer.

A louder explosion was heard in 1929 when the Lord Chief

Justice, Lord Hewart, published his book *The New Despotism*. It
was a bitter, some said hysterical, attack on those bureaucrats
whose goal was 'to subordinate Parliament, to evade the courts
and to render the will, or the caprice, of the Executive un-
fettered and supreme'; men who wanted to get rid of the Lord
Chancellor, use the judges to give advance opinions on hypo-
thetical cases and reduce them to the level of departmental
solicitors. 'Administrative law is administrative lawlessness,' said
Lord Hewart. He cited numerous Acts in which the Minister
was given 'power to remove difficulties' in any way he chose,
in other words to amend Acts of Parliament as he thought fit.
The Lord Chief Justice was especially contemptuous of the
motion – much canvassed in that decade – that there should be a
Ministry of Justice, with a politician at its head empowered
to appoint judges (Lord Birkenhead had also opposed this
idea, notably in his *Points of View,* putting his case less
excitedly).

Whitehall was unamused by the Lord Chief Justice's broadside. The Lord Chancellor set up a committee to ascertain
whether the Executive was exceeding its powers; it discovered
no enormities. Lord Hewart is said to have changed his views
completely in later years, conceding that a welfare state was
unworkable without some sort of administrative law and expressing regret that he ever wrote *The New Despotism*.* He
did not live to hear Aneurin Bevan boasting in 1946 how he had
made it impossible for judges to 'sabotage' his National Health
Service, and contending that no Minister could accept responsibility for a service if all its employees were able to appeal to the
courts.† Since then the doctrine that 'the gentleman at Whitehall knows best' has received one or two setbacks, notably at
Crichel Down. In 1958 a Conservative Lord Privy Seal, Mr R.
A. Butler (Lord Butler), moving a Bill to give a right of appeal
to the courts from tribunal rulings, said, 'The zeal for State
control and planning has tilted the scales in favour of the
State and against the individual citizen. We are now restoring
the balance.'‡ As to whether that balance has been restored the
newspaper reader must judge for himself. As these lines are
written the judges are being belaboured for their failure to

*Robert Jackson: *The Chief*.
†*Hansard,* July 23, 1946.
‡*Hansard,* July 3, 1958.

stand up for the common man against the Executive. Lord Hewart may have been right the first time.

Before World War One there were only about one thousand divorces a year in England. This did not reflect a wide state of connubial bliss, nor was it evidence of the nation's continence. For one thing, a wife had not yet won the right to divorce her husband for adultery. The main factor which kept the divorce rate down was that the Divorce Court was still 'quite beyond the reach of the poor', as the Royal Commission on Divorce admitted in 1912. This injustice caused no overwhelming distress in Parliament, where many Members held the view that cheap divorce was like cheap gin – the public were better off without it. Some persons of humble means, wishing for a divorce, would save up for years until they had enough money to make the necessary visit to London; others merely resorted to cohabitation, bigamy and other practices of which, the Commission said, 'it is lamentable to hear'. The Lord Chief Justice, Lord Alverstone, who gave evidence, held the old-fashioned view that divorce jurisdiction should not be entrusted to the lower courts. A county court judge, he thought, could probably determine the facts on adultery, but was he competent to deal with cruelty, aggravation, condonation and collusion? Only 'a strong and experienced court' was fit to handle such matters. Lord Alverstone regretted that the Divorce Court was beyond the access of the poor, but he did not want to see any changes of procedure which would make divorce 'easy'. This, it could be argued, was a question not for a judge but for the Legislature.

World War One produced, in Lord Birkenhead's words, 'thousands of inconsiderate marriages' and the rush of divorce business was such that emergency measures had to be taken. King's Bench judges were sent to help out in the Divorce Court and, by an Act of 1920, judges of assize began to try divorce cases. They found the task unwelcome. In a criminal court the judge knew where he was; now he found himself sitting in a court of morals, administering a narrow illogical code handed down not by judges but by saints and prophets. In 1917 Lord Sumner had said it was mere rhetoric to argue that Christianity was the basis of English law, but the Christian ethic nevertheless pervaded the matrimonial courts. The Lord Chancellor did not disguise his contempt for the divorce laws, which he called inhuman and immoral, the worst of any civilised country. In particular he detested the Church's compromise of judicial separation, a state which he said led only to vice. A young wife separated from her husband by law was expected to remain chaste for the rest of her life. 'Human nature in the warmth of youth has repelled these cold admonitions of the cloister; and I, for one, take leave to say with all reverence, that I do not believe that the Supreme Being has set human nature a standard which two thousand years of Christian experience has shown that human nature, in its exuberant prime, cannot support.'* In 1923, having left the Woolsack, and become president of the Divorce Law Reform Union, he made a speech to a Caxton Hall meeting which possibly pained his late brethren in the Divorce Court. 'There was no chicanery, no trick, which our judges had not been compelled to employ in administering the laws of divorce,' he said. 'That was not true of the Bench in any other department of the law.' In every other branch they were allowed to apply fine judicial minds to the problems before them, But in administering the laws of divorce they had to adopt a series of humiliating compromises, for which the Legislature alone was responsible.†

In that year, thanks to a Bill pioneered by Lord Buckmaster, an Englishwoman at last secured the right to divorce her husband for adultery. A dissentient voice was that of Lord Braye, who knew only one reason for dissolving a marriage. 'Catholics,' he said, 'had a court and there sat a judge for whom, and beyond whom, there was no appeal and that judge was Death.'‡ The first woman to be 'named' in a divorce suit did not emerge until 1926; she was the licensee of a hotel in Norfolk.

Conspicuous among the judges who assailed the divorce laws was Mr Justice McCardie, who protested that judges were expected to decide petitions in the interests of public morality, which was as difficult to determine as public policy. It involved considerations of sociology, whereas by tradition a judge's duty was to determine questions of fact and law. Not that Mr Justice McCardie had any objection to flying a sociological kite from time to time. As early as 1920 he allowed himself to doubt, openly, whether public morality was advanced by allow-

*Hansard, March 24, 1920.
†The Times, April 12, 1923.
‡Hansard, June 27, 1923.

ing the break-up of a marriage when one party had committed adultery but refusing a dissolution when both had sinned. Might not public morality be better served by granting a divorce than by refusing one? In the petition before him he was obliged to deny a decree. 'I regret this result,' he said, 'but I must administer the law as it stands.' Mr Justice McCardie thought the office of King's Proctor a repulsive one. Like some of his colleagues, he resented being asked to put a cash value on an adulteress; and he confessed to great difficulty in understanding 'how a man of sensitive honour and of recognised rank can seek to recover financial solace for the dishonour of his wife's body.' This sort of claim, he said, was peculiar to Anglo-Saxon countries and foreigners were baffled that English law should allow it. He found time for lighter comments. How was it, he wondered, that a wronged husband was often infinitely more dashing than the cited Lothario? The paramour and the bigamist were often drab and dreary fellows, but presumably, said the Judge, they had the knack of evoking sympathy in women's hearts.*

Mr Justice Swift did not hide his belief that the divorce laws he had to administer were wicked and cruel. He was wary of the wife who declined, ostensibly for religious reasons, to free a guilty husband. What a judge had to determine was whether such a wife might be acting maliciously, or from a notion that she would receive better financial terms from a judicial separation. Mr Justice Swift believed that divorce was rapidly becoming a relief for the guilty rather than a remedy for the innocent. In 1925 his disgust drove him to suggest that petitioners should be allowed to parade before the Registrar of Births, Marriages and Deaths and announce that they no longer desired to be married. The Lord Chief Justice, Lord Hewart, went a step further and suggested that divorces should be handed out at the post office, like dog licences, but half-a-crown cheaper.† He resented 'his' judges being asked to spend laborious days scrutinising hotel bills and listening to chambermaids with superhuman powers of memory. In 1934 he complained in Parliament about the loading of divorce work on to circuit judges, a burden 'never contemplated by those who accepted judicial office before that decision

*George Pollock: *Mr Justice McCardie;* Albert Crew: *The Judicial Wisdom of Mr Justice McCardie.*
†Robert Jackson: *The Chief.*

was taken'.* His belief that most of the work could be relegated to judges or officials in the lower courts deeply offended the permanent judges of the Divorce Court. So did any impression propagated by the King's Bench judges that divorce work was a form of slumming.

Some judges were quietly cynical about the whole procedure, though not so cynical as counsel, who would take stop-watch bets as to whether they could get a decree in an undefended case in less than a minute.† More conscientious judges found the work repulsive. They would become short-tempered with the tribe whose function is to peer through fanlights to watch other people going to bed; they would be saddened by the sight of children brought into court to testify to their parents' adultery. 'I used to sit in savage boredom,' wrote Lord Justice MacKinnon, 'listening to the sordid stories, occasionally interjecting, "That will do. Decree nisi and costs." ' He could not conceive why such cases were not heard by county court registrars. He mentions a strong-minded vacation judge who refused to go through the formality of making decrees absolute, with the result that another judge had to be called in.‡

The 'Herbert Act' of 1937 did something to diversify the proceedings, for petitioners were now able to offer, as grounds for divorce, desertion, cruelty and insanity; but it did much to increase the flow of work. However, relief was not far off. Following the Denning Committee's report in 1947 authority was given for certain county court judges and Queen's counsel to sit as Divorce Commissioners. They were to be addressed as 'My Lord' instead of 'Your Honour'. Lord Alverstone might not have cared for this compromise, but the public have shown no dissatisfaction with the system, other than to cherish a resentment that they must continue to hire a barrister as well as a solicitor. This, they suspect, is the real reason why divorce work must never be allowed to pass into the hands of the post office.

It is wrong for judges to curry favour with the public. However, in the Great Depression, they seemed to go out of their way to curry disfavour, by resisting a twenty per cent cut in their £5,000 salaries under the National Economy Act, 1931. An

---

Hansard, December 11, 1934.
†John Parris: *Under My Wig.*
‡F. D. MacKinnon: *On Circuit.*

Order in Council said the cut was applicable to 'offices in the
service of His Majesty' and 'persons in His Majesty's service',
and it was ingeniously argued that this excluded judges, who
were not civil servants and whose independence should be preserved inviolate. Informed that the public would know what to
think of this argument, the judges remained adamant, though
some of them professed to be willing to share in the common
sacrifice, if only it did not present a threat to their integrity.
Collectively, the judges addressed a memorandum to the Prime
Minister, marking it 'Private', which did not prevent the Lord
Chancellor from reading it out in the Lords. 'We believe,' the
memorandum said, 'that the respect felt by the people for an
English judge has been partly due to his unique position, a
feeling which will survive with difficulty if his salary can be reduced as if he were an ordinary salaried servant of the Crown. If
the salaries of the judges can be reduced almost *sub silentio* by
the methods recently employed, the independence of the judiciary is seriously impaired. It cannot be wise to expose judges
of the High Court to the suggestion, however malevolent and
ill-founded, that if their decisions are favourable to the Crown
in revenue and other cases their salaries may be raised and if
unfavourable may be diminished.'* These statements now seem
so far-fetched as to be ludicrous; but few bodies of intelligent
men are capable of advancing other than unworthy arguments
when they fancy their financial well-being to be impaired. In
the Lords the Marquess of Reading said that, having been a
judge, he found it a little surprising to be told that a judge was
not 'in His Majesty's service',† and the country no doubt shared
his bewilderment. On assize the judges had always been treated as
the Sovereign's representatives and they remained seated for the
Royal toast ('Sit down, you fool,' said a Victorian judge to an
inexperienced colleague, '*we* are the Queen!') The public
learned without consternation that a judge, thanks to taxation,
was able to spend only £2,700 of his salary. At one stage the
judicial 'shop stewards', among whom were Mr Justice
Macnaghten (son of Lord Macnaghten), Mr Justice Maugham
and Mr Justice Avory, threatened to present a Petition of Right.
Early in 1932 Stanley Baldwin, Lord President of the Council,
said in the Commons that he had reassured the judges that there

Hansard, July 27, 1933.
†*Ibid.,* November 23, 1933.

was no intention of altering their status; all of them, he said, were ready to share the nation's burdens.* More than a year later, pressed by Sir William Davison to rescind the cuts, he said, 'I do not see why a judge should be excused his cut any more than I am.'† He was unmoved by a report that the judges, according to Mr Justice Avory, were 'performing their duties under the shadow of a grievous wrong'. The cuts were restored when the nation's fortunes improved.

The year 1933 saw the abolition of the grand jury, that long-established captive audience for judicial wit, wisdom and prejudice. A committee which had been inquiring into the business of the Supreme Court – its members included the Master of the Rolls and other judges – decided that the public interest would not suffer if what had gone on for seven hundred years were now to cease. Magistrates and stipendiaries considered cases so thoroughly that the work of the Grand Inquest of the Nation was supererogatory. There is no doubt that attendance on grand juries caused a good deal of delay and inconvenience. In 1931 some 22,272 citizens were called on to serve in this role; and at the Old Bailey grand juries had to attend ten sessions a year. In the latter part of World War One they had been dispensed with and no noticeable miscarriages of justice had occurred. However, several judges did not care to see this link with the past severed and said so from the assize Bench. At Lewes the grand jury were so impressed by Mr Justice Avory's tribute to their usefulness that they made a 'presentment' saying it would be a pity if they were abolished. The Judge said he would forward it to the appropriate quarter.

*Ibid., February 26, 1932.
†Ibid., July 12, 1933.

19

THE LAST INDIVIDUALISTS

If it is true that 'he is the best judge whose name is known to the fewest readers of the *Daily Mail*', then the early decades of this century produced a good many undesirable judges. Obviously a judge cannot always be blamed for the publicity he incurs. If he shuts down his court on Derby Day, as Mr Justice Hawkins used to do, he must not complain if the press pursue him. By contrast, it was just bad luck that Mr Justice Bucknill had to sentence to death a fellow Mason, the poisoner Seddon; his tearful exhortation to 'make your peace with the Great Architect of the Universe' has long since passed from the front pages into popular legend. Presumably it was not the way this Judge would have wished to be remembered. But many judges of those days were born to the headlines; they had a colour, a port and a presence – perhaps also an arrogance – rarely seen today. Sometimes they qualified for worse than headlines. Sir Rufus Isaacs (Lord Reading) ascended the Bench as Lord Chief Justice with a rank-smelling albatross round his neck in the shape of Kipling's poem 'Gehazi', which commemorates his involvement in the Marconi scandal. 'Future generations,' writes Charles Carrington, 'are likely to remember the name of Rufus Isaacs chiefly because he was Kipling's Gehazi, as they remember Hervey because he was Pope's Sporus and Buckingham because he was Dryden's Zimri.'* Lord Reading is not wholly forgotten as a Viceroy of India.

Some of the headline judges, like Lord Birkenhead and Lord Carson, owed their notoriety to the political passions in which they had previously wallowed. Lord Birkenhead's appointment

*Charles Carrington: *Rudyard Kipling*.

as Lord Chancellor, in 1919, caused grave misgivings in the King, who doubted whether this was the right man for the second highest post in the land; and *The Times* thought it was carrying a joke too far. Everyone knew 'F.E.'s' views on Ireland and on trade unionism; everyone knew him for a careerist; everyone knew of his acerbities as a counsel, his knockabout performances on the platform and in Parliament, his controversial press articles and the extravagances of his private life. How could a man like this settle down and distil the pure essence of equity? How could he keep discipline in the Lords? Yet lawyers agree that he was a correct and dignified Lord Chancellor and that his judgments command respect. It was his boast that the word 'laughter' never appeared in reports of actions over which he presided. If he reported for duty trailing the atmosphere of the Sporting and Deauville Casino, the worldliness evaporated as he robed.

In 1922 Lord Birkenhead retained his dignity under heavy provocation in a dispute with Lord Carson over the right of a judge to talk politics. Carson was a lord of appeal and, as a peer, was entitled to take part in debates in the Lords; but the custom had grown up that the lords of appeal should not speak on party matters. One or two of them had broken the rule. In 1922 Lord Carson addressed a public meeting with his usual political virulence on an Irish Bill, presumably well knowing that in his judicial capacity he might have to consider matters arising from this measure. As Lord Chancellor, Lord Birkenhead was obliged to criticise his colleague's conduct. Lord Carson, he agreed, was 'a special case', but that did not entitle him to stand on a platform and taunt the Government or deliver a crude political speech on Government policy. He regretted that Lord Carson was not there to hear that opinion. If Lord Carson was entitled to behave as he did, 'was there anything to prevent the whole body of judges from distributing themselves in political hordes all over the country, supporting and opposing candidates, impeaching or defending the policy of the Government of the day?'[*] Two days later Carson was in his place, having worked up a spirited brief for himself. He pointed out that there were four categories of peers entitled to hear appeals: the Lord Chancellor, who was 'the most political person we have'; the former Lord Chancellors, who by tradition had a

[*]*Hansard,* March 27, 1922

right to take part in political matters; peers with experience of high judicial office; and lords of appeal in ordinary, like Carson. Those in the first three categories did not corrupt the administration of justice by indulging in political behaviour, so why should the lords of appeal? In the Commons, he said, sat various recorders, among them Sir Ernest Wild at the Old Bailey – 'Why is he not tainting justice if I am?' What about chairmen of quarter sessions, licensing justices, justices of the peace? 'Why is my honour to be besmirched any more than the honour of a justice of the peace?' Once again the Lord Chancellor rose from the Woolsack to announce his disapproval and, incidentally, to give a definition of the function of a Lord Chancellor. The office, he agreed, was an anomaly and violation of constitutional theory, 'but it was considered convenient and desirable that there should be a connecting link, a high judicial personage, who was not divorced from membership of the Cabinet and would be able to impress his political colleagues with the view of the judiciary and the legal profession, while at the same time he would be able to keep his judicial colleagues in contact, not with party issues, but with those public considerations from which they thought it not wise completely to divorce the judicial Bench'. If, went on Lord Birkenhead, Lord Carson's arguments were followed to their logical conclusion, a lord of appeal could finish up as a leader of the Opposition and the Lord Chief Justice could busy himself at the hustings; it was tantamount to saying that 'every judge in this country should be entitled to fling himself into the Parliamentary strife from which the progress of generations had secluded him'. It was not a question of judicial independence being tainted; 'it is necessary that the public should be under no delusion'. Viscount Finlay disagreed with the Lord Chancellor; the appeal lords, he said, were appointed to strengthen the House and should enjoy all its right and powers.* That Lord Carson was in the wrong would now be widely conceded. Judges of the High Court did not fail to note that they were in a unique category, totally forbidden any political utterances : above them, appeal lords could get away with an occasional outburst, at a cost, and below them sessions chairmen and justices of the peace could indulge in passionate politics because there was no hope of preventing them.

*Hansard, March 29, 1922.

Lord Birkenhead: he thought Britain's divorce laws 'inhuman and immoral'

Mr Justice Avory: the archetype of a stern 'red judge'

d Goddard: 'a mistake to
eve that all criminals are
juided, or uneducated or
rtunate people'

The New Judge, by Spy,
in *Vanity Fair*

An Old-Fashioned Judge,
by Quiz, in *Vanity Fair*

'Company Law' by Spy,
in *Vanity Fair*

The need to ensure that 'the public should be under no delusion' led Lord Birkenhead to move against the City Recorder,
Sir Ernest Wild, who showed reluctance to resign his seat for the
Upton Division of West Ham. He was the nominee not of the
Lord Chancellor but of the Court of Aldermen. Sir Ernest
argued that other City Recorders had also occupied seats in the
Commons, but the difference was that he was sitting for a
division over which he had jurisdiction as a judge. Lord Birkenhead held it most desirable that the link should be severed,
since 'the functions of a judge and the functions of a Member
of Parliament appear to the Lord Chancellor to be incom-
patible'; but he agreed that recorders of quarter sessions, faced
with only a fraction of the work of an Old Bailey judge, could
reasonably sit in the Commons. Sir Ernest Wild made a
personal statement in the House and then did the Lord
Chancellor's bidding.

If Lord Birkenhead was against levity in court, Mr Justice
Darling sometimes appeared to be all for it. Once a judge gets a
reputation for some indulgence, the press can be relied upon
to fasten on to it and never let go. Mr Justice Darling was no
irresponsible *farceur*; he could conduct a murder trial with all
requisite dignity. His career gave the lie to those members of
the Bar who, when he was appointed, derided him as one of Lord
Halsbury's political errors. At times his jokes were undoubtedly
misplaced. Experience shows that a jesting Pilate does not necessarily command the respect of a jury; he certainly does not inspire the confidence of the litigants, who may be risking all
on a point of honour. Moreover, a jesting Pilate encourages
others to match their wits against his; or even tempts counsel
to act as a 'feed'. When Sir Patrick Hastings was appearing for
George Robey, the comedian, Mr Justice Darling asked, 'In
what way is your client celebrated?' and the reply (which sounds
like a pre-arranged one) was, 'My Lord, perhaps my client
could best be described as the Darling of the music halls.' No
pains would be spared to clear the way for a quip. During a
gang trial in which evidence was given by three brothers called
Sabini, old hands at the Bar sensed that a rib-tickler was on the
way. They had to wait until the summing up, when the Judge
said the brothers were probably descended from the Sabine
women, and then added, as if it had just occurred to him, 'I

H

always understood that the ladies settled down quite comfortably and made excellent wives and mothers.'* Mr Justice Darling should have learned his lesson during the Pemberton Billing prosecution, a lubricious episode which did much to distract the nation from the final death grapple on the Western Front in the summer of 1918. It is only fair to say that almost any other judge would have been in difficulties, for Noel Pemberton Billing, Independent Member of Parliament for East Hertford-shire, chose to conduct his own defence and wildly abused the traditional licence accorded to those who dispense with counsel. When the trial began the M.P. objected to the Judge on the grounds that he allowed an element of levity into his court and that this had been the subject of criticism in press and Parliament by himself. Mr Justice Darling replied that he had read none of it, that people could not choose their own judges and that no one could exclude a judge by writing about him beforehand. Pemberton Billing was accused of defaming the actress Maud Allan, who had appeared in Wilde's *Salome,* but the basic issue was speedily lost when he began to question wit-nesses about a German 'Black Book' said to contain the names of 47,000 British subjects of doubtful loyalty and even more doubtful morals. The Judge tried to prevent witnesses from naming persons supposedly listed in this directory, but the defendant would simply shout out 'Is So-and-So's name in it?' and the witness would shout 'Yes.' What, asked the Judge plaintively, could one do in the face of behaviour like this? At one point Pemberton Billing pointed dramatically to the Bench and asked, 'Is Mr Justice Darling's name in it?' The answer from the woman in the box was, 'It is.' She added that the war was unlikely to be won while the Judge sat there. There was much hubbub, punctuated by cries of 'Is Mr Asquith's name in it?' and 'Is Mrs Asquith's name in it?' The answers were 'Yes.' The witness was ordered from the box but did not move. When Pemberton Billing had momentarily quietened, the Judge said, 'Have you finished asking questions of that character?' The reply was, 'I have not.' There was a further rebuke, after which the defendant asked, 'Are you determined to go on trying this case, my Lord?' and was ordered, 'Resume your examination.' A few moments later Pemberton Billing said, 'It will take more than you to protect these people, my Lord.' This time he was

*Travers Humphreys: *Criminal Days.*

warned if he did not conduct himself properly there would soon
be an end of the case altogether.

Even in this nightmare of a trial, with judicial authority
tottering and baseless charges of unnatural practices being hurled
at almost every public figure, the Judge could not curb his
inclination to jest. After reading some 'flamboyant' passages
from *Salome,* he said, 'This is high art. Of course, that is why I
cannot understand it.' On learning that a witness had plans to
tour *Salome* in a neutral country as a type of British art, the
Judge remarked, 'I can imagine that if he did the country
would declare war on us.' When a witness mentioned Lloyd
George, commending him for having sacked many inefficients
from office, counsel objected to the introduction of the Prime
Minister's name; but the Judge said, 'I do not like to deprive
Mr Lloyd George of a testimony to his character.' One of the
counsel complained of an echo in the court ceiling, which
inspired Mr Justice Darling to tell the story about 'the prisoner
in that court who received seven years and collapsed, because
he added the sentence to the echo and thought he had received
fourteen years'. Throughout the trial the gallery applauded and
hissed as if at a play. At one point the Judge found it necessary
to issue a warning that the next person who laughed would be
ejected, which drew from Pemberton Billing the question, 'May
we laugh at your jokes, my Lord?' The answer was, 'No, you
may not.' On another occasion the Judge accused the defendant
of playing to the gallery, which was met with, 'I cannot help
what happens in the gallery any more than you can help laughing at your own jokes.' Indignantly, the Judge exclaimed, 'You
have insulted me to my face now.' So it went on. Lord Alfred
Douglas was ejected after he had risen, his arms waving, and
shouted that the Judge was a 'damned liar'. When finally the
jury brought in a verdict of not guilty, all those in the gallery
were turned out for applauding.

Mr Justice Darling's press cuttings on the trial can have
brought him little pleasure. The *Daily News* described it as 'one
of the most sinister and humiliating events of these times',
exceeding 'in its frenzied silliness anything ever conceived in the
fertile brain of Titus Oates'. The Judge had 'bandied words of
forcible feebleness' with a man who had tried to treat him as a
criminal; 'we can recall no case in the past in which the administration of justice has been so helpless in dealing with so gross an

outrage'. Not even a 'certificate of character for Lord Grey' by the Judge pleased the *Daily News*; none of those named were in need of 'patronising' defence from the Bench.* In *The Times* the trial was described as a scandalous one, conducted with 'astonishing levity' and 'flippancies and joking of the kind which Mr Justice Darling has made his own'.† However, the *Morning Post* declined to join in the chorus against the Judge. If he had erred, it said, he had erred on the side of fairness. It was as hard for a judge to silence an accused person as it was for a man to silence a woman. No reasonable person could contend that a judge 'should have had the strength to anticipate and prevent the successive explosions of stinkpots which have horrified and scandalised the country'. The only alternative would have been to hold the trial *in camera*, which would have set afoot worse scandal.‡ Many must have wondered how Pemberton Billing would have fared if he had come up before Mr Justice Avory.

The severest comment on Mr Justice Darling was contained in a Max Beerbohm cartoon in which the Judge is handing his black cap to the usher to have bells sewn on it. It may or may not have been his sense of humour which caused him to be passed over in the selection of a Lord Chief Justice. On learning the name of the venerable colleague who was appointed, he is said to have commented, 'I suppose I am not old enough.'

Though not one of the larger-than-life judges, Mr Justice McCardie secured for himself a good deal of press attention chiefly through his comments on social and matrimonial matters. Some of his views on divorce have already been noted. In 1924 he figured in a political row and was publicly rebuked by the Prime Minister, Ramsay MacDonald. Summing up in a libel action the Judge expressed the view that General Dyer, who gave the order to fire on the mob at Amritsar, acted rightly in exceptional circumstances and was wrongly punished by the Secretary for India. Whether it was essential for Mr Justice McCardie to say what he did in his summing up is a subject on which lawyers have opposing views. George Lansbury demanded that an address be presented to the King asking for the Judge's dismissal as unfit for his duties, but the Prime Minister took the view that however unfortunate the words

*June 5, 1918.
†June 5, 1918.
‡June 6, 1918.

might have been they did not constitute a moral delinquency justifying extreme action. 'His Majesty's Government,' he said, 'will always uphold the right of the judiciary to pass judgment even on the Executive if it thinks fit, but that being the right of the judiciary it is all the more necessary that it should guard against pronouncements on issues involving grave political consequences which are not themselves being tried.'* Ministerial cheers greeted this statement and Lansbury withdrew his motion.

To the press, Mr Justice McCardie was the 'Bachelor Judge' as inevitably as Dean Inge was the 'Gloomy Dean'. Though he had a reputation as a liberal thinker, his comminations on spendthrift wives have an early Victorian ring about them. In a 1923 judgment he said, of such a wife, 'She threw herself beneath the fatal curse of luxury. She forgot that those who possess substantial means are trustees to use them with prudence, charity and propriety. She forgot that ostentation is the worst form of vulgarity. She ignored the sharp menace of future penury . . . She sought felicity in the ceaseless change of trivial fashions. Self-decoration was her vision, her aim, her creed. I observe no record of any act of beneficence . . .' He continued to pursue the butterfly in this fashion, ending up by saying that unlike 'the most gracious portion of English womanhood' this wife had sacrificed 'the privileges of social service for the allurements of ignominious folly'.

In similar actions he dwelt on the merciless excesses of the fashion industry and debated such questions as 'How much of a man's income is his own and how much is to be regarded as the perquisite of his wife's dressmaker?' Part of the reason why a woman squandered money on dress, he thought, was because her function in society was largely utilitarian; men were the leaders in all spheres and women merely the decorations of social life. Hence a reasonable indulgence in dress was necessary to counterbalance their inferiority complex. Married men, as well as editors, were grateful for such observations as, 'The overgenerosity of a husband rarely leads to happiness and may often lead to financial tragedy.'†

The spendthrift wife was to be regretted, but there were worse evils; and high among these Mr Justice McCardie ranked the mentally defective mother, capable of producing a long string

Hansard, June 17, 1924.
†Albert Crew: *The Judicial Wisdom of Mr Justice McCardie*.

of mentally defective children. The eugenist in him mutinied. He
was for sterilising the mentally unfit, a doctrine now dismissed as
Hitlerian and unthinkable. The abortion laws, in his view,
called for relaxation, though hardly for as much relaxation as
they have now received; termination of pregnancy he described
as 'a crime for the poor but only a surgical operation for the
rich'. Most of the nation's economic ills, he held, could be – and
could have been – prevented by spreading birth control knowledge where it was most needed. He did not need a grand jury
on which to try out these ideas; he was in demand as a public
speaker.

Mr Justice McCardie's sociological views were not always
relished by the appeal lords, one of whom, Lord Justice Scrutton,
rebuked him severely in a judgment on the 'Helen of Troy'
enticement action of 1932. The less sociological knowledge that
was brought into the examination of legal questions the better,
said the Lord Justice. 'If there was to be a discussion of the
relations between husband and wife he thought it would come
better from judges who had more than theoretical knowledge
of husbands and wives. He was a little surprised that a gentleman
who had never been married should, as he had in another case,
have proceeded to explain the proper underclothing that ladies
should wear and he thought that these things were better left
out of the discussion of legal questions.'

The tone of this rebuke earned Mr Justice McCardie some
sympathy at the Bar, but his subsequent action dispersed it. At
the start of a hearing he announced, 'If there be an appeal I
shall not supply any copy of my notes until I am satisfied that
Lord Justice Scrutton will not be a member of the court which
tries the appeal . . . I regret that it has become my duty to
administer this public rebuke to Lord Justice Scrutton.'

This outburst was by no means ignored in the press. In
Parliament there was a motion to deplore 'conduct calculated
to lower the prestige of the judicature', but it was not discussed.
The Master of the Rolls, Lord Hanworth, on taking his seat in
the Court of Appeal, observed that for a judge to withhold his
notes in such circumstances would be 'a serious inroad on the
rights of suitors who desired their case to be reheard'; mildly, he
added that he was sure all his brother judges would wish to
maintain the traditional co-operation. That afternoon Mr Justice
McCardie announced in court that he deemed it his duty to act

as the Master of the Rolls had indicated. His conduct over the years had become moody and ill-balanced. In the year following this clash, his private life in disarray, he shot himself. At Birmingham Assizes in 1934 a litigant who complained that a judgment by Mr Justice McCardie had been delivered when he was of unsound mind received the shortest of shrift from Mr Justice du Parcq.*

Lord Justice Scrutton in earlier years had offended the Bar by his ill-tempered behaviour in court. Finally the Bar rebelled, as the Irish Bar had rebelled against the Earl of Clonmel. A junior barrister named Alfred Chaytor was retained by the leading solicitors of London to make a formal protest to the Judge in open court, a task he discharged with tact and credit. The Judge listened without comment, but took the hint.†

The name of Lord Chief Justice Hewart was well-known, not only to readers of the *Daily Mail,* but to those of the *News of the World,* in which he wrote well-paid articles on controversial subjects like law reform and hanging. When it was suggested to him that this was no way for the Lord Chief Justice of England to behave, he replied that he wrote in his capacity as a peer of the realm. In 1935 Stanley Baldwin, questioned about Lord Hewart's press articles, said it was obviously undesirable that judges should write on matters of controversy, or on questions which they might have to decide judicially, but the limit had to be left to the discretion of the judge.‡ Lord Hewart continued to be seen in the company of Sir Emsley Carr, proprietor of the *News of the World.* Other newspaper chiefs may not have resented this association (which would seem to have disqualified Lord Hewart from hearing any libel action against the *News of the World*) but they did resent his occasionally Scroggs-like views on the freedom of the press and his warning that he was tired of hearing newspapers plead that 'they did not mean what they obviously did mean'.§

All rebuffs were lost on Lord Hewart. He had risen from draper's son to peer of the realm and rejected any notion that just because he was also Lord Chief Justice he should preserve 'an austere and pensive silence' on matters of public interest.

*The Times, July 17, 1934.
†D.N.B.
‡Hansard, June 24, 1935.
§Robert Jackson: *The Chief.*

For that reason he grumbled at the pressures which forced him to resign from a committee on electoral reform. Was it not his duty as a peer to 'treat and give council' on affairs of state?* His most famous saying was, 'It is of fundamental importance that justice should not only be done but should manifestly and undoubtedly be seen to be done'; but not all agreed that his conduct in court was always in keeping with this dictum.

Lord Hewart was not the only judge of the period who fell foul of the press. Mr Justice Swift's conduct in the sedition trial of 1925 left him liberally ink-spattered. It was a prosecution which invites comparison with the sedition trials of the Napoleonic years; indeed, the charges were brought under the Mutiny Act of 1797. This time the foreign power suspected of trying to subvert the realm was Russia and much was made of the alleged acceptance by British Communists of Moscow gold. Twelve Party members, among them Walter Hannington, Harry Pollitt, William Gallacher and J. R. Campbell, were charged with conspiracy to publish seditious libel and to seduce members of the Forces from their allegiance. No soldier entered the box to say that efforts had been made to undermine his loyalty, the prosecution relying entirely on seized documents. Mr Justice Swift imposed prison sentences on all twelve, after giving some of them a chance to repudiate their allegiance to Communism in order that they might be bound over. This they refused to do. There was sharp criticism of the action of the Judge (a 'bewigged puppet', said the *Daily Worker*) in trying to coerce men into changing their political views. In Parliament Ramsay Mac-Donald introduced a motion saying that the prosecution was a violation of free expression. The Speaker tried to check criticism of the Bench, but Will Thorne contrived to say, 'The Judge was a notorious Tory to start with' (he had been a Conservative M.P.). Sir William Joynson-Hicks, Home Secretary, said the men were prosecuted not for holding the views they did, but for seeking to alter the constitution by violent and unconstitutional means. He quoted a passage from Erskine in his defence of Thomas Paine, which is not wholly irrelevant to the present day. Of a would-be revolutionary, Erskine said:

'If indeed he holds out to individuals that they have a right to run before the public mind in their conduct; that they may oppose by contumacy or force what private reason only dis-

Ibid.

approves; that they may disobey the law because their judgment condemns it; or resist the public will because they honestly
wish to change it – he is then a criminal upon every principle of
rational policy as well as upon the immemorial precedents of
English justice.'

The motion was defeated by 351 votes to 127.* A protest
demonstration was held in the Queen's Hall, London, and
Labour Members of Parliament ostentatiously used seditious
language in hope of prosecution, but without success.

Three years later criticism of Mr Justice Avory by the *New
Statesman* resulted in proceedings for contempt. Commenting on
a libel action brought against Dr Marie Stopes, Clifford Sharp,
the editor, wrote : 'The serious point in this case is that an individual owning to such views as those of Dr Stopes cannot
apparently hope for a fair hearing in a court presided over by
Mr Justice Avory – and there are so many Avorys.' Lord Hewart
heard the subsequent proceedings and decided that Sharp's
words meant what they said, but that perhaps he did not intend
them to have such a meaning. If they had been so intended, he
would have been sent to gaol.† As it was, he was ordered to pay
costs. Because of this and other clashes with the Bench, the press
began to show a certain reluctance to criticise judges; which
was a bad thing for both judges and the press.

In fact, there were not 'so many Avorys'. There was only one.
This archetype of a stern 'red judge', nurtured amid the villainies
of the Old Bailey, was the man most feared by the thug and the
professional criminal, to whom he would award 'the cat' along
with long stretches of penal servitude. He was known as a
'hanging judge'; unfairly, since the law provided only one
sentence for murder and it was not suggested that he summed
up with bias. Lawyers agreed that 'he was a good man to come
up before if you were innocent'. Mr Justice Humphreys has said,
'On the whole I should think that Avory's sentences were on the
lenient side.'‡ Severe in aspect, unmellifluous, quick to suppress
'scenes' and 'breezes', the Judge looked on depravity as depravity
and punished it as such. To a Bournemouth chauffeur in the
dock he said, 'It is a foul and brutal murder. You also shall die.'§

Hansard, December 1, 1925.
†Edward Hyams : *The New Statesman.*
‡*Criminal Days.*
§Gordon Lang : *Mr Justice Avory.*

Like many judges of his generation he distrusted psychiatric evidence. After the murderer Ronald True (tried by another judge) had been reprieved, Mr Justice Avory told the grand jury at Exeter that it was doubtful whether the crime wave would abate 'if the infliction of the penalty of the law is to be left to the discretion of Harley Street'. Cynicism over medical evidence had been sharpened over the generations by all those compensation cases in which a railway company could always find three doctors to rebut the evidence of three doctors produced by the claimant; and judges still remembered the Staunton murder case of 1877, in which four hundred doctors publicly drew attention to the insufficiency of medical evidence on which four persons were convicted, as a result of which three were reprieved and one was freed. Mr Justice Avory was still on the Bench in his eighties, after a quarter of a century's service as a judge. His efficiency dismayed those who wanted to see a compulsory retiring age for judges.

One of the last of the rugged school of judges was Lord Chief Justice Goddard, whose views on the merits of birching and capital punishment are still fresh in memory. His advocacy of these measures was conducted not only in court but in Parliament and even at mayoral banquets. His campaign could be described as a political one, in so far as he doubted the wisdom of Parliament in weakening the penalties for murderers. As one who had watched the parade of knavery for fifty years, he held that the punitive element of a sentence should not be overlooked, and his belief was one in which vast numbers of his countrymen concurred, though they never got a chance to say so. As a result Lord Goddard became that unusual figure – a Lord Chief Justice with a large post-bag. This no doubt convinced many liberals that Bacon had been right: there was nothing so much to be dreaded as a popular judge. The members of the Royal Commission on Capital Punishment, which sat from 1949 to 1953, found him an unusually outspoken witness. 'You have to deal with a great number of very wicked people in this world,' he assured them. 'It is quite a mistake to believe that all criminals are misguided, or uneducated or unfortunate people.' He said he thought the royal prerogative of mercy was being wielded a little too freely. He saw no reason for not hanging women murderers. He disagreed strongly with the system which allowed doctors appointed by the Home Secretary to find a man insane when the jury had found him fit to plead. The mentally disturbed, in his opinion, did not necessarily lose all sense of responsibility. Asked about the murderer Ley, reprieved as a paranoiac, Lord Goddard said, 'I should have thought it very proper that he should have been hanged . . . he could make his peace with God, I think, quite well.' When it was suggested that, in the medical view, Ley's disease had altered his personality sufficient to make such wickedness possible, the Lord Chief Justice said, 'If that is the medical point of view I am afraid, frankly, that it does not appeal to me at all. If that was the case I think it was one of the reasons why he should have been put out of the way.' In a debate in the Lords in 1953, on the Royal Commission's findings, Lord Goddard said he would resign if Parliament gave effect to a recommendation which would have given the last word in a murder trial to medical witnesses and defence counsel, with the prosecution bound to silence. Lord Goddard's views did not escape criticism in the newspapers; but the press handled him, in the main, with care especially after he had gaoled the the editor of the *Daily Mirror* for contempt and threatened to put the directors behind bars next time.

Like Mr Justice Avory, Lord Goddard was still on the Bench in his eighties. When he retired, in 1958, the qualities for which he was praised included – to the surprise, possibly, of radicals – a wide-ranging humanity, a sense of humour and a lack of pomposity. Among lawyers this survivor of the Victorian Bar had always commanded strong respect; they commended his brisk dispatch of business and readiness to 'put on a white sheet' if he felt he had been wrong in law. In commercial cases he showed great wisdom and common-sense. His term of office seemed to justify the policy of conferring the chief justiceship on a first-class lawyer who had risen through the judiciary rather than awarding it automatically to an ambitious attorney-general (when appointed he was a lord of appeal in ordinary). Those who disliked his penological ideas knew that he spoke not from a thirst for vengeance but from a conviction that the law's first function was not to reform the criminal but to protect the public. His belief that the causes of crime today are the same as they were in Old Testament days is probably widely shared outside the communications industry.

*   *   *

Self-importance, eccentricity, fussiness – these qualities are less evident on the Bench than of old. There is no Mr Justice Croom-Johnson to send for the commanding officer of a Royal Air Force station and order him to ground his aircraft during the assize, or to direct that the streets be barricaded outside the court-house to keep traffic away.* It must be a long time since a judge has imposed a summary fine on a sheriff for some fancied dereliction. But judges still retain some of the weaknesses that have always characterised their occupation; they fall, or appear to fall, asleep; they criticise the clothes of witnesses, sometimes not without justification; they over-interrupt; and they clash with juries whose minds seem insufficiently agile. In 1957 the Court of Appeal was told that plaintiff's counsel in an action before Mr Justice Hallett at Chester Assizes had been unable to cross-examine because of the excessive number of judicial interruptions. The Judge's name appeared 544 times in the transcript of the evidence and each entry might represent two or three supplementary questions. In 1960 the Court of Criminal Appeal quashed the conviction of three men tried before Mr Justice Stable at Nottingham Assizes, their grounds being that, contrary to the principles of common law, the Judge had set a time limit for the jury, non-compliance with which would have meant that they would have been unable to separate until the court sat again next day. After a summing-up of an hour and a half the jury had twice returned to court for further directions and on the second occasion the Judge told them that he had twice disorganised his travel plans 'pretty considerably' and did not propose to do so any further. 'In ten minutes I shall leave this building,' he said, 'and if by that time you have not arrived at a conclusion in this case you will be kept all night and we will resume this matter at a quarter to twelve tomorrow. May I suggest to you that you go back to your room, that you use your common-sense and do not worry yourselves with legal quibbles. That is what you are brought here for.' Five minutes afterwards the jury brought in a verdict. Before the appeal court, counsel argued that this was a reversion to the old days when juries were imprisoned until they made up their minds and that 'the Judge tried to shock the jury into a verdict so that he could catch his train'. The Court of Criminal Appeal ruled that any such ultimatum was 'a disservice to the cause of justice'; it

*John Parris: *Under My Wig.*

also pointed out that in such circumstances jurors had the right to spend the night in a hotel.* With these views *The Times* agreed, pointing out that this Judge was normally 'exceptionally liberal and humane'.

The post-1945 years saw some curious examples of the judicial tribunal, set up to investigate matters of corruption, security and morals. Ironically, the Act authorising tribunals had been introduced in 1921 by that foe of ministerial despotism, the future Lord Hewart. As Attorney-General in charge of the Bill he was criticised for giving excessive powers to a Government department. A Minister, it was pointed out, would be able to set up an inquiry into any matter that exercised him and the tribunal would have the powers of a High Court judge to send for documents and witnesses. In practice the judicial tribunal, though it took away a judge from his bench and turned him into a Government inquiry agent, had a limited usefulness in sifting facts from scandalous rumour. In 1936 Mr Justice Porter probed much-publicised allegations into a Budget 'leak', with the result that an indiscreet Cabinet Minister, J. H. Thomas, retired from public life. In 1948 a tribunal under Mr Justice Lynskey uncovered, at great trouble and expense, the operations of the middle man, Sidney Stanley, who had wormed his way into Westminster. It made mildly scandalous reading in dull times. The Vassall Tribunal of 1962, set up to investigate security, left the press angry and bruised, for two reporters were gaoled for refusing to disclose the sources of their information. Lord Chief Justice Parker ruled that in matters of security the citizen should put the State's interest foremost. It was a good subject for polemics; but the nation did not regard this as a revival of Stuart oppression. In totalitarian lands the fuss must have seemed baffling. In 1963 a tribunal under Lord Denning investigated the Profumo-Ward scandals. The leader of the Liberal Party, Mr Jo Grimond, was one who thought the inquiry foolish. 'Since when,' he asked, 'have the people of this country had to call in a High Court judge, however eminent, in order to carry out a roving commission in the private lives of various individuals, so that we may be informed whether we are behaving ourselves or not? Can you contemplate Mr Gladstone requiring advice on this subject? Disraeli would have laughed himself silly . . .' The Report, for which hundreds queued, did not

*The Times, January 13, 1960.

spare the Ministers of the Crown. Mr Harold Macmillan rue-
fully quoted 'Albert and the Lion' and said 'Somebody had to
be summonsed.' It is not very clear why the Tribunals Act of
1921 had to be set up in the first place, but the sponsors had
opened the way for some increasingly bizarre entertainments.

In the 1960s began a sporadic campaign to make solicitors
eligible for appointment as judges. The number of judges was
constantly increasing (it has doubled in the last thirty years) but
they were still drawn exclusively from the Bar. Not all the existing judges were happy in their work, or happy with their pay;
according to Sir Winston Churchill, in 1954 several of them
had applied to return to the Bar. In 1961 Lord Chorley and
Lord Silkin tabled an amendment to the Criminal Justice
Administration Bill which would have made a solicitor of the
High Court of not less than ten years standing eligible for the
High Court Bench. Denying any personal ambition to be a
judge, Lord Silkin argued that in the ranks of solicitors were men
of great wisdom, experience, integrity and objectiveness who
were as well qualified to be judges as any members of the Bar;
and he said he could name High Court judges who had been
put to work which they had never done before in their professional lives, though he did not suggest they had been incompetent at it. The Lord Chancellor, he suggested, should allow
solicitors to ascend the judicial ladder by way of the county court
to the High Court, thus making the county court an intermediate
station, not a terminus. Since 1945 only five county court judges
had been promoted to the High Court. Lord Denning was
against establishing any sort of career ladder. 'An able man, ambitious to reach a High Court judgeship, does not accept a county
court judgeship,' he said. He thought it was the experience
judges had gained as barristers which enabled them to give
summings-up which were the envy of the world. The Lord
Chancellor, Lord Kilmur, repeated what he had said a year
previously, when he had appointed eight judges : he could, he
insisted, have found twenty-four suitable candidates. He contended that solicitors who wanted to become judges could
always transfer to the Bar for that purpose, as Mr Justice Lynskey
had done. The amendment failed.*

That year the Streatfeild Committee on the criminal courts
devoted some thought to the rigours of the judicial life. In 1956

Hansard, November 23, 1961.

Crown Courts had been set up in Liverpool and Manchester to speed the flow of criminal trials, but the Committee were against an extension of the system. They had been impressed by the views of judges and lawyers who said that 'the full-time criminal judge was in danger of becoming stale and even prosecution-minded as a result of taking nothing but criminal work', and that the risk increased if he sat each day in the same court. He lacked daily contact with other judges. Socially, it was impossible for him to forget that he was a judge, under the necessity of avoiding 'local associations which might impair his impartial position'. His contacts 'took on an embarrassing one-way character and he had to look elsewhere for his normal social outlets'. Moreover, the attitudes of a full-time judge necessarily became matters of common knowledge and discussion, which the Committee thought 'unfortunate'. Some of these arguments were rather reminiscent of the objections produced by Lord Lyndhurst to the establishment of county courts. The Committee made further recommendations: that records should be kept so that judges could see the effects of their sentencing; and that judges should visit gaols more often.

In 1965 the High Court welcomed an appointment which, a generation earlier, would have seemed an unbearable drollery. The newcomer was the first woman judge: Mrs Justice Lane. As a commissioner she had been addressed as 'his Lordship' and it seemed that she was now fated to be addressed as Mr Justice Lane. Would she be made a knight or a dame? Would she be addressed as 'brother'? The *Solicitors' Journal* made the point that Britain had long been ruled by queens without finding it necessary to address them as kings. Eventually the Lord Chancellor directed that the new judge should be addressed as Mrs Justice Lane.

The call to make judges of solicitors was repeated, in 1969, in the Report of the Royal Commission on Assizes, under Lord Beeching. Charged with finding ways to decrease the law's delays, the Commission recommended some fundamental changes. Unlike the Streatfeild Committee, it was prepared to see an extension of Crown Courts, which would take all criminal work not handled by local magistrates. It urged the abolition of about half the existing assize centres (which still numbered sixty-one); the creation of a new Bench of Circuit Judges; the setting up of a second-tier Bench of 175 judges, for criminal and civil cases, made up of county court judges and other existing judges, plus some forty new appointments; and the replacing of some three hundred recorders and chairmen of quarter sessions by 120 part-time recorders. The Commissioners believed that solicitors should be eligible for appointment as circuit judges and recorders. They were struck by the anomaly that solicitors acted as chairmen of quarter sessions but could not sit in county courts; and they thought that the Bar's potential for providing judges was at present limited.

There was some gentle teasing of the Bench in the Report. 'The movement of judges,' it said, 'has the advantage of ensuring that if they do occasionally develop idiosyncracies as a result of the exalted seclusion in which they live, their foibles move with them and do not become a source of irritation or amusement to any one sector of the community.' The Commissioners discussed the traditional notion that 'the periodic visible presence of "the red judge" is a reassurance to the righteous and a deterrent to the evildoer,' but thought that, as things were, the presence of the judge was most noticeable where it was least important. In small towns, where crime did not reach an extravagant level, there might be the traditional parade of coach, trumpeters and pikemen; but in large cities, where crime required to be deterred, the judge was whisked through the traffic in such a way as to cause minimum inconvenience to the community and entered the court-house through a side door. The Commissioners refused to credit the assize ceremonial with 'such deterrent effect as to justify a judge's presence for little other purpose'. They also noted that it was becoming increasingly difficult to find butlers and cooks willing to move round the judicial circuits; that court accommodation was sometimes such that the judge's retiring room was 'not much bigger than a cupboard and may indeed serve the charwomen in that capacity when its distinguished occupant is gone'; and that the littering of court buildings with brass band music stands and the apparatus of boxing rings was 'nationally discreditable'.

It is perhaps an unhappy moment at which to leave 'the red judge', as he hurries through the side door of the court-house, trips over a music stand and robes himself in a broom cupboard. Yet perhaps a broom cupboard is just the place to concentrate his mind on those large questions which, according to the press, the judge of today should be asking himself: Questions like: Am I behaving like a judge or a civil servant? Am I supinely acting as an arm of the administration? Am I taking every opportunity to interpret the statutes in favour of the individual? Am I prepared to give an honest judgment at the cost of being dubbed political? Is it my duty to oppose the apparent wishes of a democracy in its more tyrannous moods?

Among other questions for the broom cupboard might be: Am I doing all I can to shorten the law's delays? Am I checking those garrulous counsel who threaten to 'encroach on eternity'? Might it not be a salutary thing if, for once, I tried to emulate Lord Ellenborough and went through the list (in Mr Justice Talfourd's phrase) 'like a rhinoceros through a sugar plantation'?

If the judge is robing himself for a criminal trial, he may well be reflecting on the eternal problem of punishment. Parliament has decided that he shall no longer emerge from the broom cupboard to sentence a man to death. It has also decided that most of the prison sentences he imposes shall be suspended ones. For grave offences, there is nothing to stop him from sending men to serve periods of thirty years or more (the spy, Robert Blake, was sentenced to forty-two years by Lord Chief Justice Parker); but the Executive retains the power to shorten his sentences and ignore his recommendations. A century ago, Mr Justice Stephen complained that there was an element of the fox-hunt about a criminal trial. All the excitement was confined to the chase; nobody cared what happened to the quarry. Legal niceties were explored almost to infinity, but the judge was left only a few moments to decide on sentence and it was as easy to say six years as four. Now, the judge is obliged to take many factors into account, but sentencing remains an inexact science, despite judicial conferences on the subject. 'The Christian judge,' says Lord Longford, 'in the full knowledge that he also is a sinner like the man in the dock, judges with love and then does all he can to help the prisoner repay.'* Lord Goddard held it an eminently Christian duty to 'avenge' crime, in order to show the community's detestation of it. Today mention of vengeance or retribution causes such widespread scandal that some judges prefer to talk of the 'denunciatory' value of a heavy sentence. In the heat engendered from such controversies it has been suggested that the task of sentencing offenders should be taken away from

The Idea of Punishment.

judges and handed over to panels of sociologists and psychiatrists. It is an idea which seems to stem from the belief that almost any social worker, or for that matter any television playwright, knows more about the springs of human nature than the man who spends his life watching frailty and depravity pass before him. If judges are to be dismissed, as an Earl of Carlisle once dismissed them, as 'legal monks, utterly ignorant of human nature and of the ways of men, governed by their own paltry prejudices,' they are entitled to reply, as Lord Chief Justice Kenyon did, that judges see more of life than if they were shut up in gaming houses or brothels.*

It could be, and no doubt will be, argued that a judge who is too remote from life to be entrusted with sentencing must also be debarred from presiding and summing up. Those who have never seen a judge in action – and a surprising number of citizens go to their graves without entering a court of law – should perhaps not wait too long to rectify the omission.

*Lord Campbell: *Lives of the Lord Chief Justices.*

INDEX

Abbot, Mr Justice (Lord Tenteden), 137, 171
Abinger, Lord (James Scarlett), 142, 154, 163–4, 205, 206
Absalom and Achitophel, 71, 120
Ailesbury, Earl of, 149
Alderson, Baron, 13, 157, 159, 160, 161, 163–6, 178, 206
Alfred, King, 15–16, 17, 77, 128
Allybone, Mr Justice, 92, 98–9, 178
Alverstone, Lord, 216, 219
Anatomising, of murderers, 146
Andrews, Archie, 56
Anglo-Saxon Chronicle, The, 17, 19–20
Appeal, Court of, founded, 197–9
Appeal, Court of Criminal, founded 198–9
Appeal, lords of; lords justices of, 198
Appeal lords, and politics, 223–4
Army, judges and, 121, 180
Ashhurst, Mr Justice, 123–4, 135, 136
Askew, Anne, 37
Asquith, Herbert, 202–3, 206, 226
Assizes, see Circuit
Atkinson, Lord, 211
Attainder, Bills of, 34

Attorney-Generals, promotion to judge, 205
Audley, Baron, 36–7, 51
Audley, Lord, Earl of Castlehaven, 60
Avory, Mr Justice 220–1, 228, 223–4, 235; portrait, 224
Aylesbury, 159, 178

Bacon, Francis, 11, 45, 46, 47–9, 50–3, 104, 106, 197, 200, 234; disgrace of, 50–3
Bagehot, Walter, 185–6
Baggage, judges', 178
Baldwin, Stanley, 220–1, 231
Ballantine, Serjeant, 167–9
Baron, judicial title, 22, 193
Barrington, Sir Jonah, 176
Barristers, on circuit, 133, 179; clashes with Bench, 12, 84, 173–6, 231; judges revert to, 70–1; qualifications for judgeships, 10, 238; threatened by country courts, 193–4; wiles of, 24–5; see Counsel, Serjeants
Basset, Ralph, 13, 17
Bastwick, Dr John, 59
Battle, trial by, 17–18
Baxter, Richard, 84
Bealknap, Sir Robert, 28, 29
Beaumont, Sir John, 39
Beck, Adolf, 199
Bedlow, William, 75–80
Beeching Report, 239–40

243